TROUT FLIES OF STILLWATER

The Natural Fly, its Matching
Artificial Fishing Technique
and Modern Fishing Methods

Also by John Goddard

TROUT FLY RECOGNITION
Published by Adam & Charles Black

WHAT FLY IS THAT?
Published by the British Field Sports Society

THE SUPERFLIES OF STILLWATER

BIG FISH FROM SALTWATER

Published by Ernest Benn Ltd

Trout Flies
of Stillwater

JOHN GODDARD, F.R.E.S.

WITH COLOUR AND OTHER PHOTOGRAPHS BY THE AUTHOR
AND DRAWINGS BY CLIFF HENRY

FOURTH EDITION

ADAM & CHARLES BLACK · LONDON

FOURTH EDITION 1979
FIRST PUBLISHED 1969
SECOND EDITION 1972
THIRD EDITION 1975
REPRINTED 1977, 1983
BY A. AND C. BLACK (PUBLISHERS) LIMITED
35 BEDFORD ROW LONDON WC1R 4JH
© 1969, 1972, 1975, 1979 JOHN GODDARD

British Library Cataloguing in Publication Data

Goddard, John
  Trout flies of stillwater – 4th ed.
  1. Trout fishing – Great Britain 2. Fly
  fishing
  I. Title
  799.1'7'55   SH688.G7
  ISBN 0–7136–1878–7

ISBN 0-7136-1878-7

*Printed in Great Britain by
J. W. Arrowsmith Ltd
Bristol*

CONTENTS

ILLUSTRATIONS

ACKNOWLEDGEMENTS

I should like to take this opportunity of thanking all those who have either directly or indirectly assisted me in completing this book. In particular I should like to pay tribute to the following:
To the Editors of *Trout and Salmon* and *Angling*, the late Ian Wood and Mr. Brian Harris, for permission to reproduce certain sections from articles written for these magazines. To Dr. Paul Freeman and other members on the staff of the Entomological Department of the British Museum of Natural History. I would also like to specially thank Mr. Peter Ward of the same department for his additional assistance out of hours, and also for the wonderful coloured photographs of two species of Aquatic Moths—The Water Spider and the Greater Water Boatman, that he has so kindly provided for this book.
I must also thank the various Water Authorities and private individuals who so kindly allowed me access to their waters for the collection and study of insect and fish life. In this respect I feel I must particularly mention Mr. Alex Behrendt of Two Lakes near Romsey, and Mr. Kennedy Brown, late of the Bristol Waterworks Company whose help and personal assistance was invaluable. To Capt. Terry Thomas, Messrs. John Veniard, Barrie Welham, Fred J. Taylor, Vic Evans, and Dick Walker, whose friendship I have enjoyed over the years and whose help and opinions are always much respected.
I am also deeply indebted to Mr. David Jacques, the noted author and angler entomologist, for his assistance and advice in checking the final MS. of this book, and for the incalculable number of hours spent with me at home and in the field experimenting, debating (and arguing) the many aspects of insect behaviour. Also to my constant fishing companion, Mr. Cliff Henry, the well-known amateur fly-tyer for his help and encouragement at the fly-tying

bench, and for his valuable and dedicated assistance in collecting specimens for study and photographing.

And last, but not least, I must extend my sincere thanks to my secretary, Mrs. Betty Campbell, for her cheerful devotion to the monotonous task of typing and re-typing what to her must have been a dry-as-dust treatise.

AUTHOR'S PREFACE

This book has been written for the stillwater fly-fisherman in an effort to provide a reasonably simple method of identifying most of the common insects and other fauna found in or on many of our lakes, reservoirs and ponds. I have also endeavoured to inform the reader at what times of the day and season these insects, etc., are to be expected. This aspect is most important, as unlike the river dry fly fisherman who is able to identify by sight the insects on which the trout are feeding on the surface, the species on which the trout may or may not be feeding in stillwaters are, in many cases, out of sight below the surface. Under these conditions the best chance of hooking a trout is to fish a pattern that is most likely to represent the natural that could be most in evidence at that particular time. That there are blank days on stillwater, we all know, as most of us have experienced our share, but I am quite certain that these can be reduced considerably by an increase in our knowledge of the natural fauna on which trout feed, coupled with the ability to produce an artificial pattern that is a reasonably good imitation and fished in the correct manner.

As far as the dry fly river fisherman is concerned, exact identification of particular *species* is often of prime importance, but to the stillwater fly-fisherman, this is not always necessary. This is indeed fortunate, as most stillwaters harbour a far larger number of different species than rivers. Therefore, in this volume, I have in most cases felt that it was sufficient to differentiate between Families and Genera but seldom between *species*.

It will no doubt be appreciated that certain insects are common to both still and running water, and as I have already dealt extensively with all species of interest to the angler that inhabit the latter in my previous book *Trout Fly Recognition*, I have included in this present book several chapters from it that are applicable to both.

Finally, I should like to make it quite clear that this is basically a book about flies, both natural and artificial, and about fishing techniques, but it does not cover comprehensively either casting, equipment or tackle, as of course, there are already many excellent books on these subjects. If in this book I can convey to my readers a little of the knowledge and happiness I have derived from the study of this subject I shall have achieved my object. I sincerely hope that it will help to make their fishing days more interesting and successful.

INTRODUCTION

The enormous increase in the popularity of reservoir trout fishing in the last fifteen years has placed a new and vital importance on the study of stillwater insects. In fact for centuries men have observed the lake flies which make trout rise but never before has a study of this kind been undertaken in such depth.

John Goddard brings exceptional talent to this work. To begin with, he is both a skilled and experienced trout fisherman and one as well armed in the techniques of stillwater as in those used on a river. He also has the gifts of acute observation and great patience, and has used these to extend existing knowledge by practical study at the lakeside, by breeding many insects in his tanks at home and by long hours spent at the microscope. Above all he has been able to reinforce these studies by his skill in photography. The splendid colour plates are not only a valuable aid to identification: they reveal too the quite extraordinary beauty of some of these insects.

This is essentially a practical book and the reader can wade in as deeply as his fancy decides. For the serious student of entomology there is much food for thought, much of it new. As a work of reference for the growing army of reservoir fishermen it is an invaluable aid to identification and to the selection of the right artificial. Not least important is the sound advice it contains on the strategy and tactics of stillwater trout fishing.

John Goddard's previous book earned him his rightful place among the great angling entomologists of the past—Ronalds, Halford, Skues, West, Mosely, Dunne, to mention but few. This place in both the literature and the history of angling is further secured by this fine book.

CAPT. TERRY THOMAS

CHAPTER I

STILLWATER FISHING

During the past few years stillwater fly-fishing has enjoyed an increasing popularity, undoubtedly due to more waters becoming available. We are indebted to the various Water Authorities and Boards for the majority of these, as fortunately for the angler, they have finally realized that a steady and remunerative income is to be earned from the angler for fishing in their reservoirs. This fact, combined with present-day thinking by most local authorities to provide as many recreational facilities as possible, means that more and more stillwaters will become available in future.

One of the first and certainly the most famous of these is without doubt Chew Valley lake in Somerset. When this comparatively large sheet of water first opened in 1956 the fishing was incredibly good and within a very short time was advertised as the finest trout fishery in Europe. It retained this reputation for a number of years, and even today the fishing is still very good. The chief architect of the success of this particular venture was Mr. Kennedy Brown of the Bristol Waterworks Company, and as a result he is now in constant demand by other authorities throughout the country in an advisory capacity, and I think it should be realized that fly-fishermen in general owe him a considerable debt of gratitude. I have quoted this particular case as an example, but would like to point out there are also many other personalities that have achieved success in this field equally worthy of our gratitude.

More recently we have seen the opening of another new water at Grafham in Northamptonshire, where the first two weeks of trout fishing can only be described as fabulous; during this period even inexperienced fly-fishermen were taking the limit bag of eight trout, most of which were in excess of two-and-a-half pound. Furthermore, quite a large percentage of fish over four pounds and some over five were taken in this period, and when one considers that none of these fish were more than about three years old, the growth rate can only be considered as phenomenal. Unfortunately, this honeymoon

I

period (some referred to it as the duffer's fortnight) did not last for long and by the end of its first season this water had settled down to giving limit bags only to those fishermen with sufficient experience to attain them.

From the above it will doubtless be apparent that most new reservoirs which are constructed by flooding agricultural land and stocked with trout enjoy a period varying between several months to several years where the size and condition of the trout are well above average. This variation is usually due to two factors, (a) the richness, or otherwise, of the newly flooded land and (b) the spasmodic rise and fall of the water, and the consequent regularity with which any shallow areas are left high and dry to fructify in the open air under the direct rays of the sun, thus reinvigorating its complement of living vegetation. A further contributory factor that usually leads to a quick deterioration in the condition of trout stock is the infiltration of unwanted coarse fish.

It is interesting to note that although the fishing and the size of most of the trout in many of these man-made waters tend to deteriorate, there are occasionally exceptions to this general rule. Three of these in particular that come to mind are: Two Lakes in Hampshire, a private fishery run by that genial expert on trout culture, Alex Behrendt, and his wife Katharine. The size of the trout in this fishery has in fact increased over the years, and in this case it would seem to be due to correct fishery management plus particular reference to the culture of the correct living creatures on which trout thrive. In fairness to other managements I would like to point out that these lakes are comparatively small, and to carry out the same type of programme on very much larger waters may be a formidable proposition.

The second exception is Hanningfield reservoir in Essex. This is a very large sheet of water and has now been stocked with trout for several years. In this case also the fishing and average size of the trout has improved tremendously since it was first opened to anglers several years ago. This, at first sight, would not appear to be a particularly promising reservoir as there does not seem to be a large annual rise and fall in water level, and it is therefore a little difficult to acertain the reason for the excellent results that have been obtained here. Originally, the trout were introduced into this water to combat the very large number of insects that had become established and which were proving a nuisance to both the water authority and the surrounding inhabitants. Perhaps the fact that the aquatic insect population had become firmly entrenched before trout were introduced has proved to be the answer in this case. On the other hand, a further factor may be the high alkalinity of the water, combined with the extremely large amount that is pumped in daily.

Finally, I would mention a slightly different example. Many of the lakes and reservoirs in Wales are of a barren nature or have waters high in acid content. These conditions are naturally not conducive to the growing of large trout. Consequently, the majority of these waters, although well stocked and providing good fishing, rarely produce large trout. Yet a reservoir opened some time ago near Port Talbot in South Wales has over the past two seasons produced an astonishing number of very large trout!

Apart from reservoirs, other potential sources of trout fishing are the many gravel pits dotted around the countryside, and over the past few years many of these suitable for rearing trout have been acquired either by clubs or private syndicates. As in the majority of cases these types of waters are dependent on constant restocking to provide the maximum sport, it is to the ponds, lakes and lochs in the more inaccessible parts of these islands that we have to look for our natural trout fishing. A fair proportion of such waters hold a good head of naturally bred trout, but usually the average size of these is considerably lower than in those waters that are carefully restocked. Nevertheless, there are a few noted exceptions, most of which are either in Scotland or Ireland. Typical of these are such famous waters as Loughs Corrib, Mask and Conn.

During the last two decades considerable progress has been made in fishing techniques and tactics as applied to stillwater fishing, consequently many new artificial patterns of flies have been developed, and a considerable number of these have now proved to be very popular and killing patterns under the right conditions. In my opinion we are now, like the river fly-fisherman at the beginning of this century, on the threshold of an era where our whole approach to stillwater fishing may be influenced by discoveries and methods yet to be introduced. In substantiation, the advances in river fly-fishing in the last seventy-five years corresponds in no little measure to the vast fund of literature that has been published over the same period, during which, at least until 1953, very little of value had been written on stillwater fishing, with correspondingly little progress being made in its technique.

If anyone should require further proof of this it is only necessary to compare the development of artificial flies since the beginning of the century and up to the last war. Let us first consider river angling.

Literally hundreds of new patterns have been published and developed, many of which are now virtually household names. Among these are many that were perfected by such angling giants of their day as the immortal Halford, Skues and Lunn. In contrast, I have been unable to discover many examples of significant lake patterns that have appeared in the same period. Apart from a few excellent modern ones developed in the last few years, nearly all the famous patterns of lake flies with which we are so familiar, such as the Peter Ross, Alexandra, Butcher, Teal Blue and Silver, and Silver Doctor—to mention just a few—were developed in the last century. None of these patterns are, or were, intended as close imitations of natural flies or insects, although undoubtedly some of them do loosely simulate certain naturals and are no doubt taken by the trout as such. Before I proceed further, let me assure the reader that I am not in any way decrying any of these artificials as, after all, they have stood the test of time and many are excellent killing patterns under the right conditions. I personally refer to most of these types of artificials as "general patterns", and even today some of them will be found in my fly box. However, I do feel that the future of stillwater fishing probably lies in a combination of close imitation plus correct presentation.

In addition to the types of artificials mentioned above, there are also a legion of what I term fancy patterns or lures that were popularized during the same period; I have little time for these, but this is purely a personal viewpoint and I should not like to feel that I am influencing other anglers against their use if they feel so justified. As most of these are very colourful and fairly large, I think that many of them originated from salmon or sea trout patterns, as it must be remembered that our forbears consistently fished for salmon and sea trout as well as for brown trout in many of the Scottish and Irish stillwaters even as we do to this day.

At this stage, I feel that the phrase "stillwater" should be clarified. The modern trend seems to be to refer to all bodies of water, whether they be lakes, lochs or reservoirs,, etc., as stillwater. It must be appreciated, however, that this is a generalization, as of course nearly all areas of water, except for small stagnant ponds, have some movement of water, caused by inlets, outlets, wind or temperature.

The modern approach to lake fishing (in future, for the sake of brevity, where applicable I shall refer to all reservoirs, lakes, lochs, etc., as stillwater) really began with T. C. Iven's book *Still Water Fly Fishing*, published in 1953, although I think it only fair to point out that the first tremors probably started way back in 1924 with R. C. Bridgetts' book, *Loch Fishing in Theory and Practice*, in which he constantly emphasizes the necessity of recognizing the food on which trout feed and the importance of applying this knowledge in a sensible way to the patterns of one's choice. More recently we have seen the publication of a book by C. F. Walker entitled *Lake Flies and their Imitation*, an excellent work which I look upon as the first major step forward in the history of stillwater fishing.

To the beginner, on his first attempt to fish stillwater (unless trout are actually rising), the prospect may appear to be most disheartening, and under these conditions—if he has no one present to advise him and has a blank day—he is often, unfortunately, turned away from this type of fishing for life. I would, therefore, strongly recommend the erstwhile beginner to ensure that at least on his first outing he is accompanied by a fly-fisherman experienced in this particular art, although I must point out that even the expert does have the odd blank day. Unfortunately, the image of the stillwater fisherman that has existed over the years is that of either the boat fisherman constantly casting and retrieving a short line along the surface with no apparent rhyme or reason, or the bank fisherman standing up to his thighs in the water all day casting a long sinking line with monotonous regularity. It is not to be denied that in fact a fair percentage of anglers do fish in this manner and catch fish, and if they obtain a maximum of enjoyment by so doing it would be a disservice to influence them otherwise. However, it is a great pity that this image persists, as it is very far from reflecting the true enjoyment that is to be found by or on our stillwaters.

Without doubt, persistence and patience are two very important words in the lake fisher's vocabulary no matter how he fishes, although this applies in particular to anglers who fish by the two methods described above. It is probably true that many of these anglers catch their quota of fish and some, on occasion, may even do better than the expert who endeavours to present an imitation in the correct manner, but on balance my money would be placed on the latter every time. On many occasions I have heard the view expressed that lake fishing is purely "chuck it and chance it", as, except when the trout are rising, the fisherman has no idea of their location. This is far from the truth, as an angler who is familiar with the stillwater he is fishing will know from past experience where the fish are most likely to be under given conditions. Apart from this, most bodies of stillwater have certain features that to the experienced eye will be obvious lies for fish under certain conditions. These are weed beds, shallow banks in deep water, deep channels or ditches in shallow water, old hedgerows or the flooded roads that often form part of the bed, inlets, outlets or areas in the vicinity of natural springs which feed some stillwaters. The list is unending, but as a typical example I would like to relate a personal experience that happened several years ago. At the time I was on a week's fishing holiday in the West Country, and during most of this period I concentrated on trout fishing on a local reservoir. This was in late summer and the fishing was not particularly good and, although I had managed to get a few nice trout during the evenings, the mornings and afternoons had been disappointing. Despite my own lack of success and that of many other anglers with whom I passed the time of day, it was particularly noticeable that one or two fly-fisherman in a relatively restricted area along one bank were enjoying consistently good sport during this dour period. Upon closer examination I observed in this area what appeared to be some tree stumps showing slightly above the surface of the water and determined to return early the next morning to give this spot a try. I was fortunate next day in obtaining a place, and had an excellent day's sport, grassing several very nice trout of grand proportions. My earliest suspicions that they were tree stumps and roots were confirmed, as before I commenced fishing I was able to wade out to within a rod's distance of the nearest of them, to find that they were harbouring vast shoals of sticklebacks. Using an artificial stickleback pattern, success was assured. Many times since I have fished this particular spot in this reservoir, but it only fishes consistently well during the latter part of the summer, when the sticklebacks are most in evidence.

Since the early days of fly-fishing, stillwaters have been looked upon as the beginner's happy hunting grounds, and no angler of experience would deny that on certain days trout in stillwater almost give themselves up. On these occasions the beginner is as likely to do as well or even better than the expert, depending largely on luck. Circumstances such as this seldom, if ever, apply on the river, as the expert will rarely depart with an empty creel, whereas the beginner will often fish hard for days on end with nary a single fish to reward his efforts. No doubt it is this fact, and this alone, that has given rise to this opinion. It is most unfortunate that this appraisal of stillwater fishing still prevails, although in latter years it seems to be on the wane, due no doubt to increased interest in the subject. The fact that most bodies of stillwater do provide occasional days when the fish are easy is just as well, as it does ensure that the inexperienced angler is given a certain amount of encouragement. On the other hand, blank days are far more prevalent on stillwater than on rivers and on these occasions it is usually the expert who will get the odd fish. From the small amount of literature available on this subject it would appear that blank days were far more prevalent earlier in the century than they are nowadays, and doubtless this is due to the progress in recent years in fish culture and in the understanding of the entomology of stillwater which has resulted in many new artificial patterns being developed.

As suggested, it is my view that the slow advance in the technique of lake fishing until comparatively recently can largely be accounted for by the lack of interest in the insects and other fauna which, after all, provide the bulk of food for the trout. It would, therefore, appear that at least a working knowledge of entomology should increase one's chances of success. Some anglers may deem it necessary to make a fairly detailed study of this subject, and although I must admit that this can become most absorbing and fascinating, a little basic knowledge should suffice for the average fly-fisherman. Therefore, I trust that this book will provide enough information for the enthusiast without confusing the uninitiated.

In the preface I mentioned that this was to be basically a book on flies and, except for suggesting fishing methods to be used in conjunction with definite species of insects, I intended to keep it this way. However, I felt it prudent before proceeding with the entomological aspect to give a short résumé of various facets of stillwater fishing that may be of some interest to the beginner or to those experienced river fisherman who have decided to try their hand at this particular branch of our sport.

CHAPTER II

BOAT, BANK AND CASTING

Boat Fishing

Over the years much controversy has raged as to whether boat or bank fishing is more successful. Experience emboldens me to suggest that on average more trout are caught by the boat angler, but the bigger ones are usually caught by the angler from the bank, and this seems to be the view expressed by most competent fishermen. Both these methods of fishing require completely different techniques, and although the boat angler may be rather restricted in the way that he fishes his flies, he does cover during a day's fishing a much greater area of undisturbed water, and is able to fish large areas that are inaccessible to the bank angler; hence his heavier creel on most occasions. Some fly-fishers prefer boat fishing and some prefer bank fishing and a few can enjoy both equally. Nowadays I do not mind either, in contrast to my former preference for bank fishing. Perhaps, as one gets older, the little luxuries of life become more desirable, and there is no doubt that the boat is far more comfortable and less fatiguing than the bank. Some hired boats are equipped with a drogue, a most useful item, as not only does it slow the rate of drift but virtually eliminates yawing. Also the direction of drift may be controlled to a certain extent according to the position at which the drogue is attached to the boat. Normally it is secured to the side of the boat, but in high winds it is a good idea to secure it to the bow. The boat will then drift slower and be more stable. When used in this manner one angler sits in the bow and one in the stern, facing in different directions, each casting at an angle over his right shoulder. In this way each angler will also find he can cover a very wide arc on his side of the boat.

Most anglers are aware of the frightening effect that vibration has on fish, and this is particularly applicable when fishing from a boat; for this reason movement should be minimized as far as

8

possible, and it is a good idea to wear soft shoes. The use of these also reduces possible damage to your line, as in the process of being retrieved, it inevitably lies in the bottom of the boat.

It is usual when boat fishing to be accompanied by a friend and, providing one's sole aim in life is not to catch as many trout as possible in a day's fishing, the companionship can add greatly to the enjoyment. I would, however, respectfully suggest that one's companion in a boat is chosen with a little care, as to have an inexperienced fly-fisher in the close confines of a boat with you is, to say the least, risky, as a team of relatively large lake flies on the end of a cast can be quite dangerous. It should be made quite clear, tactfully of course, to whomever is with you that the cast should always be made at right angles to the boat; the only exception to this rule is during a surface rise, when you may require to cast to a fish in any direction. Under these circumstances the back cast must be kept high, and also both of you must be quite certain of each others' intentions. At dusk, during a late evening rise, this can be a little tricky and it is, therefore, an advantage to observe a prearranged verbal signal which will give advance warning that one is about to change the direction of the cast.

As previously mentioned, one is rather restricted in the method of fishing a fly from a boat, and over the years there has been little advance in technique. The old loch fishers of days gone by usually advocated a long, light rod which allowed them to fish a reasonable length of line without false casting or fatigue, working, no doubt, on the principle that the longer your flies are fishing the better your chances, and so far as any stillwater fishing is concerned this is sound common sense. The long rod also allows you to bounce your top dropper along the surface in a most enticing manner. An expert fishing in such a manner is indeed a pleasure to watch but, unfortunately, nowadays one sees less and less of this style of fishing, the modern trend seeming to favour a shorter rod with frequent false casting to achieve distance, and in many cases you will find an angler standing up and casting from a boat. This presents a much larger silhouette and more movement than a seated angler, and merely puts down fish over a larger radius. Another point which probably only a few anglers realize is that the extra rhythm required for false casting will invariably cause the boat to rock, and this in turn sends out waves in a radius from the boat which is often sufficient to put a trout down. Should anyone doubt this statement, let them take a boat out on a flat calm when fish are rising well, and they will find that the area of water around the boat which often seems empty of rising trout will be broadened considerably when standing up to cast.

The wind is as important a factor in boat fishing as it is in bank fishing. Probably most experienced boat fishers will agree that a steady breeze is preferable to a flat calm, and during such latter conditions it is a good idea to try to locate a slight ripple, which may indicate an area that is receiving a slight breeze from some direction. The edge of such a ripple is often well worth fishing. When the winds are strong, foam or wind lanes tend to form and, as the trout sometimes follow them in their search for food, it often pays dividends to fish along them.

The sun as well as the wind is an important factor in boat fishing, and when it is directly behind you when on the drift, the trout often "come short" and are difficult to hook. A longer, or an across-wind roll-cast instead of one down-wind, will often prove effective in overcoming the problem.

The successful boat angler relies first of all on the correct choice of artificial fly, and combines this with an intimate knowledge of the water he is fishing, particularly where fish are to be found at any given time under any existing conditions.

Finally, it is worth mentioning that a new technique which seems to be gaining converts is the use of a sinking line and a lure cast to maximum distance and retrieved at speed from either an anchored or drifting boat. That this method catches fish is not to be denied, but it has no appeal for me. However, fishing a team of pupae or a nymph from an anchored boat with a floating or sink tip line, can under the right conditions be very rewarding.

Bank Fishing

These days, with the increasing popularity of stillwater fishing, the banks of our more popular waters are often crowded with lines of fishermen, sometimes barely twenty yards apart. Wading, which is fairly general, has created a paradox because the disturbance sends the fish further from the bank, thus making it necessary for the angler to wade out still further, which in turn drives the fish still further away; this consequently has created a necessity for casting greater distances in order to be successful. This seems a great pity, because if bank anglers could be pursuaded not to wade at all it would be possible on many occasions to catch trout quite close to the shore. Unfortunately, human nature being what it is, one or two anglers in a crowd will always be found disregarding a code of behaviour, and naturally if one or two wade, all must wade.

Many times in the past, when I have been fortunate to find a secluded section of bank, I have fished from and along it without entering the water and caught some very big trout. This can be particularly rewarding in the latter part of the season when there are not so many anglers about, and the larger trout are feeding on sticklebacks. It is significant that I have caught trout in water so shallow that it barely covers their backs as they voraciously pursue the shoals of fry right into the margins of the lake. When fishing the banks in this manner the angler should always be watchful of his movements and where possible utilize any available background to obscure his whereabouts, or he will find that he is putting down more fish than he is able to cover.

The bank fisher, when wading, should always remember that it is a very easy matter to scare the fish out of casting range either by careless wading or clumsy casting. One often observes the bank angler walking out into the water as if he has a train to catch and, on doing so, sending out a bow wave like a barge! Not content with this he then commences to cast, laying the line down on the water so hard that every self-respecting trout departs for the other side of the lake. Wading should always be executed very slowly, carefully placing one foot in front of the other with the minimum of disturbance. It is also circumspect to transfer your weight slowly to the forward foot, or alternatively to use a specially made wading net fitted with a long shaft, as many lakes have potholes or areas of soft mud and it is a very simple matter to take one step forward and find oneself submerged.

It is a good practice, when commencing to cast from whatever position has been selected, to start off with a short line and while fishing between casts to gradually lengthen it successively until the desired distance is attained. Simultaneously one should cover a frontal arc to ensure that the maximum area is thoroughly worked with your flies. Furthermore, an angler's silhouette is so reduced when standing in the water up to his thighs that it is not surprising that, with care, rising trout can be approached quite closely. Of course, care should also be taken in casting and, particularly when fishing a short line, to use a side cast to reduce the movement of the rod against the skyline.

During the evening rise, which is often of short duration, it is a good idea to carry spare flies and accessories in either a haversack over the shoulder or, better still, a hip bag on a belt which can be slid around to the front when required. In addition to this it is necessary to provide some means of retaining any trout caught, and this can be accomplished by fashioning a simple wire hook and hanging it from the bag ring or belt. The angler, thus equipped, obviates the necessity of returning to dry land after netting a trout, thereby creating a disturbance and also wasting precious time. Unfortunately, in some cases, part of this operation may be in vain if you have anglers on either side of you who do not observe the same care.

It has already been stated that the bank fisherman has far more scope in the presentation of his flies to the trout, but I do not intend to elaborate on this for the moment. The different techniques to be used for relating natural creatures to their imitations will be explained in later chapters.

Due to variable conditions it is difficult to suggest any set pattern of rules to assist the bank fisher in the locating of fish throughout the season or even during a single day, but to generalize I would venture to suggest the following. During the early spring, before the water has warmed, it is usually better to concentrate in the areas of deeper water. The same applies if the weather turns cold towards the end of the season. On hot summer days it also pays to fish the deeper areas during the day and concentrate on the shallows in the early morning and late evening. Many lakes, or particularly reservoirs, are deep at one end and shallow at the other, and in most cases the shallows fish better in the evenings during warmer weather of summer. Some lakes, lochs or more often reservoirs, are featureless and offer few, if any, obvious trout-holding areas. Despite this, waters of this nature often have very localized favourite spots for no apparent reason; these can usually be located by excessive wear on the bank in such places, and are always well worth trying.

The direction of the wind can also play an important part in the movement or location of trout. In most lakes trout tend to face or travel upwind against the surface drift of the water, because any insects in or on the water surface are being brought towards them. It will, therefore, be apparent that in a cross-wind both trout and their food are continually moving across the angler's front, and this presents him with first-class opportunities. However, the majority of anglers prefer to fish with the wind behind them, as it requires less expertize and in any case it is less fatiguing. Unfortunately, this can often prove to be bad tactically as, particularly in strong winds if the lake or reservoir be deep, the colder deoxygenated water may be forced up on to this shore off which the wind is blowing. Consequently, it is unlikely to hold many trout for the angler to catch. Under these circumstances the fisherman would be well advised to try one of the other shores. When the wind is blowing towards the bank and bringing food and the hungry trout with it, the angler who has mastered the knack of casting into the wind may have not only a fishing advantage but the boon of sole possession of a large stretch of bank. Occasionally the direction of the wind may change at short notice from that described above, and when it does may prove the exception to the general rule as many insects, terrestrial or aquatic, that have been congregating along the shoreline or among the bankside vegetation, will then be gradually blown into the lake, and when this happens the observant angler will derive much benefit from it. Wind can also form eddies, particularly if the lake has any prominent headlands, and these are always good spots to fish. Finally, it is worth remembering that for evening fishing a west bank is often favourite, because the sun is usually off the water earlier along this bank.

Casting

There are several excellent books available on this subject and I do not intend to discuss technicalities, but from the tactical point of view there are several points worthy of mention.

In the first place, false casting should always be kept to a minimum, whether boat or bank fishing, particularly in bright weather when the line throws its inevitable shadow on the water, as at times this may scare fish into believing that one of the many natural winged predators is in the vicinity.

The boat fisher relies mainly on the floating line, although the present-day trend is to use, on occasions, a sinking or slow-sinking line, but whichever type of line is used it is sensible to use as light a line as possible to allow delicate presentation and also in an effort to eliminate the sag which tends to form on the retrieve between rod tip and flies, particularly when boat fishing, with consequent loss of touch.

The bank fisher is at home equally with either the sinking or floating line, although most have a preference for one or the other. In addition to the sinking line which is used for retrieving along or near the bed of the lake, and the floating line for fishing the surface or sub-surface, there is also a sinking-tip line now available which is very useful for fishing in midwater, or along the bottom in shallower water.

Many discriminating anglers prefer to use a floating line, and use a sinker only when the conditions are such that it is absolutely necessary. A floater gives far greater control of the artificial flies in use and enables waters of depths up to the length of the leader to be successfully fished. Indeed, the only time it is essential to use a wet line is during the colder weather or on very hot, flat, calm days when the trout are lying deep, or particularly when retrieving fast and deep, flies or lures such as imitation sticklebacks or fry. The length and type of leader used will vary from situation to situation, but a good average length is about 9 ft. Some authorities suggest one style of leader, while others another, and as there are many variations from a standard tapered leader to fancy double or even forward tapered leaders that one can make up oneself, the choice must be dictated by personal preference. If the leader is required to float, a light application of mucilin is recommended. A heavy application, which will cause a noticeable wake when the leader is retrieved, is a mistake. When fishing a sunken fly it is highly desirable for the leader and flies to sink as quickly as possible, and to this end I have yet to find a better medium than ordinary commercial Teepol. This can be carried in a small screw-top bottle, and when fishing commences the flies on the leader are immersed in the liquid one at a time, and the liquid can then be spread from the flies along the leader with finger and thumb. Modern fly lines require little attention or dressing, although it is a good idea to wipe down occasionally a sinking line with Teepol or a floating line with mucilin.

Apart from the normal double or forward tapered fly lines in use today, there is a type of line that has been fast gaining in popularity for stillwater fishing, and this is called a shooting head, made in both sinking and floating styles. The first of these lines are now commercially available, but for many years anglers have made these themselves from part of a standard fly line. In this latter case the head is composed of the front section of a standard double-taper fly line, and can vary in length, according to personal choice, from 8 to 15 yds. or more. The cut length is then whipped on to a nylon monafilament backing of about 20 lb. test. These shooting heads, in vogue in this country since comparatively recent times, have been used in the U.S.A. for many years and undoubtedly originated there. I myself have been using one since 1956, and in the intervening years I have occasionally come across others using them but, of course, they are now very common. My own preference at times is for a head of about 10 to 11 yds. in length and preferably cut from the front part of a forward taper line, as opposed to a double taper which, in my opinion, does not turn over so well as a forward taper. In addition, I find I can put it down more lightly on the water, particularly against a wind. The length of head used will vary from person to person, depending on the type of rod and a combination of physical and casting ability. If the head is too short the distance you are able to cast will be rather limited but, on the other hand, if the head is too long, while distance can be achieved it will be at the expense of fatigue and poor presentation. With a well-balanced shooting head distances in excess of 30 yds. can be maintained all day without too much effort, or 40 yds. if used in conjunction with the double-haul technique, but in spite of this and other advantages some fly-fishermen look upon them with disapproval.

These days a certain percentage of anglers use a shooting head for all aspects of lake fishing, and I have even seen them used all day from a boat. Under the right conditions they are an extremely

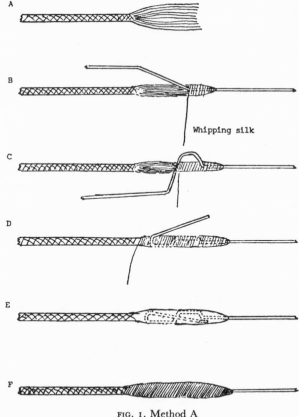

FIG. 1. Method A

useful weapon in the bank fisher's, or on occasions boat fishers, armoury, but where distance casting is not absolutely necessary they should seldom be used, particularly when fishing the dry fly, or on very bright, calm days, as they have grave disadvantages compared to a normal fly line owing to the difficulty of the inexperienced caster laying a shooting head lightly and delicately on the water. This is not to infer that it is almost impossible, but it does require considerable expertize. However, two of the most important benefits of a shooting head lies in the fact that it practically eliminates false casting, and allows you to fish areas where your back cast is restricted.

The shooting head should be spliced to not less than a 100 yds. of about 20 lb. test monofilament backing. Some types of nylon are preferable to others, but the choice must be left to the personal preference of the angler. Some anglers use a plastic bucket strapped to one leg, in which they coil the nylon backing, while others use a line raft, or tray, and although undoubtedly their use does increase

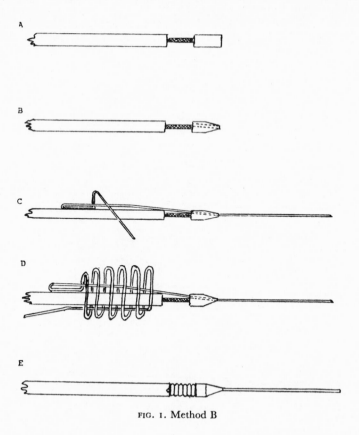

FIG. 1. Method B

the distance you can cast, many anglers do not consider the inconvenience caused by these gadgets makes it worth while.

Finally, I should like to mention three methods of attaching your leader or backing to the fly line. Methods A and B show you how to permanently attach the leader to a silk or plastic line, then attaching or detaching your flies as required. Method C is intended for the fisherman who prefers to tie and detach the leader, complete with flies, from a selection of leaders carried in a cast or leader carrier. This latter method has much to commend it, particularly when a quick change of flies is required, or when a bad tangle occurs at dusk.

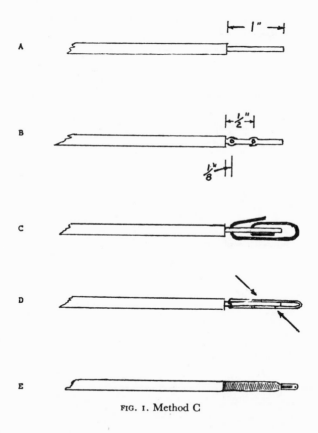

FIG. 1. Method C

Another alternative which I also practice is to carry a spare rod with me. During the day this is very useful particularly when bank fishing for either alternative use with a sinking or sink tip line or another floating line similar to that fitted to the main rod but with a different selection of flies. In the late evening once I have decided upon the method of fishing and type of flies, I fit the spare rod up in the same way. I then have a duplicate outfit ready for instant use should I require it.

Unfortunately even the best fishermen acquire some dreadful tangles at night for various reasons. Probably the most common cause is the small rainbow that takes a fly on a dropper—this nearly always results in a wonderful birds nest of leader and flies by the time he is netted. When this type of incident occurs the full benefit of a spare rod or made up leaders will be appreciated.

I have already discussed leaders earlier in this chapter but since writing the original edition of this book I have been engaged upon some interesting research into these and also fly lines. So far as the former are concerned I now tend to use much longer leaders 14 to 16 ft. overall and according to the records I have kept my catches have been better since using the longer leaders. Of course, it is almost impossible to prove or disprove any theory such as this conclusively, but apart from improved bags of fish it seems logical to have as long a leader as one can manage thereby allowing maximum distance between artificials. Using standard 9 or 10 ft. leaders I now feel the artificials are too close together or too near to the fly line and this may appear suspicious to a trout.

I have a friend who has access to certain laboratory equipment, including an extremely delicate unit for measuring decibels of sound through water. He fitted this to a long tank of water and carefully tested various sounds made by the fishermen and his equipment. The most astonishing results of all these tests was the relatively high proportion of sound or vibration made by a fly line hitting the water after the angler's cast. The worst offenders were floating lines particularly torpedo or forward tapers in the heavier weights. Naturally the lighter the line and the smaller the diameter the less the noise.

Following on from this he then carried out a series of tests between the new plastic coated lines and the old fashioned type of silk lines. This seemed to prove that the smaller equivalent diameter of the silk fly lines made less sound when hitting or alighting on the water. We had, the previous year, carried out a series of carefully controlled tests over a whole season using modern plastic coated lines and the old style silk lines, and the latter certainly accounted for far more fish particularly from a boat. I am sure we can all recall calm still days with plenty of trout rising, but no matter how careful one is every fish you cast near goes down. I am now reasonably certain that this is due to this line slap as I call it, and although it cannot be avoided completely it can most certainly be minimized by using as light a line as possible and better still if it is silk. Following this train of thought we have also found that the longer leaders we now use for the reason previously discussed also assist to minimize the sound of the line hitting the water to the trout, as naturally the longer the leader the further the actual fly line from the trout and the less noise it will hear.

Although some fly fishers still use silk lines the majority now seem to prefer the more modern plastic coated lines as these do not require constant greasing to keep them floating. By trial and error I have now discovered a method of treating ordinary silk lines which allows you to fish with them for several hours without the tiresome task of regreasing. I use Barbours waterproofing compound which can be purchased in tins from most fishing tackle retailers. If a brand new line is to be treated proceed as follows.

First of all it is necessary to find a shallow round container slightly larger in diameter than the coiled fly line (the lid of an old tin will suffice). Cover the bottom of the container with enough water-proofing compound to cover most of the line when melted, then place in a hot oven for about an hour after the heat has been turned off. Remove the line from the oven and container and uncoil. The line should then be stretched out taut in the garden on a warm sunny day. At least twice during the day it should be rubbed down thoroughly with a felt pad impregnated with the same Barbours compound. After this it should only be necessary to rub it down with the same compound after returning from each fishing trip. It is however still necessary to remove the line from the reel when not in use and transfer to a line winder. If one fishes hard over a long period it may of course be necessary to give it an occasional rub down.

N.B. If an old line is to be treated it will be necessary to thoroughly clean and degrease before commencing.

CHAPTER III

FLY FISHING METHODS

Artificial flies may be fished in many different ways, but the two basic ways are wet and dry.

Broadly speaking, most lakes or reservoirs may be divided under either of two headings: upland or lowland. Such waters as Chew Valley, Blagdon, Ravensthorpe and Eyrebrook, are typical lowland waters and, being of an alkaline nature, often based on rich limestone or other subsoil, have an abundance of underwater life, harbouring large quantities of shrimp, snail, corixa, caddis larva and other forms of life. In waters of this nature the trout wax far and often grow to a very large size, but they are basically bottom or midwater feeders and it consequently requires an abnormal amount of insects on or in the surface film to bring about a general surface rise. Under these conditions the wet fly is usually the better proposition, except when surface activity is fairly widespread. The upland lakes and lochs in the hilly country of Wales and the North, on the other hand, are often of an acid nature. These waters are not so rich in bottom or midwater fauna, and consequently a relatively small amount of surface hatching or even terrestrial insects blown on to the water will often bring the fish up, and on these waters a dry fly may often prove as effective as a wet fly.

The Dry Fly

This style of fishing may be practised equally well from a boat or the bank, but in both cases success is usually dependent on some surface activity. It must be appreciated that there are many different types of natural insects to which trout will rise, and as the artificials of many of these require individual techniques, this aspect will be dealt with fully in a later chapter. It will doubtless be realized that when trout appear to be feeding on the surface it does not necessarily mean that they are actually doing so, as they may equally well be taking nymphs or pupae hatching in the surface film. In most cases it is possible for the experienced lake fisherman to tell the difference by the rise form, but it is seldom easy and the beginner is liable to have a little difficulty until experience provides the answer. To a large extent the best dry fishing is dependent upon the right weather conditions as well as a rise of fish to surface food. A gentle breeze which provides a good ripple on the water, especially when the air is crisp and when the sun occasionally peeps through the fleeting clouds, will probably prove ideal. Bright, sunny or heavy overcast days seldom provide good bags, and very bright, hot cloudless days with a flat calm are certainly not conducive to good fishing with either the wet or dry fly. While wet, windy conditions often favour the wet fly fisher, they are not the best medium for good dry fly fishing as even with liberal use of floatant it is no easy matter to keep the fly on the surface where it belongs, and from a boat where one has a fast drift to contend with it is generally impossible. On sunny days it will be particularly noticeable that the most likely time for a trout to take will be when an odd cloud covers the sun for a brief interval. Over the years I have found this situation to be so consistent that I always expect activity when the sun is covered briefly in this manner.

When stillwater fishing, if possible, it is always a good policy, whether from bank or boat, to have two rods made up, one for wet fly fishing and one for dry. Most boat anglers prefer the floating line and in consequence both rods are usually equipped with normal double tapered lines, while for bank fishing one rod is usually equipped with a shooting head. It is also a good idea to have various leaders made up with flies or nymphs ready for use; should a tangle occur, particularly in poor light, lengthy unravelling time can be avoided if the spare leaders are held on a leader or cast carrier, available for instant use.

Some authorities advocate the use of wet flies in conjunction with a dry fly on the leader, but it seems the majority of anglers prefer to fish a single dry fly. Another choice facing the fisherman is whether or not to use a floatant on fly or leader. When fishing with a dry fly it is in most cases important that it cocks well and floats high in the water. To achieve this the leader can be greased with a floatant such as lanolin or mucilin, and the fly can also be treated with one of the many floatants or sprays available from tackle shops. Mucilin, which can be lightly applied with finger and thumb, is also a good medium for anointing the fly, particularly for some sedge patterns which have to be fished with movement, which drowns a dry fly far quicker than anything else and which to a large extent is prevented by an application of mucilin. The use of floatants, which form a film of oil around the fly and leader, in calm conditions may well cause a taking trout to refuse at the last moment and is avoided by many experts. If one is of this school of thought, the answer lies in frequent false casting, combined with the occasional use of amadou to dry your fly thoroughly. A compromise between the above methods is to use floatants sparingly only when conditions make their use essential, and this is probably the best solution.

When dry fly fishing in stillwater, observation of the movement of trout on the surface is of utmost importance. Providing the actual rise is observed it is often possible to tell in which direction a trout is travelling. In some cases, particularly if the fish shows its head and tail, it is quite easy, and in other cases, if the trout is moving along just under the surface fairly fast, the direction can be ascertained by the shape of the rise. On many occasions, however, it is exceedingly difficult and only experience will tell. Some fly-fishermen of my acquaintance have this talent to a very high degree, and can forecast the direction with uncanny accuracy, but for myself I am quite elated if I prove to be correct twice out of three. This problem is most complicated during a widespread general rise, and at its simplest when a solitary trout on a beat is observed rising in a more or less straight line at frequent intervals. In such a situation as this, if the fish is in range the fly can be cast to alight in the estimated position of the next rise. Most authorities seem to believe that in stillwater trout tend to move up-wind, and my own observations so far substantiate this, and therefore if one is uncertain of the direction being taken by a rising fish it is always a sound proposition to cast a few yards up-wind of the last rise. However, there are exceptions to all rules, and some trout seem to favour a more or less stationary position a few feet under the surface, waiting for wind or surface drift to bring food into their window before rising. Consequently, when I am uncertain of direction, I always drop my fly as speedily as possible near the centre of the rise, and with practice it is amazing how quickly this can be achieved. If this does not produce a take within a couple of seconds I then re-cast and drop the fly about five yards up-wind, but experience teaches that even when we feel we can estimate the position of the next rise, our cast should be somewhat short in order to prevent lining the fish and putting it down, which will almost certainly happen when the surface is calm or unruffled. Remember, if it is not put down you will probably have two or three chances to cover him before he is out of range.

Without a doubt, one of the most difficult features of the dry fly on stillwater is to know when to strike. Over the years much argument has raged on this point and, as no two anglers seem to agree, I venture to suggest the following. On stillwater, trout generally take a fly on the surface in a much more leisurely fashion than on a river and, consequently, the fisherman would be well advised to hesitate for a second or so before striking. The larger the artificial being fished, the longer the hesitation. Alternatively, if one's eyesight is good it is an excellent plan to watch the cast or line a few feet from the artificial or rod tip and strike when you see a positive draw. This delayed strike is one of the most difficult features for a river angler—who is used to an instantaneous strike on fast water—to master. There is good reason for the longer hesitation on stillwater compared to running water, for on the latter the insect is very quickly removed out of reach by the current, and so the trout must act quickly; whereas, in contrast, the stillwater trout is well aware that its prey will probably await its pleasure, and that therefore it can take its time.

No description of dry fly fishing would be complete without a mention of dapping, or blow line fishing as some call it. Apart from informing the reader that this can sometimes be a very thrilling form of fishing, demanding the use of a very long light rod in conjunction with a live insect and a floss silk line, I feel I can do little better than make reference to that excellent book *Loch Trout*, by Col. H. A. Oatts, where a whole chapter is devoted to this particular style of fishing.

The Wet Fly

While some anglers prefer to. use a dry fly on a lake whenever possible, most are confirmed wet fly fishers and in many cases rarely consider even using a dry pattern; this is, of course, a pity, as the successful fisherman should be prepared to alter his method of angling at a moment's notice according to conditions. As the dry fly is usually restricted to periods when trout are rising, it will be appreciated that its use is far more limited than the wet fly, which can virtually be fished at all times under all conditions and, furthermore, it can be fished at varying depths, just under the surface, midwater or along the bottom. For this reason, and also because it embraces not only general wet flies but also nymphs, lures and various other patterns, its scope is exceedingly wide. From the above it will be quite apparent that the claim for wet fly fishing as the most efficient method of killing trout in stillwater is not without considerable justification. This form of fishing may be practised equally well from a boat or from the bank, although, as previously stated, the boat fisher is very much more limited with his style of presentation and corresponding range of patterns that can be successfully used. In most cases the boat angler favours the use of a floating fly line with his wet flies, while the bank fisher sometimes prefers a high density fast sinking or slow sinking line, although I myself favour a floater on most occasions. When fishing from a boat in rough conditions the wet fly angler, due to his flies fishing in or near the surface because of the inevitable fast drift, will probably find himself limited to the use of mainly general patterns. On the other hand, on calm, windless days, he has almost as much scope as the bank angler, and many methods may be used. Another alternative is to anchor the boat, when, in theory at least, it should be possible to emulate the style of the bank angler. In practice, however, this does not seem to work out, and personally I never feel I have the same control or fish so well using the bank technique from a boat.

The bank angler has far greater scope both in respect of methods of fishing and varieties of artificials he can use, though many of these artificials are tied as imitations to represent specific insects and must be fished in a certain way. The methods of fishing standard or fancy patterns also varies greatly. With nearly all stillwater imitations animation is of utmost importance, and this can only be imparted by the way they are fished, although it must be pointed out that the type and quality of materials from which they are tied can assist in this respect. This fact has no doubt led to the present popularity of hair or fur-dressed patterns, as these have more built-in life than tinsel or feather. Some anglers rely on the surface ripple to impart animation to their flies when being retrieved, but others accomplish this either by movement of the rod tip or by variation in speed of retrieve. Other factors also play a part, such as the depth at which your flies are fished or whether you retrieve in a series of small jerks or alternative long and short pulls, or by sink and draw, which is a very effective method. Whichever way is adopted, some anglers seem able to impart a little extra something to the flies which will produce a trout where others fail. In practice the above methods should be regulated according to the specific pattern being fished, but if a general pattern is being used, each of the methods may be tried over a period, devoting sufficient time to each until success is achieved. When the taking method has been discovered the angler should persevere with it until such time as conditions have obviously changed or a period has elapsed with no results.

As mentioned above, the depth at which one fishes can also be of importance, and the following system can be adopted. Cast out your line and allow your flies to sink while slowly counting to, say, five, then slowly retrieve and examine your flies carefully for particles of debris or weed, which should confirm, if present, that maximum fishing depth has been reached. If your flies are clean, repeat, but increase your count by two, and keep on increasing till bottom is located; alternatively, if the bed of the lake is weedy, constant plucks on the line as you retrieve will tell you that your flies are as near bottom as it is possible to fish. Once bottom has been located by this counting method it is a simple matter to predetermine the depth at which you fish your flies by the number to which you count before the retrieve is commenced. By this same counting method it is also possible to ascertain and maintain the fishing depth at which the trout are found to be feeding.

When fishing the dry fly it is seldom necessary to fish more than one artificial on the leader, but when fishing wet it is often desirable to use two or three patterns. Some waters do have restrictions in this respect, and insist on a one-fly-only rule, which in this case must be observed. On the other hand, on many of the Scottish lochs it is sometimes the practice when boat fishing to use four or even more artificials. When fishing with more than one general wet pattern most authorities on the subject insist that these should be attached to the leader in a predetermined position. In a few cases many experts are in agreement over the position of certain patterns, and good examples of these are the Peter Ross on the point, and the Mallard and Claret on the top dropper. In most cases the experts are far from unanimous, and for this reason it would be of little value to pursue this subject further. The distance between flies on the leader is also another controversial point, and is best left to the discretion of the individual angler, although this aspect, in addition to length of leader, is dealt with later in the book in relation to specific artificials.

The wet fly fisher should be on the alert for a take at all times, and for this a high degree of concentration should be maintained, particularly when bank fishing. Unlike fishing the dry fly where the take on the surface is obvious, the take of the wet fly underwater is usually impossible to observe. In some cases the take is quite savage and the trout will literally hook itself with little or no assistance from the angler, but at other times the take can be so gentle that only the experienced angler will know that a trout has, in fact, accepted his fly. In the latter case the only indication is a slight drawing of the line, and this is rarely felt. Probably the best answer to gentle takes such as this is to watch the fly line on the surface of the water, and to strike immediately any check or movement is noticed. In conditions where the light is not good it is advisable to watch the loop of line hanging down from the rod tip to the water.

One little hint which cannot be emphasized too strongly is, never to hold your rod pointing directly along and parallel with your fly line. How often the stillwater trout fisherman is heard to state, "and I was broken on the take by a huge trout", and in nine cases out of ten it is due to the above fault; and furthermore, if the truth were to be known, it was probably only an average sized trout anyway. When the rod and line are in one straight continuity, a trout may break the cast with little effort, and I have indeed observed personally a leader with a 12 lb. point broken with ease because of it by a trout of about 3 lb. This is largely an oversight of the bank angler, as when retrieving, seated in a boat, the angler's rod tip is pointing slightly upwards automatically. It is surprising how many fly-fishermen are in fact guilty of this fault, including many experienced reservoir fishermen. It is no uncommon sight to see a whole line of bank anglers fishing in this way. The answer is quite simple. When retrieving, always stand at a slight angle to the direction in which you have cast, so that your rod forms a slight angle to the line. This will allow the natural flex of the rod to absorb the initial shock from a fast moving trout should it take your fly. Alternatively, you may prefer to hold your rod upwards at an angle but, while this is equally effective, many anglers prefer the former method, where the tip of the rod may be held within an inch or so of the water surface. With the latter method the tip of the rod is high in the air, with a resulting belly of line which is subject to every vagary of the wind; apart from this, it is equally important to avoid too much slack line.

Lure Fishing

Today this style of fishing has become very popular on many of our stillwaters, and it is no uncommon sight to see a whole line of bank fishermen so engaged. Depending on the depth of water and presumed location of the trout, either a floating, slow sinking or sinking line may be used. It is usual to fish only one fly or lure on the point. This method of fishing is regarded by many fly-fishermen as tantamount to spinning, and while I am personally inclined to agree that its use can be abused, I feel it can be justified when fishing a lure that is meant to represent fry or sticklebacks on which trout are obviously feeding. To fish such a lure correctly requires considerable art and experience.

Unfortunately, such lures, even when fished incorrectly, prove to be attractive to some trout by virtue of their size and the speed at which they are usually retrieved. This fact undoubtedly accounts for their popularity among some anglers and it is a fact that, providing persistence is maintained, it usually results in a fairly high quota of takes. This applies particularly after restocking before the trout have become educated, and even more so on a new reservoir for the first season or so. Generally speaking the older and more established, or harder fished a water, the less effective lure fishing becomes. In any case it is a very monotonous method of fishing and unless used selectively requires little imagination or technique.

Many of the lures in use today come under the heading of Bucktail or Streamer flies and are not really tied to represent any particular living aquatic creature. Some of them have double or even treble hooks tied in tandem and are really fearsome looking creations. When one considers that some anglers fish three or more of these lures on the same leader, either from the bank or from a boat, it will be realized why in certain circles this style of fishing is frowned upon. Personally, I derive too much pleasure from the pursuit of natural representation of flies, on which the fish may be feeding, even to consider this style, and I am inclined to believe that trout take this type of lure only either out of irritation or because of the primeval or predatory urge to pursue a creature endeavouring to escape. The technique of fishing these lures is a combination of distance casting and physical endurance, hardly the proposition for the thoughtful angler.

However, this method should not be condemned out of hand purely on these grounds, as we are all entitled to enjoy our selected style of fishing. What is objected to is the fact that a method based largely on physical prowess and little else lacks interest and is capable of little development and, consequently, kills the desire in many anglers to pursue the imitative style of fishing where there is so much to be learned and so much to enjoy.

By the Waterside

Many of us have an enquiring mind and are keen to improve our catches, and although there are many ways in which this can be achieved, one of the more important and certainly one of the most interesting is to undertake a study of the insects on which trout feed.

Undoubtedly, the quickest way to further one's knowledge in this direction, provided the angler has the basic will to learn, is to make a habit of regularly collecting a few specimens at the waterside on every outing, and then take them home for study and identification at leisure. Within a comparatively short time it will be found that you will be able to recognize the more common species at the waterside as you encounter them. Once an angler has learnt to identify most of the more prolific species of insects, and to match the corresponding artificial to the natural, his chances of success must obviously be increased.

The collection of the natural insects need take little of the angler's time, and in any case it will often provide him with an added interest during those dour periods that are often encountered. The only equipment that the budding collector needs is a small, fine mesh net for capturing specimens either in the water or on the wing. This can be purchased at any aquarist shop and can quite easily be adapted to screw into a landing-net handle. A watertight screw-top jar for retaining aquatic species of insects and a second screw-top container for adult winged specimens. For these latter insects the inside of the jar should be lined with blotting paper to absorb moisture which would otherwise damage these relatively delicate winged flies. As it is difficult to retain more than three or four specimens in an open-top jar at a time, due to the fact that the original captures tend to escape as fresh specimens are introduced, I have adapted a very simple item to solve this problem. Purchase a small-size plastic paraffin funnel from an ironmongers, cut off the long spout at the base of the funnel and trim off the top section until it is a press fit into the top of the jar. Your collecting jar will then operate as a minnow trap. The insects can be tapped into the container, but it is virtually impossible for them to escape (see photograph opp. p. 182).

One other aspect that is closely allied to the collection of live specimens and also of considerable value, particularly to the stillwater trout fisherman, is the spooning out of captured trout to study their stomach content. This, of course, is done in an effort to discover on what particular species of insects the trout are feeding at the time, and can be of considerable importance in deciding the choice of pattern to be fished. Of course, in some cases the stomach content will be nil, but it takes so little time to spoon a trout that nothing is really lost by so doing. From the dry fly fisherman's point of view it is, of course, rarely necessary to carry out this operation, as in most cases the insect on which the trout is feeding can be observed on the water. On lakes or reservoirs, however, where various forms of underwater life are often the order of the day, it can often mean the difference between a good bag of fish or an indifferent one and, therefore, the first fish caught should always be spooned out even if subsequent fish are not.

It is possible to purchase a proper marrow scoop, although they are not always easy to locate. Alternatively, it is fairly simple to make one or, temporarily, a long-handled teaspoon with the sides of the spoon trimmed can be used. The spoon or scoop is pushed down the trout's gullet as far as it will go, and is then twisted from side to side or completely turned over and then withdrawn. The contents of the scoop should then be emptied into a shallow container of water for examination. In many cases it will be found that much of the stomach content is digested beyond recognition, but insects that the trout have most recently fed on will usually be recognizable, and these, of course, are of prime importance and the specimens to which the artificials should be matched. Fuller details on collecting and also photography are given in the appropriate chapter later in the book.

Conclusions

As it is not always easy to pick out the more important points from a mass of other information, I am listing them below in the hope that they will provide a quick reference of do's and don'ts for the newcomer to stillwater fishing.

1. Choose one's fishing location carefully, taking advantage of any natural holding areas.

2. When fishing from a boat avoid noise and excessive movement.

3. Do not stand up to cast from a boat, unless absolutely necessary.

4. Avoid unnecessary false casting.

5. Never wade unless you have to, but if you have to, wade carefully and quietly.

6. Always take advantage of background or cover, where possible, when bank fishing.

7. A cross-wind is usually most favourable for the bank fisher.

8. Use floatant sparsely on flies and leaders when necessary.

9. Do not strike too quickly when fishing the dry fly.

10. When wet fly fishing watch the line on the water or at the rod tip for indication of a take.

11. Never point your rod directly along your line when retrieving your fly.

12. Periodically check your hook for damage and *always* after losing a fish.

On waters where the trout are difficult to catch but free rising it is often good practice to bide one's time and only cast to individual rising fish rather than to fish the water. For this style of fishing concealment is of utmost importance and it is essential to use a light rod and line with a fine cast and point in conjunction with a single fly. This also applies on all waters when trout are rising and feeding in a flat calm. Under these conditions at certain times of the year trout become preoccupied feeding on *Caenis*, smuts or exceedingly small midge pupae and are often notoriously difficult to tempt. It seems the best chances of success are assured by using the above mentioned method combined with a general pattern such as a Hare's Ear, or specialized patterns like my own Last Hope or Small Hatching Midge tied on the smallest of hooks. It should also be mentioned with this style of fishing correct presentation and very accurate casting are essential.

CHAPTER IV

THE FOUR MAJOR GROUPS OF INSECTS

CLASSIFICATION

The entomological Orders of Ephemeroptera, Diptera, Trichoptera and Plecoptera include many of the insects which are of importance to the fly-fisherman, and for simplicity these Orders can be described as Upwinged flies, Flat-winged flies, flies with Roof-shaped wings, and Hard-winged flies. The latter are of less importance to the stillwater fisherman than the previous three.

The first step in the identification of any given fly is to establish to which of the following groups the specimen belongs:

1. The Upwinged flies (Ephemeroptera)

All flies in this Order have a segmented body, two or three long tails and two large upright transparent or opaque wings. Almost all have two small hindwings.

2. The Flat-winged flies (Diptera)

The flies in this Order have two rather short transparent wings which lie flat along the top of the body. They have no tails and in general appearance, though not always in size, are somewhat similar in many cases to the common house-fly.

3. Flies with Roof-shaped wings (Trichoptera)

These flies have four wings, and when at rest the wings lie close along the body in an inverted V-shape. The wings appear to be soft, as they are covered completely in very tiny hairs. They are without tails.

4. The Hard-winged flies (Plecoptera)

The wings, of which there are four, are long and rather narrow when the fly is at rest and lie flat along and slightly over the body, (although in some species they are rolled around the body) they are

31

hard and shiny or horny. Some of the larger species have tails. The wings of the male of many of these larger species are often very short and useless for flight.

A simplified explanation of the life cycle of flies in these Orders may be of value and I have therefore decided to include this, as I feel in any case that it should be of considerable interest.

THE UPWINGED FLIES (*EPHEMEROPTERA*)

Flies in this Order are known as the Upwinged flies. To coin a phrase in popular use, when a hatch of these is discussed "they look like a fleet of elfin yachts as they breast the ripples, drifting along with the wind".

The Egg

The egg stage is the first in the life cycle of flies of this Order. Eggs of most species are deposited by the adult female on the surface of the water, when they sink to the bottom and attach themselves naturally to weeds, stones, etc., although some species, such as certain of the Baëtis Genus found on some rivers, crawl down projecting weeds, stones, posts, etc., and deposit the eggs directly. The egg stage of development lasts anything from a matter of days to many months, according to species and time of year.

The Nymph

The nymphal stage is the second in the cycle, following the hatching out of the egg. This period may last from two to twelve months or even longer, according to species and the time of year the egg was laid. During this stage the nymph lives on or near the bottom. Some species hide in or on various weeds, others cling to stones and rocks, while certain other species actually burrow in the lake bed.

As the nymph develops and grows larger, it casts its skin at intervals, as this becomes too small. The growing nymph feeds mainly on decaying vegetable matter.

The Sub-imago or Dun

When the nymph is fully grown it is at last ready to change into the winged insect known as the sub-imago, or dun. This emergence takes place fairly rapidly. The mature nymph ascends to the surface, where the nymphal case splits and the fully winged fly emerges on to the surface film, resting on this film while its wings dry and it gathers strength to fly off.

On hot, dry days or in windy conditions, this emergence is very rapid, as the wings dry very quickly and the insect flies off almost at once. The dun is slower to take wing on wet, damp, cold days or when there is a heavy surface film. Certain species seem able to become airborne much faster than others. The dun stage usually lasts between twelve and thirty-six hours, much less in the case of flies belonging to the family Caenidae, where the transpositions from nymph to dun and dun to spinner may both take place in a matter of minutes.

The Imago or Spinner

The final stage in the life cycle of flies of this Order is after the change from the rather dull-looking dun to the beauty and perfection of the imago or spinner. It is during this final stage of its life, which may last only a matter of hours, that the fly engages in the procreative processes before it dies. The spinner can easily be distinguished from the dun as the latter is rather drab or dun-coloured, as its name implies. The wings are dull and opaque, and the trailing edges are usually lined with very fine hairs which can be clearly seen under a low-power magnifying glass. On the other hand, the spinner's body is very bright and shiny, with transparent shiny wings, now devoid of the fine hairs (except Caenis) along the trailing edges; the tails and forelegs are also considerably longer.

The final stage of transposition from dun to spinner is accomplished fairly quickly in much the same way as the earlier stage from nymph to dun. This usually takes place in the bank herbage, anything from a few hours to a day or two after the appearance of the winged dun. The change from dun to spinner can actually be observed, with patience. If a dun can be successfully taken home alive, it should be deposited in a cool place, or better still kept overnight in an ice box or refrigerator, which usually results in slowing or halting the metamorphosis. On the following morning, place the fly in a warm spot in direct sunlight, if possible, and within a fairly short time, if you are fortunate, the final transformation can be observed.

Duns at rest hold their wings upright and together, and usually the first indication of the forthcoming transformation is when the wings open out until they are spread wide apart. The dun sometimes spends several minutes in this position, quivering slightly from time to time, before the wings finally appear to fold slowly along the body. It is at this stage that the skin splits along the top of the thorax, and the fully adult fly or spinner emerges.

The cast-off skin retains the shape of the original insect, with the exception of the wings, which are too frail.

The fly now, as a spinner, is able to mate, and copulation usually takes place in flight. After this act, the spent male dies over land, but in some cases dies over and falls on to the water. The female, after extruding and depositing her eggs, usually dies in or on the water.

Finally, it should be explained that all flies in this Order have either two or three long tails, a segmented body, six legs and upright wings. Most of them have two large forewings and two smaller hindwings. In some cases the latter can be clearly seen, as in the Mayfly or Blue Winged Olive, but in other species, such as the Small Spurwing, they are so small that a magnifying glass is required to detect them. In a few species the hindwings are absent altogether.

THE FLAT-WINGED FLIES (*Diptera*)

This is an extremely large Order of insects, which includes all the true flies, such as House-flies, Mosquitoes, Dung-flies, Crane-flies, etc., and is considerably larger than all the other three Orders put together.

Of the flies in this Order that are of interest to anglers, the majority are aquatic. They can be divided into three main sections: Crane-flies, terrestrial flies and Midges. The latter, it should be mentioned, are by far the most important Family to the stillwater fisherman.

Crane-flies

The adult flies, often referred to as Daddy-long-legs are very common at times on many of our stillwaters. Many species are terrestrial and are of little interest to anglers. A few pass their larval stage in damp ground adjacent to water, while others, aquatic by nature, spend both their larval and pupal stages in the water. They vary greatly in size, some species having bodies well over an inch long.

Midges and terrestrial flies

Most of the flies in these two sections are smaller than the larger Crane-flies of the previous one. The eggs of the Midges are usually laid by the adult females on the water surface, in small or large clusters, forming rafts or beads of eggs which become attached to weed or other projections.

The small larva which at length emerges swims to the lake bed, where it lives in the mud or silt. Eventually the larva transforms into a pupa which is of the free-swimming variety, similar to the last instar nymphs of the Olives. When the adult fly is ready to emerge the pupa ascends to the surface, where it remains suspended for some little time in the surface film (depending on weather and water temperature). The winged insect then emerges and flies away.

All flies in this section are fully adult immediately after emerging from their pupal case, and pass only through the one-winged stage before they mate and die. It should be noted that Black Gnats, Hawthorn-flies, etc., are terrestrial, and are only of interest when blown onto the lake surface.

All flies in the Diptera Order are tailless, and have two short, flat transparent wings similar to the common House-fly, which belongs to this same Order.

FLIES WITH ROOF-SHAPED WINGS (*TRICHOPTERA*)

The Caddis or Sedge-flies

This again is a fairly large Order of flies, about 190 different species having been recorded in these islands. Many of these are of little interest to the angler; some are very small, while others are very uncommon or locally distributed.

However, the species of Sedge-flies that are common are important indeed to anglers. They have roof-shaped wings, four in number, which are covered with a layer of tiny fine hairs. These are sometimes difficult to see with the naked eye but show up clearly with a magnifying glass. Superficially, they are similar to moths, but these latter have a covering of tiny scales on their wings instead of hairs. Also Sedges, when at rest, are considerably slimmer, particularly across the thorax.

Many Sedge-flies have particularly long antennae, in some cases over twice the length of their bcdies. The mouthparts include two pairs of jointed protuberances called palps, which are set one behind the other. The front ones, the "maxillary palps", sometimes vary between male and female, and in a few families the male palps consist of three to four segments and the female's of five segments. In most families, however, both male and female palps consist of five segments.

The female Sedge-fly lays her eggs in one of three ways according to the species:

(*a*) On the water surface.
(*b*) By crawling under water and depositing the eggs.
(*c*) On herbage or vegetation overhanging the water.

The several hundred eggs are often laid in one gelatinous mass which adheres to any vegetation or underwater obstruction with which it comes in contact.

There are four well-marked stages in the life of the Sedge-fly: egg, larva, pupa, and the adult winged fly.

The Eggs

These begin to hatch into larvae after ten to twenty days and most species construct cases to protect their relatively soft bodies.

The Caddis Larvae

These are a familiar sight to most anglers, as practically every clump of weed pulled from the lake bed will have its attendant host of Caddis cases in various shapes and sizes. In days gone by these used to be a popular bait with bottom fishermen, and even today are still much used in Ireland. The larvae form their tubular cases (see Plate 5, No. 55) from all manner of debris from the bed of the river or lake, including particles of gravel, shells, bits of leaf, decaying vegetation and even small sticks. In fast flowing water the larvae usually choose heavy materials such as small stones, gravel, etc., to help prevent them being swept away by the current. On the other hand, the species found in stillwater tend to use semi-buoyant materials which facilitate movement.

The majority of flies in this Order form cases as described, but a few free-swimming species form shelters on the undersides of stones or plants. After the larva is fully developed, it pupates within its case or shelter, and after a period varying from days to weeks, according to species and the time of year, during which it does not eat, the pupa emerges. At this stage it is still enclosed in its pupal envelope and is equipped with a pair of powerful paddle-like legs which enable it to swim to the surface, or to climb up plant or weed stems above water where it hatches out into the fully adult fly. In some species the pupa swims directly to the surface, where it immediately hatches out. Large Cinnamon Sedges are typical of this latter group, and many anglers will be familiar with the disturbance they cause as they hatch on the surface and skitter about in a frantic effort to become airborne.

Sedge-flies in the winged state, perhaps because they are able to absorb liquid, live for a much longer period than flies of the Ephemeroptera group.

Finally, it should be noted that most of these flies mate while at rest, and therefore it is usually the female of the species that is sometimes taken by the trout when she returns to lay her eggs.

THE HARD-WINGED FLIES (*PLECOPTERA*)

Commonly called Stoneflies, this is a small Order of flies consisting in Britain of a little over thirty different species. Nevertheless, where they occur in abundance, they may be important to anglers. This is mainly in the North Country lakes that have gravelly or stony beds. They are, of course, found in some of our southern lakes but seldom in sufficient quantities to be of interest to anglers.

The flies in this group vary considerably in size, from the large Stonefly, which is well over an inch long, to the small Needle-fly, the smallest British fly in the Order. They all have four wings and when at rest the wings are long and narrow and lie close to the body. These wings are hard and shiny, prominently veined and considerably longer than the body of the fly, except in some males as mentioned earlier. They are poor fliers and in flight appear considerably larger than they really are. The adult fly is like its nymph counterpart, active on its feet.

The life span of the insects in this Order varies considerably, the average being about a year, but in some cases lasting as long as two to three years.

The Egg

The time taken for the eggs to hatch out, again, varies from a few days to many weeks. The nymphs of Stoneflies are very robust and active creatures. Many anglers will be familiar with some of the larger nymphs in this group, which are popularly known as creepers, and in some circles are much in demand as bait for bottom fishing.

These nymphs can easily be distinguished from the nymphs of the Ephemeroptera as they have only two tails, and the two antennae on the head are quite long. In the latter stage of the life of these nymphs the wing cases are quite prominent. When the adult winged fly is ready to emerge from its nymphal case, the mature nymph crawls on to dry land, where metamorphosis takes place. The life of the Stoneflies in the winged state can be anything from a few days to a few weeks, according to species, and they never wander very far from water, and mate at rest.

In many of the larger flies in this Order, the wings of the male are little better than stumps, and these insects are quite incapable of flight. Also, species found at high altitudes often have shorter wings than those in lowland areas.

The females return to the water to lay their eggs, and the method of doing so varies a little according to the species. So far as can be ascertained, however, they all lay their eggs actually on the surface. With some of the larger species, they will alight on the water and release the eggs while swimming or fluttering along. In doing so they create quite a disturbance, and make an attractive target for any hungry trout in the vicinity.

Other species fly out over the water and literally fall down on the surface, releasing all their eggs in one mass, while some dip up and down on the water in a similar manner to some of the Upwing spinners, depositing a few eggs at a time. The eggs, when released by the female on the surface, sink to the bottom, where they attach themselves to stones, rocks, etc.

The Classes or Orders of interest to fly-fishermen are as follows. They are listed according to importance.

Diptera	Midges, Gnats, etc.
Trichoptera	Sedge-flies
Ephemeroptera	Upwinged flies.
Plecoptera	Stoneflies.
Crustacea	Shrimps, Water-louse, etc.
Hemiptera	Water-bugs, Corixids, etc.
Coleoptera	Beetles.
Megaloptera	Alder-flies.
Lepidoptera	Moths, etc.
Hymenoptera	Wasps, Ants, etc.
Odonata	Dragonflies and Damselflies.
Arachnida	Spiders.
Neuroptera	Lacewings, etc.
Orthoptera	Grasshoppers.

All the above, with the exception of Crustacea and Arachnida, belong to the Class Insecta.

For the fly-fisher intending to make a superficial study of entomology, it is important to note that all insects are divided into Orders, which in turn are divided into Families, and then into Genera, and finally into the Species. The following table shows how two different Orders of insects are classified.

	MAYFLY	BLACK GNAT
CLASS	*INSECTA*	*INSECTA*
ORDER	*EPHEMEROPTERA*	*DIPTERA*
FAMILY	*EPHEMERIDAE*	*BIBIONIDAE*
GENUS	*EPHEMERA*	*BIBIO*
SPECIES	*DANICA*	*JOHANNIS*

CHAPTER V

THE UPWINGED FLIES (EPHEMEROPTERA)

IDENTIFICATION

In the opening stages of Chapter IV, the life cycle of this Order has been dealt with fairly concisely, and it is not felt necessary to elaborate too deeply for fear of confusing the reader. However, there are many other features and facts about this interesting and fascinating group of flies which, if explained in a straightforward and simple manner, can be of considerable interest to the angler. It is therefore proposed to deal with them step by step as we go along.

It should first be explained that although the winged flies in this group are important from the fisherman's point of view, they are not necessarily of so much importance from the trout's point of view, as they may not form a substantial part of its diet. Trout feed on a great variety of food: Snails, Shrimps, Crayfish, Caddis and the larvae of other aquatic insects such as Midges. In addition, trout are not averse to feeding on the smaller specimens of their own kind. Minnows, Sticklebacks and the fry of other fish also form an important part of their diet in many waters, as do the nymphs of the Ephemeroptera and Plecoptera insect Orders. On occasions, also, trout are fortunate in coming across such tit-bits as Tadpoles, Caterpillars, Beetles, Wasps, and various other land-bred creatures which find their way on to or into the water. Therefore, with this large variety of food to choose from, it is sometimes surprising that they ever bother to rise at all to small Ephemeropteran duns or spinners. It is very fortunate for the fly-fisher that trout feed regularly on these and other surface flies; they do so probably because during the summer, when these flies are most in evidence, they are easier to obtain than other wholly aquatic organisms. Another possibility, of course, is that these adult flies supply a deficiency in the trout's diet and are necessary to its well-being, for perhaps it looks upon them as either an *hors-d'oeuvre* or a dessert. In 1933 K. R. Allen carried out a survey on trout in Lake Windermere, and he states:

"The results suggest that when all classes of food are available the trout will feed on the surface rather than on the bottom, and that, if no surface food is present, they will feed on the temporary bottom fauna rather than on the permanent bottom fauna." It would seem, however, that this statement should only be accepted as a generalization, as this would depend to a large extent on conditions and also the particular species of trout concerned.

Let us now consider the physical structure or characteristics of flies in this Order:

The Head

This is often wider than its length, the major portion consisting of the eye structure; there is no mouth as such, the duns being incapable of eating or drinking. This may account for their very short life span in the final winged state. The head also has a small pair of antennae like miniature horns, which are usually plainly visible.

The Eyes

The head carries a pair of large compound eyes or oculi, one on each side, and in most cases the eyes of the male are considerably enlarged and extend over the top of the head. These have probably evolved to enable it to locate the female of the species, which usually approach the male swarms from a higher level.

The Thorax

The head is connected by a short neck (prothorax) to the thorax of the fly, which is made up of three segments. The middle segment is by far the largest and carries the forewings and the middle pair of legs. The front segment carries the forelegs and the rear segment the hindwings (if any) and rear pair of legs.

The Abdomen

This, the main body of the fly, is divided into ten distinct segments. The last segment carries the tails and the ninth segment carries the claspers of the male fly. The top of the abdomen will be referred to as the dorsum and the under surface as the venter.

The Tails

They are usually long and slender. In some species there are two and in others three. In many cases these tails are very short when the dun is freshly hatched, but they rapidly lengthen with age. In the spinner stage the tails are usually considerably longer.

The Wings

As previously explained, these are fairly large with extensive veining, and are always carried upright. Most of the flies in this group have hindwings of various sizes and shapes, but four species have no hindwings at all.

The Legs

These are six in number, the front or anterior legs being normally longer than the remaining four, which are referred to as the median and posterior legs respectively. The anterior legs of the males are usually a little longer than those of their female opposites; in the spinner stage they are often longer still. Each leg consists of five main joints; the most important of these are the femur (thigh joint), tibia (shin joint) and tarsus (foot).

So much for the physical structure of these flies, but before we proceed further let us consider from the angler's point of view the simplest way of determining the sexes. This can be achieved by two methods, the first of which concerns the eyes. In the male these are usually very prominent, and to clarify this the following sketches should be studied.

FIG. 2. Eyes of a typical female.

FIG. 3. Eyes of a typical male.

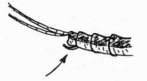

FIG. 4. Showing claspers of male fly viewed from the side.

FIG. 5. Showing close up of male claspers viewed from under.

The first sketch shows the eyes of a typical female, and the second those of the male. (See Figs. 2 and 3.)

It must be pointed out, however, that to identify the males by the eye characteristics alone is not conclusive. In certain of the larger families of flies in this Order, this difference in structure is not so apparent. Therefore, for conclusive evidence, the second method is infallible. All male flies in this Order have a pair of forceps or claspers to enable the male fly to attach itself to its chosen mate during copulation. These are situated underneath the fly just behind the tail on the ninth segment (see Figs. 4 and 5). They can usually be seen with the naked eye, but a small magnifying glass will show them quite clearly. In conclusion, it should be noted that in nearly all cases the male fly is smaller than the female of the same species.

DIFFERENCE IN SIZE AND COLOUR

It is probably not generally realized how much variation it is possible to find in the colour and size of Ephemeropteran flies of the same species. This, of course, can greatly increase the difficulties of positive identification, as we automatically tend to recognize certain flies by their general size and colour. Therefore, these variations must be kept very much in mind. Fortunately these seem to occur only occasionally, and it is possible to work to average sizes and colours in most cases with reasonably accurate results. Let us first discuss the question of colour.

Colour

As a general rule the temperature of the air is thought to affect the coloration; the colder the day, the darker the colour of the fly. To follow this temperature effect further, flies that hatch in the spring or early in the year are darker than flies of the same species that hatch during the summer. Then, when the weather begins to get colder in the autumn, the colour is again darker. Another point also to be borne in mind is that the male is usually darker than the female. Apart from the above, the colours of the same species of fly can vary in different localities. However, where a colour variation does occur, it is more a lightening or darkening of the basic colour. Little has been written on the subject of size and coloration in the past and during the preparation of this book hundreds of colour photographs have been taken and many thousands of specimens have been examined and it has been during this time that these variations have been noticed.

Having dealt briefly with colour as applicable to the duns, let us now consider colour in respect of spinners. With these the variation in colour seems to be very much greater, and is much more noticeable in certain species than in others. Whether or not air temperature plays much part in coloration in the spinners is not definitely known, but it is generally accepted that the older the spinner the darker the colour. This is particularly noticeable in the females, and they seem to darken very rapidly after copulation. Although this progressive darkening with age seems fairly constant, it does not bear any relation to the final colour of any particular spinner, as this seems to depend more on the original colour of the spinner when it changes from the dun stage. So far as I have been able to ascertain, the exact cause of this variation in colour is unknown. Dr. Michael Wade suggests that mutant factors might ensure a mixture of colours in each generation, so that against different coloured backgrounds some will be less conspicuous to predators and thus more likely to survive.

Difference in Size

Fortunately, from the point of view of identification, this variation in size seems to be the exception to the rule, and it is only the odd fly here and there that is either very considerably smaller or larger than the norm. If there is a variation it is more likely that the specimens will be smaller than normal rather than larger. It is quite common to encounter complete hatches of the various species in this Order that vary in size slightly. Once again one can only theorize on the reason for this, and in all probability it is simply a lack or an abundance of food during their early stages of life under water.

It must also be borne in mind that a small variation in size can be accounted for by a natural tendency of all living creatures to differ in this respect. To give a comparison of this as against human beings, half a millimetre difference in the length of a Pond Olive (which is quite common) would be roughly equivalent to a difference in a man's height of about eight inches. Therefore, a variation of up to one millimetre or more would not be abnormal in a fly.

MATING AND FLIGHT

Mating

Although this was dealt with superficially in Chapter II it is felt that a little more detail would be of general interest. In most cases mating takes place in the air. Once a male has located a female of the species, he approaches her from underneath, and with the aid of his forceps (claspers) he attaches himself to her. Copulation then immediately takes place, during which the female endeavours to keep both herself and her mate airborne. The pair may slowly sink towards the ground, but in most cases copulation has been effected before they actually reach it. After mating has taken place the female will usually fly out over the water in preparation for laying her eggs, and the male will return to its swarm, possibly preparatory to mating with other females. Eventually the males, when fully spent, will return inland, where they die. Few males actually fall spent on the water in any quantity.

Flight

The male spinners of the Ephemeroptera usually form themselves into swarms of varying size. Each swarm may be composed of several dozen or even several hundred individuals. Each different species seems to have its own favourite area or locality for swarming. Also, apart from the location of the individual swarms, the actual flight pattern or behaviour of flies of the different species varies. From the above it will be apparent that with experience the keen observer may eventually be able to recognize and identify some of the different species of spinners while in flight or by their location. For the angler, a little knowledge of the behaviour of these spinner swarms can be useful. Spinners are very susceptible to a change in weather conditions, especially to a drop in temperature, and indeed on cold days they are often absent. Also, if a cold wind blows up in the evening, bringing about a temperature drop, the swarms which might have formed throughout the afternoon will suddenly disappear to await a more favourable opportunity. This may not arise until the next day.

On some stillwaters the banks vary between open grassland and sheltered woodland. In inclement weather, the exposed open areas will be deserted, and the spinner swarms may then often be located in the sheltered lee of the trees and shrubs.

The following name key includes all the more common species of upwinged flies found on stillwater. Scarce or localized species have not been included for fear of confusing the reader.

DETAILED NAME KEY FOR THE EPHEMEROPTERANS OF STILLWATER

CURRENT ANGLING NAME	OLD ANGLING NAME	ENTOMOLOGISTS' NAME	POPULAR NAME FOR SPINNER
MAYFLY	Green Drake	*Ephemera danica*	Spent Gnat.
BLUE WINGED OLIVE	Blue-winged Olive	*Ephemerella ignita*	Sherry Spinner.
SMALL SPURWING	Little Sky-blue or Pale Watery	*Centroptilum luteolum*	Little Amber Spinner.
LAKE OLIVE	Lake Olive	*Cloëon simile*	Lake Olive Spinner.
LARGE SUMMER DUN	—	*Siphlonurus lacustris*	Large Summer Spinner.

CURRENT ANGLING NAME	OLD ANGLING NAME	ENTOMOLOGISTS' NAME	POPULAR NAME FOR SPINNER
POND OLIVE	Pond Olive	Cloëon dipterum	Pond Olive Spinner or Apricot spinner.
YELLOW MAY DUN	Little Yellow May dun or Yellow Hawk	Heptagenia sulphurea	Yellow May spinner.
DUSKY YELLOWSTREAK	Dark dun	Heptagenia lateralis	Dusky Yellowstreak spinner.
CLARET DUN	Claret dun	Leptophlebia vespertina	Claret spinner.
SEPIA DUN	—	Leptophlebia marginata	Sepia spinner.
AUTUMN DUN	August dun	Ecdyonurus dispar	Autumn spinner.
CAENIS OR BROADWING	Angler's Curse or White Midge	Caenis and Brachycercus spp.	Caenis spinner or Broadwing spinner.

In my previous book, *Trout Fly Recognition*, I dealt with the Upwinged flies very comprehensively, as to the river fly-fisherman they are of prime importance, and due to the fact that there are many more species inhabiting rivers I felt it was necessary to provide several keys to simplify positive identification. So far as the Upwinged species of flies that are found on stillwater are concerned, I do not feel that these keys are necessary, as there are but a dozen species that are sufficiently common to be listed.

It is interesting to note that in all of the earlier books written on lake or lock fishing only two or three separate species were recognized. R. C. Bridgett's book on loch fishing is of particular interest in this respect, as he provided more information on natural flies of stillwater than any previous author. Even so, on the Upwinged duns he only specifically mentions four types: the Medium Olive, in three different colours—light, medium and dark—and the Pale Watery dun. From his description this latter fly is without doubt the species we now know as *Caënis*. The Light Olive was probably the Small Spurwing, the Medium Olive either the Lake or Pond Olive, and the Dark Olive I should think may have been either the Claret or Sepia Dun.

Of course, the greater knowledge we now have of this subject does not necessarily make better fishermen of us, but at least it provides us with the opportunity to present an artificial that is a better imitation.

Although it is a little dangerous to rely too much on size or coloration for positive identification, as these two points can be of considerable assistance the following size references will be used, combined with a detailed description of each species.

SIZES OF UPWINGED FLIES

FIG. 6.
Group 1. Very large.

FIG. 7.
Group 2. Large.

FIG. 8.
Group 3. Medium large.

FIG. 9.
Group 4. Medium.

FIG. 10.
Group 5. Small.

It is fairly simple to identify most of the commoner species of Upwinged flies that inhabit stillwater providing the following points are borne in mind before proceeding to the detailed descriptions that follow.

The Dun

The colours are usually rather drab and the wings are often opaque or coloured. The trailing edge of each forewing is fringed with very fine hairs.

The Spinner

The colours are usually brighter or shiny. The tails are often considerably longer than in the dun, especially in the case of males. The wings are nearly always transparent and shiny, and no longer have the fine hairs along the trailing edge (except in the case of *Caenis* spinners).

These are the main points to look for when a quick identification is required:

(1) Number of tails (two or three)
(2) Number of wings (two or four)
(3) Shape of hindwings, if any
(4) Venation of wings

(5) Size
(6) Coloration

Occasionally the genitalia will need microscopic examination for positive identification, but this can be left until the angler is more proficient; it is not, however, dealt with in this book.

The reader must be on his guard against two things. First, occasionally an insect loses a tail, and consequently a three-tailed fly can look as if it possesses only two. In one species the hindwings are very small and can easily be overlooked.

FIG. 11. Showing forewing and upright hindwing with slight costal projection.

FIG. 12. Showing single intercalary veins and small narrow hindwings—with spur shaped costal projection.

FIG. 13. *C. luteolum*

FIG. 14. *E. ignita*

FIG. 15. *L. marginata.*

FIG. 16. *H. sulphurea.*

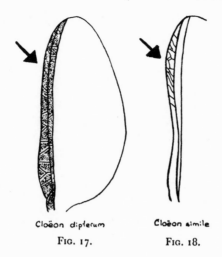

Cloëon dipterum   Cloëon simile

FIG. 17.   FIG. 18.

The above sketches depict the difference in shape between the hindwings of various species, and differences in venation on forewings between two other species.

It should be noted that *Caenis* spp., the Pond Olive and Lake Olive, have no hindwings.

Some of these features are tabulated below in a simple form which should assist to a quick identification.

SPECIES	SIZE	NO. OF TAILS	HINDWINGS	CONSTANT FEATURES
MAYFLY	Very large—Fig. 6	Three	As Fig. 11	Marks on dorsum, see Fig. 19
BLUE WINGED OLIVE	Medium large—Fig. 8	Three	As Fig. 14	
SMALL SPURWING	Medium to small—Figs. 9 or 10	Two	As Fig. 13	See Fig. 12
POND OLIVE	Medium to medium large—Figs. 8 or 9	Two	Absent	Two parallel red lines along ventral segments. ♀ Also see Fig. 17
LAKE OLIVE	Medium—Fig. 9	Two	Absent	See Fig. 18
LARGE SUMMER DUN	Large to very large—Figs. 7 or 6	Two	As Fig. 11	
YELLOW MAY DUN	Medium large—Fig. 8	Two	As Fig. 16	Yellow Wings
DUSKY YELLOWSTREAK	Medium large—Fig. 8	Two	As Fig. 11	Yellow streak each side of thorax in front of forewing root
CLARET DUN	Medium large—Fig. 8	Three	As Fig. 15	Hindwings buff-coloured

SPECIES	SIZE	NO. OF TAILS	HINDWINGS	CONSTANT FEATURES
SEPIA DUN	Medium large—Fig. 8	Three	As Fig. 15	
AUTUMN DUN	Large—Fig. 7	Two	As Fig. 11	Wings heavily veined giving a mottled appearance
CAENIS SPP.	Very small—Fig. 10	Three	Absent	Wings very broad

The following detailed descriptions of the Upwinged flies have been provided to assist in positive identification. It is emphasized that the colours given are as seen on the majority of specimens that I have myself examined. Apart from the fact that colours of these flies vary greatly, many of us describe colours as we see them in different ways, and my interpretation of these colours may not be in accordance with other authorities. Most species of Upwinged flies of interest to stillwater fishermen have been included in these descriptions. It should be noted that generally the female is larger than the male.

In the following descriptions the body of the fly is in many cases divided into two parts—the DORSUM (top) and the VENTER (underpart). Where it is not divided the coloration is overall.

In many cases the rear edge of the body (abdomen) segments are of a different colour from the rest of the body segments. For simplicity, in the detailed descriptions these lighter or darker areas round the body where particularly noticeable are referred to as "ringing" or "joinings".

The true colour of the eyes of the male duns may not be apparent when freshly hatched. It is therefore advisable to let a short period elapse before examining freshly hatched specimens.

Before proceeding with the detailed descriptions I should like to make it quite clear that, although I have included twelve species in this list of stillwater Upwinged flies, only six are common or abundant in many localities. These are as follows:

The Mayfly	*Ephemera danica*
The Pond Olive	*Cloëon dipterum*
The Lake Olive	*Clöeon simile*
The Sepia Dun	*Leptophlebia marginata*
The Claret Dun	*Leptophlebia vespertina*
Angler's Curse	*Caenis spp.*

The remaining six species are probably more localized, but as they are often abundant in areas where they occur I felt it prudent to include them.

There are also a few other comparatively scarce species and these are given a brief mention in the next chapter.

Ephemera danica (THREE-TAILS)

DUN

Mayfly, male

EYES: Very dark brown.
WINGS: Heavily veined brown on a grey (tinged yellow) ground, with dark markings.
BODY: Dorsum—greyish white with brown blotches.
Venter—greyish white with constant brown marks.
LEGS: Dark brown.
TAILS: Dark grey to black.
SIZE: Very large.

Mayfly, female
(Plate 13, No. 138)

EYES: Black-brown.
WINGS: Grey tinged blue-green with dark markings. Heavily veined blackish. Yellow tinged along leading edge.
BODY: Dorsum—yellowish cream with constant brown marks.
Venter—slightly paler with brown markings.
LEGS: Creamy olive with black tinges.
TAILS: Very dark grey to black.
SIZE: Very large.
Remarks: The thorax is a distinct pale orange colour, and they have large upright hindwings with a costal projection. (as Fig. 11)

SPINNER

Spent Gnat, male
(Plate 13, No. 139)

EYES: Black-brown.
WINGS: Transparent with brownish tint. Heavily veined brown with several almost black patches.
BODY: Dorsum—creamy white, last three segments brownish.
Venter—Cream with brown marks and grey ringing, last three segments brown.
LEGS: Forelegs black-brown, remainder dark olive brown.
TAILS: Dark brown.
SIZE: Very large.

Spent Gnat,   EYES: Black-brown.
    female   WINGS: Transparent but with a bluish tint. Veined brown
                            with several almost black patches.
          BODY: Dorsum—pale cream. Three tail segments with
                            brown streaks.
                            Venter—cream with brown markings.
          LEGS: Dark olive-brown.
          TAILS: Dark brown.
          SIZE: Very large.
          Remarks: The thorax of these spinners is sooty-black, and
          the forelegs are very long.

Ephemerella ignita (THREE-TAILS)

DUN

Blue Winged Olive, EYES: Red.
     male   WINGS: Dark blue-grey.
                  BODY: Orange-brown, varies to an almost olive-
                        brown in some specimens, last segment
                        yellowish.
                  LEGS: Brown-olive. Feet dark grey.
                  TAILS: Dark grey, ringed brownish.
                  SIZE: Medium-large.
                  Remarks: A most distinctive fly. Brownish body
                      with three tails and dark blue-grey wings.
                      Once correctly identified, not likely to be con-
                      fused with any other fly.

Blue Winged Olive, EYES: Dark greenish-black.
    female   WINGS: Dark blue-grey.
 (Plate 2, No. 11)   BODY: Early in June the body is a bright green-
                        olive, but through the season it darkens
                        to a dull grey-olive and late in the year
                        to a rusty brown-olive.
                  LEGS: Dark olive. Feet grey.
                  TAILS: Pale grey-brown, ringed dark brown.
                  SIZE: Medium-large.
                  Remarks: Both dun and spinner have upright
                      hindwings with costal projection. (Fig. 14).
                      The forewings are also large for the size of the
                      fly and are backward raked.

ILLUSTRATIONS
IN
COLOUR

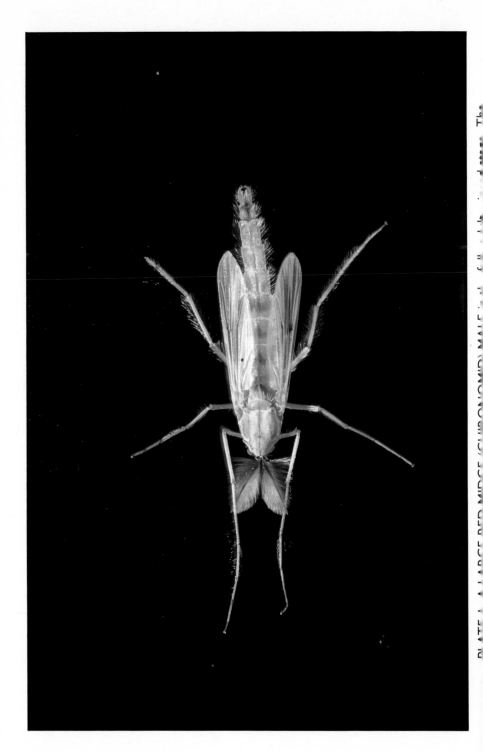

2. LAKE OLIVE-FEMALE
    Cloëon simile

3. SEPIA DUN-FEMALE
    Leptophlebia marginata

4. POND OLIVE-FEMALE
    Cloëon dipterum

5. LAKE OLIVE-MALE
    Cloëon simile

6. SEPIA DUN-MALE
    Leptophlebia marginata

7. POND OLIVE-MALE
    Cloëon dipterum

8. CLARET DUN-FEMALE
    Leptophlebia vespertina

9. SMALL SPURWING-MALE
    Centroptilum luteolum

10. AUTUMN DUN-MALE
    Ecdyonurus dispar

11. BLUE WINGED OLIVE DUN
    FEMALE   *Ephemerella ignita*

12. DUSKY YELLOWSTREAK
    SPINNER-FEMALE
    Heptagenia lateralis

13. YELLOW MAY SPINNER MALE
    Heptagenia sulphurea

14. BROADWING SPINNER
    Caeniś Spp.

15. POND OLIVE NYMPH
    Cloëon dipterum

16. B.W.O. NYMPH-MALE
    E. ignita —
    x 1·6

PLATE 2. DUNS AND SPINNERS × 1

17. LAKE OLIVE SPINNER FEMALE
Cloëon simile

18. SEPIA SPINNER FEMALE
Leptophlebia marginata

19. APRICOT SPINNER FEMALE
Cloëon dipterum

20. LAKE OLIVE SPINNER MALE
Cloëon simile

21. SEPIA SPINNER MALE
Leptophlebia marginata

22. POND OLIVE SPINNER MALE
Cloëon dipterum

23. CLARET SPINNER FEMALE
Leptophlebia vespertina

24. SHERRY SPINNER FEMALE
Ephemerella ignita

25. AUTUMN SPINNER FEMALE
Ecdyonurus dispar

26. CLARET SPINNER MALE
Leptophlebia vespertina

27. LITTLE AMBER SPINNER
FEMALE
Centroptilum luteolum

28. YELLOW MAY DUN FEMALE
Heptagenia sulphurea

29. SEPIA NYMPH
Leptophlebia marginata

30. MAYFLY NYMPH
Ephemera danica

31. HEPTAGENIA SPP. NYMPH

PLATE 3. SPINNERS AND NYMPHS, ETC. × 1

32. LARGE GREEN MIDGE MALE
Chironomus plumosus

33. ORANGE-SILVER MIDGE
FEMALE   *C. plumosus*

34. GOLDEN DUN MIDGE
FEMALE   *C. plumosus*

35. LARGE RED MIDGE FEMALE
C. plumosus

36. ORANGE-SILVER MIDGE
MALE   *C. plumosus*

37. GOLDEN DUN MIDGE MALE
C. plumosus

38. RIBBED MIDGE FEMALE
C. plumosus

39. BLACK MIDGE MALE
C. anthracinus

40. SMALL RED MIDGE FEMALE
Microtendipes pedellus

41. RIBBED MIDGE MALE
C. plumosus

42. BLAGDON GREEN MIDGE
MALE
Endichironomus albipennis

43. SMALL RED MIDGE MALE
Microtendipes pedellus

44. SMALL BROWN MIDGE
FEMALE
Glyptotendipes paripes

45. SMALL BLACK MIDGE MALE
Polypedilum nebucolosus

46. ANATOPYNIA
Psectrotanypus varia

PLATE 4. CHIRONOMIDAE (MIDGES) ADULTS × I

47.   EMPTY PUPAL CASE
      OF MIDGE

48.   PUPA OF RED MIDGE

49.   MIDGE LARVA
      (BLOODWORM)

50.   PUPA OF ORANGE-
      SILVER MIDGE

51.   PUPA OF GOLDEN DUN
      MIDGE

52.   MIDGE PUPA VARIOUS

53.   EMPTY PUPAL CASE
      OF SEDGE-FLY

54.   MIDGE PUPA VARIOUS
      Specimen on left in early
      stage of ecdysis

55.   CADDIS OR SEDGE LARVA
      Phrygania grandis

56.   BROADWING NYMPHS
      Caenis moesta
      Top specimen is camouflaged
      with specks of lime

57.   LARGE RED WATER MITE

58.   ALDER LARVA
      Sialus lutaria

59.   DRAGON FLY NYMPH
      Aeshna spp.

60.   PUPA OF PHANTOM FLY
      Chaoborus flavicans

61.   PHANTOM MALE ADULT
      FROM UNDERWATER

PLATE 5. CHIRONOMID (MIDGE) PUPAE, ETC. × 1

62. GREAT RED SEDGE ×¾.
Phrygania grandis female

63. HATCHING SEDGE
STILL PARTLY TRAPPED
IN PUPAL CASE

64. GREAT RED SEDGE IN FLIGHT
×¾

65. THE CAPERER
Halesus radiatus

66. LARGE CINNAMON SEDGE
Potomophylax latipennis

67. MOTTLED SEDGE
Glyphotaelius pellucidus

68. BROWN SEDGE
Anabolia nervosa

69. CINNAMON SEDGE
Limnephilus lunatus

70. WELSHMAN'S BUTTON
Sericostoma personatum

71. BLACK SEDGE
Silo nigricornis

72. SMALL SILVER SEDGE
Lepidostoma hirtum

73. BROWN SILVERHORNS
Athripsodes cinereus

74. BLACK SILVERHORNS
Mystacides azurea

75. GROUSE WING
Mystacides longicornis

76. THE LONGHORNS
Oecetis lacustris

PLATE 6. SEDGE-FLIES × I

77. THE OAK FLY

78. LARGE STONEFLY NYMPH
MALE *Perlodes microcephala* x ¾

79. LARGE STONEFLY FEMALE
ADULT x ¾

80. LARGE STONEFLY MALE
ADULT

81. MEDIUM STONEFLY ADULT
Diura bicaudata

82. YELLOW SALLY ADULT
Isoperla grammatica

83. NYMPH OF
Isoperia grammatica

84. SMALL BROWN
Nemoura cinerea

85. NYMPH OF
Nemourella picteti

86. SMALL YELLOW SALLY
Chloroperla torrentium

87. NEEDLE FLY
Leuctra fusca

88. ALDER FLY ADULT
Sialis lutaria

89. HEATHER FLY
Bibio pomoni

90. HAWTHORN FLY
Bibio marci

91. BLACK GNATS
FEMALE AND MALE
Bibio johannis

PLATE 7. STONEFLIES, ETC. × 1

92. FRESHWATER SHRIMP
EXTENDED SWIMMING
Gammarus pulex

93. DAMSEL NYMPH

94. LEAF CASE OF SEDGE LARVA
Top three leaves removed
to show interior
G. pellucidus

95. PHANTOM FLY ADULT
FEMALE
Chaoborus flavicans

96. COCKCHAFER BEETLE
Melontha melontha

97. SOLDIER BEETLE
Cantharis spp.

98. SAILOR BEETLE
Cantharis spp.

99. WATER BEETLE LARVA

100. COCH-Y-BONDDU
Phyllopertha horticola

101. FRESHWATER LOUSE
Assellus spp.

102. LESSER WATER BOATMAN
Corixa punctata

103. CHINA MARK MOTH
Nymphula spp.

104. AQUATIC MOTH
Pyralidae spp.

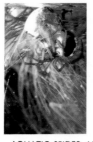

105. AQUATIC SPIDER AND
ITS BUBBLE NEST

106. GREEN LACEWING

PLATE 8. FAUNA (VARIOUS) × 1

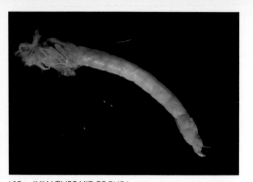

107.   IMMATURE MIDGE PUPA
STAGE I × 6

108.   MIDGE PUPA
STAGE 2 × 6 showing newly
formed wing cases

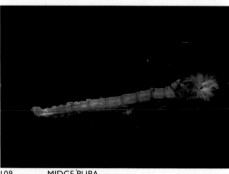

109.   MIDGE PUPA
STAGE 3 Fully developed
but with larval integument still
attached × 6

110.   ECDYSIS OF MIDGE PUPA
TO ADULT STAGE I × 2

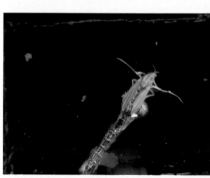

111. STAGE 2 Thorax now split and
head of adult appears × 2

112.   STAGE 3 Note orange wings
of emerging adult × 2

113.   STAGE 4 Transformation
almost complete — wings have
now lost colour × 2

114. STAGE 5 The newly emerged
adult midge × 2

PLATE 9.   CHIRONOMID (MIDGE) PUPA TO ADULT

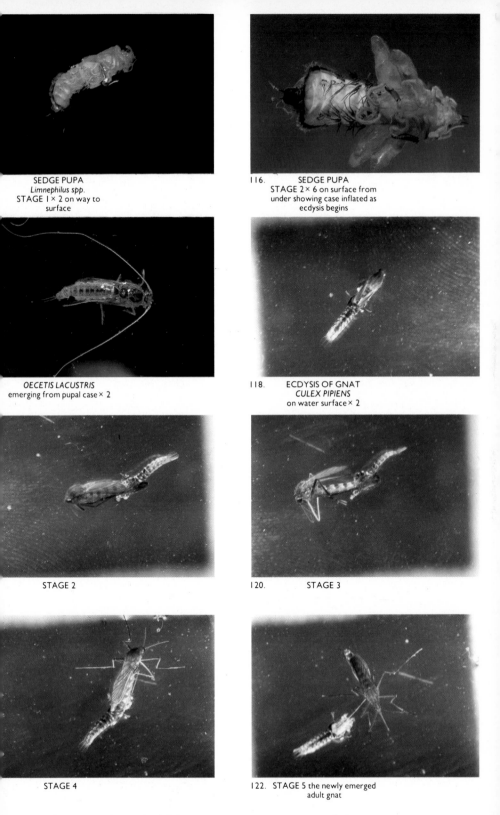

SEDGE PUPA
Limnephilus spp.
STAGE 1 × 2 on way to
surface

116.   SEDGE PUPA
STAGE 2 × 6 on surface from
under showing case inflated as
ecdysis begins

OECETIS LACUSTRIS
emerging from pupal case × 2

118.   ECDYSIS OF GNAT
CULEX PIPIENS
on water surface × 2

STAGE 2

120.   STAGE 3

STAGE 4

122. STAGE 5 the newly emerged
adult gnat

PLATE 10.   SEDGE PUPAE AND ECDYSIS OF GNAT

123.   AQUATIC SPIDER
devouring freshly caught louse

124.   GREATER WATER
BOATMAN   *Notonecta spp.*
reflected on under surface of
water

125.   FRESHWATER SHRIMP
G. pulex
feeding on weed

126.   BLUE DAMSEL
Enallagama cyathigarum
Male × 1

127.   ADULT MIDGE PUPA
that has failed to free itself
from its larval integument

128.   LARVA OF WATER BEETLE
Probably *Dytiscus spp.*

129.   EMPTY PUPAL CASE OF
ALDER FLY
Sialis spp.

130.   CLOSE-UP OF HEAD OF
SEDGE-FLY
showing the large compound
eyes oculi and the very small
whitish simple eyes or ocelli
on top of head × 6

PLATE II.   VARIOUS × 2

NYMPH OF LARGE
SUMMER DUN
Siphlonurus armatus × 2

132.   LARGE SUMMER DUN
Male *Siphlonurus armatus* ×2

LARGE SUMMER SPINNER
FEMALE
Siphlonurus armatus × 2

134.   LARGE SUMMER DUN
FEMALE
Siphlonurus armatus × 2

GREATER WATER
BOATMAN
Notonecta spp. × 2

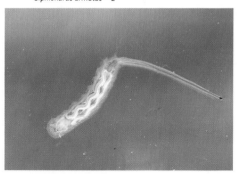

136.   LARVA OF ERISTALIS,
THE DRONE FLY × 2·5

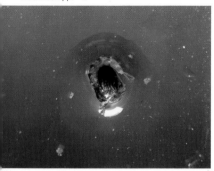

PUPA OF *Culex pipiens* × 2·5

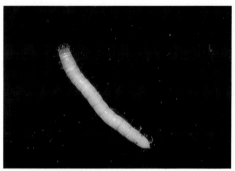

138.   LARVA OF AQUATIC
MOTH
probably *Nymphula spp.* × 2·5

PLATE 12. VARIOUS ×

139. MAYFLY DUN × 1·25
Ephemera Danica
—largest of our upwinged flies

140. MAYFLY SPINNER × ·75
Note empty chuck from which
it has just emerged

141. A COMMON SPECIES OF
DAMOSEL FLY × 1
MALE   *Agrion splendens*

142. SMALL DRAGONFLY
NYMPH × 2·5
Sympetron spp.

143. SEDGE PUPA × 2
swimming to the surface

144. COMMON WATER BUG × 2
Aphelocheirus montandoni

145. AQUATIC WORM
(ANNELIDA) × 2
Stylaria spp.
length 15mm
Habitat — water plants etc.

146. Probably *DIXA spp.* × 2·5
from stomach content of trout

PLATE 13. VARIOUS ×

147. ACE OF SPADES
David Collyer

148. APPETISER
Bob Church

149. BABY DOLL
Bob Church

150. BLACK AND ORANGE
MARABOU
Taff Price

151. CHOMPER
Richard Walker

152. DAMSEL NYMPH
Cliff Henry

153. THE GERROFF
John Goddard

154. JACK FROST
Bob Church

155. LONGHORNS
Richard Walker

156. NO. 56 THE PERSUADER
John Goddard

157. THE SUSPENDER
John Goddard
New hatching midge pupa
patterns and phantom midge
pupa on right

158. SNAIL
Cliff Henry

159. SWEENY TODD
Richard Walker

160. TADPOLLY
John Goddard

161. WHISKY FLY
Albert Whillock

PLATE 14.
A SMALL SELECTION OF MODERN STILLWATER ARTIFICIAL FLIES AND LURES

SPINNER

Blue Winged Olive   EYES: Bright red.
    spinner male   WINGS: Transparent with light brown veins.
       BODY: Dark brown to a rich red-brown on some specimens.
       LEGS: Pale brown.
       TAILS: Pale fawn with black rings.
       SIZE: Medium-large.

Sherry spinner,   EYES: Greenish brown.
    female   WINGS: Transparent with pale brown veins.
(Plate 3, No. 24)   BODY: Varies in different specimens from an olive-brown to an almost lobster-red or sherry-red.
       LEGS: Pale brown.
       TAILS: Olive-grey faintly ringed brown.
       SIZE: Medium-large.
       Remarks: The body colour of this spinner varies tremendously, even among individual flies in the same swarm.

Centroptilum luteolum (TWO-TAILS)

DUN

Small Spurwing,   EYES: Orange-red.
    male   WINGS: Very pale grey, sometimes tinged blue-white. Veins pale olive.
(Plate 2, No. 9)   BODY: Dorsum—pale olive-grey.
       Venter—olive-brown, last two segments orange-brown.

       LEGS: Brown-olive. Feet smoky grey.
       TAILS: Grey.
       SIZE: Medium to small.

Small Spurwing,   EYES: Pale green.
    female   WINGS: Very pale grey, sometimes tinged blue-white. Veins pale olive.
       BODY: Dorsum—pale brown-olive to pale watery olive.
       Venter—pale olive.
       LEGS: Very pale olive. Feet grey.
       TAILS: Grey.
       SIZE: Medium to small.
       Remarks: The flies, which appear in the early

summer, are usually darker than the pale watery-coloured specimens which are common during the late summer. The eyes of the male are normally a brighter red than any of the other olives.

Both dun and spinner have single marginal intercalary veins and very small narrow hindwings with prominent spur. (See Fig. 12)

SPINNER

Small Spurwing spinner, male

EYES: Bright orange-red.
WINGS: Transparent veins faintly olive.
BODY: Translucent watery white, last three segments pale orange-brown.
LEGS: Very pale olive.
TAILS: Pale grey-white.
SIZE: Medium to small.
Remarks: This male spinner has a very pale orange-brown thorax and is similar to the pale watery male spinner, but can be easily distinguished by its bright reddish eyes (the pale watery has yellow eyes).

Little Amber spinner, female
(Plate 3, No. 27)

EYES: Brown-black.
WINGS: Transparent veins faintly olive.
BODY: Dorsum—varies from a pale yellow-brown to a pale amber colour when fully spent. Faintly ringed cream.
Venter—is a creamy yellow with last two segments light amber.
LEGS: Pale olive-brown.
TAILS: Pale olive-white.
SIZE: Medium to small.
Remarks: The body colour of this spinner is quite distinctive.

Cloëon dipterum (TWO-TAILS—NO HINDWINGS)

DUN

Pond Olive, male
(Plate 2, No. 7)

EYES: Dull orange-brown, with two faint red lines across centre.
WINGS: Pale grey.
BODY: Dorsum—dull grey-olive, last three segments dull grey-brown.
Venter—dull grey-olive, last segment yellow.

LEGS: Pale watery-white. Faint reddish marks top of forelegs.

TAILS: Pale grey ringed brown.

SIZE: Medium.

Pond Olive Dun, female
(Plate 2, No. 4)

EYES: Dull green with two faint red lines across centre.

WINGS: Darkish grey.

BODY: Dorsum—dark brownish olive, streaked red in some cases.
Venter—green with a brown tinge.

LEGS: Pale watery olive, feet grey. Top of forelegs suffused reddish.

TAILS: Pale grey ringed black-brown.

SIZE: Medium to medium-large.

Remarks: Both dun and spinner have single marginal intercalary veins and are without hindwings. They have three to five small cross veins along top leading edge (see Fig. 17) of forewings. Also the female dun and spinner often have two parallel red lines which transverse the length of the ventral segments.

SPINNER

Pond Olive spinner, male
(Plate 3, No. 22)

EYES: Orange-red, with two faint red lines across centre.

WINGS: Transparent, with main veins along leading edge pale brown.

BODY: Dorsum—dull translucent cream, last three segments dark brown.
Venter—dull greyish cream.

LEGS: Pale grey-white.

TAILS: Grey-white ringed brown.

SIZE: Medium.

Apricot spinner, female
(Plate 3, No. 19)

EYES: Black.

WINGS: Transparent with red-brown veining. The leading edge of each wing is yellow-olive tinged red.

BODY: Dorsum—varies from an apricot colour streaked red to red-brown, tinged dark yellow.
Venter—olive.

LEGS: Forelegs olive-ringed red, remainder bright olive-green.

TAILS: Very pale grey ringed brown.

SIZE: Medium to medium-large.

Remarks: A very distinctive spinner with its ringed tail and red blotches on various parts of its body. Further unusual features are the broad bands of yellow along the leading edge of the wings and the yellow thorax.

Cloëon simile (TWO-TAILS—NO HINDWINGS)

Lake Olive Dun, male
(Plate 2, No. 5)

EYES: Green-olive suffused with medium brown.

WINGS: Smoky-grey with pale yellowish venation sometimes changing to green near front basal section.

BODY: Dorsum—reddish-brown with a grey undertone and pale ringing Venter—dark grey-olive.

LEGS: Olive-green with black feet.

TAILS: Very dark grey.

SIZE: Medium.

Lake Olive dun, female
(Plate 2, No. 4)

EYES: Olive with brown spots.

WINGS: Smoky-grey with yellowish venation, particularly along the leading edge.

BODY: Dorsum—reddish-brown with pale ringing.
Venter—grey-olive.

LEGS: Olive-green with black feet.

TAILS: Dark grey faint white rings.

SIZE: Medium to medium large.

Remarks: Both dun and spinner are similar in appearance to the Pond Olive, but to assist positive identification *C. simile* has nine to eleven cross veins (Plate 18) along top leading edge of forewings as opposed to the three to five in *C. Dipterum.*

Lake Olive spinner, male
(Plate 3, No. 20)

EYES: Dull yellow.

WINGS: Transparent veins along leading edge faintly yellow.

BODY: Dorsum—three-tail segments deep red-brown. Remainder pale brown with touches of olive.
Venter—three-tail segments yellowish, remainder grey-white.

LEGS: Forelegs femur pale yellow tibia and feet. blackish. Posterior and median legs pale yellow with black feet.

TAILS: Very long—white faintly ringed red.

SIZE: Medium.

Lake Olive spinner, female
(Plate 3, No. 17)

EYES: Olive-green.

WINGS: Transparent with all veins faintly yellowish.

BODY: Dorsum—deep chestnut-brown.
Venter—grey-olive.

LEGS: Forelegs—olive femur with blackish tibia and feet. Posterior and median legs—olive with black feet.

TAILS: White tinged red with faint red ringing.

SIZE: Medium to medium large.

Siphlonurus lacustris (TWO-TAILS)

Large summer dun, female
(Plate 12, No. 134)

EYES: Grey-green.

WINGS: Long and narrow plain grey or olive-grey tinged with sepia. Veins brownish.

BODY: Olive-brown with variable dark brown markings.

LEGS: Olive-brown.

TAILS: Light to dark brown with faint ringing visible on the lighter specimens.

SIZE: Very large.

Remarks: The male is similar but darker throughout and more strongly marked. Both dun and spinner have large upright hindwings with a costal projection. (Fig. as 11). (See Plate 12, No. 132)

Large summer spinner, female
(Plate 12, No. 133)

EYES: Dark brown.

WINGS: Long and narrow. Transparent with medium brown veins.

BODY: Dorsum—olive-brown.
Venter—greenish-grey.

LEGS: Dark greenish-black forelegs. Posterior legs light brown.

TAILS: Brown.

Remarks: The male spinner, like its
corresponding dun, is a darker and more
strongly marked version of the female.

NOTE: I am indebted to other authorities for the above description of
this particular species.

Heptagenia sulphurea (TWO-TAILS)

DUN

Yellow May dun, male

EYES: Dark blue becoming paler with age.
WINGS: Yellow with brown veins.
BODY: Dorsum—brownish yellow.
Venter—pale yellow.
LEGS: Yellow with greyish feet.
TAILS: Grey.
SIZE: Medium-large.

Yellow May dun, female
(Plate 3, No. 28)

EYES: Black-green becoming paler with age.
WINGS: Pale yellow with yellow veins.
BODY: Very pale yellow varying to a deeper yellow.
LEGS: Pale yellow with greyish feet.
TAILS: Grey.
SIZE: Medium-large.

Remarks: Similar to the Yellow Evening· dun of
rivers but larger, and of a more vivid yellow colour,
with two tails; the Yellow Evening dun has three
tails.

Both dun and spinner have upright hindwings
with a costal projection. (Fig. as 16)

SPINNER

Yellow May spinner, male
(Plate 2, No. 13)

EYES: Dark blue becoming pale blue with age.
WINGS: Transparent with dark brown veins, leading
edge smoky grey.
BODY: Dorsum—dark olive-brown.
Venter—light golden olive-brown to yel-
low-green.
LEGS: Golden brown.
TAILS: Pale brown ringed dark brown.
SIZE: Medium-large.

Remarks: A beautiful golden brown bodied spinner
with heavily veined wings. Blue eyes and exceptionally long forelegs. Similar in appearance to the
Olive Upright male spinner of running water.

Yellow May spinner, female

EYES: Blue becoming paler with age.

WINGS: Transparent, but with a pale yellow area along leading edge. Veins dark brown.

BODY: Dorsum—pale olive-yellow.
Venter—pale yellow with last two segments yellow.

LEGS: Dark olive-yellow.

TAILS: Dark grey ringed brown.

SIZE: Medium-large.

Remarks: A large yellow to pale yellow spinner with heavily veined wings.

Heptagenia lateralis (TWO-TAILS)

DUN

Dusky Yelowstreak, male

EYES: Black-brown.

WINGS: Very dark grey.

BODY: Dark greyish brown.

LEGS: Dark brown-olive.

TAILS: Greyish.

SIZE: Medium-large.

Remarks: The duns have an overall drab appearance, the predominant colour being grey.

Dusky Yellowstreak, female

EYES: Black.

WINGS: Very dark grey.

BODY: Dark greyish brown with venter slightly lighter.

LEGS: Dark brown-olive.

TAILS: Greyish.

SIZE: Medium-large.

Remarks: Both dun and spinner have upright hindwings *with costal projection* (Fig. as 11) and have a conspicuous yellow mark or streak each side of the thorax in front of forewing root.

SPINNER

Dusky Yellowstreak spinner, male

EYES: Dark brown.

WINGS: Transparent with brownish veining along leading edge.

BODY: Dark brown-olive with reddish ringing, paler underneath.

	LEGS:	Brown-olive.
	TAILS:	Brown.
	SIZE:	Medium-large.

Dusky Yellowstreak   EYES: Dark brown.
spinner, female   WINGS: Transparent with brown veining along
(Plate 2, No. 12)   leading edge.
     BODY: Dorsum—brown-olive with reddish
      rings.
      Venter—drab-olive, last three seg-
      ments orange-brown.
     LEGS: Brown-olive with red-brown patches.
     TAILS: Brown.
     SIZE: Medium-large.

Leptophlebia vespertina (THREE-TAILS)

DUN

Claret dun,   EYES: Very dark red-brown.
male   WINGS: Very dark grey with hindwing of a much
      paler shade.
     BODY: Dorsum—very dark black-brown, last three
      segments with a claret tinge.
      Venter—grey-black.
     LEGS: Dark brown-black.
     TAILS: Dark grey-brown.
     SIZE: Medium-large.

Claret dun,   EYES: Black.
female   WINGS: Very dark grey, hindwings pale buff colour.
(Plate 2, No. 8)   BODY: Dorsum—dark brown almost black with a
      claret tinge.
      Venter—brown with a claret tinge.
     LEGS: Dark brown.
     TAILS: Dark brown.
     SIZE: Medium-large.

Remarks: Both male and female duns closely resemble
the Iron Blue, but are larger, have a more claret-
brown body and have three tails. The paler colour of
the upright hindwings can be a helpful feature in
identification; they have no costal projection. (See
Fig. as 15.)

SPINNER

Claret spinner,	EYES:	Very dark red-brown.
male	WINGS:	Transparent lightly veined brownish.
(Plate 3, No. 26)	BODY:	Dorsum—dark brown with a claret tinge.
		Venter—similar but paler.
	LEGS:	Dark black-brown.
	TAILS:	Pale brown ringed with red.
	SIZE:	Medium-large.

Claret spinner,	EYES:	Black.
female	WINGS:	Transparent lightly veined pale brown.
(Plate 3, No. 23)	BODY:	Dorsum—brown with a claret shade.
		Venter—similar but paler.
	LEGS:	Brown to pale brown.
	TAILS:	Pale brown lightly ringed with black.
	SIZE:	Medium-large.

Leptophlebia marginata (THREE-TAILS)

DUN

Sepia dun,	EYES:	Very dark red-brown.
male	WINGS:	Pale fawn heavily veined brown.
(Plate 2, No. 6)	BODY:	Dorsum—dark sepia-brown.
		Venter—grey-brown.
	LEGS:	Forelegs dark brown, remainder dark olive-brown.
	TAILS:	Brown.
	SIZE:	Medium-large.

Sepia dun,	EYES:	Brown.
female	WINGS:	Pale fawn, heavily veined brown.
(Plate 2, No. 3)	BODY:	Dorsum—dark sepia-brown.
		Venter—pale brown.
	LEGS:	Forelegs brown, others olive-brown.
	TAILS:	Brown.
	SIZE:	Medium-large.

Remarks: The three tails of this fly are spread well apart. They have upright hindwings, without costal projection. (See Fig. 15)

SPINNER

Sepia spinner,	EYES:	Dark red-brown tinged dull green.
male	WINGS:	Transparent, veined light brown.
(Plate 3, No. 21)	BODY:	Dark brown ringed straw.
	LEGS:	Forelegs dark brown, others golden brown.
	TAILS:	Very long and dark brown.
	SIZE:	Medium-large.

Sepia spinner, EYES: Dark brown.
  female   WINGS: Transparent, veined light brown.
(Plate 3, No. 18) BODY: Dorsum—dark red-brown.
                     Venter—pale red-brown.
            LEGS: Forelegs dark brown, others golden brown.
            TAILS: Very long and dark brown.
            SIZE: Medium-large.

Remarks: The forewings of these spinners have a dark smoky black patch along the top leading edge.

Ecdyonurus dispar (TWO-TAILS)

DUN

Autumn dun, EYES: Deep greenish brown.
  male   WINGS: Grey, heavily veined black giving wings
(Plate 2, No. 10)   a slightly mottled appearance, with veins along leading edge brown.
            BODY: Dorsum—yellow-olive with dark brown diagonal bands along sides.
                     Venter—brown-olive.
            LEGS: Dark brown-olive with feet darker.
            TAILS: Very dark grey.
            SIZE: Large.

Autumn dun, EYES: Brown-black.
  female   WINGS: Pale fawn with heavy blackish veins, giving wings a slightly mottled appearance.
            BODY: Dorsum—yellow-olive or pale olive-brown. Sides touches of red-brown.
                     Venter—pale olive-brown.
            LEGS: Dark brown-olive.
            TAILS: Very dark grey.
            SIZE: Large.

Remarks: A rather large fly with heavily veined wings and a beige-coloured body. The forelegs of the male are very long.

Both dun and spinner have large upright hind-wings, with a costal projection. (See Fig. 11)

SPINNER

Autumn spinner, EYES: Dark brown-black.
  male   WINGS: Transparent but with veining very distinct and brownish.
            BODY: Dorsum—dark brown-red, almost mahogany colour with blackish joinings.

Venter—dark olive with last two segments yellowish.

LEGS: Brownish.

TAILS: Very dark grey-brown.

SIZE: Large.

Autumn spinner, female
(Plate 3, No. 25)

EYES: Dark greenish brown.

WINGS: Transparent but with veins a distinct brown-black colour.

BODY: Dorsum—reddish brown.
Venter—darker red-brown.

LEGS: Olive-brown.

TAILS: Very dark brown.

SIZE: Large.

Remarks: A large dark red bodied spinner, sometimes referred to as the Great Red spinner in common with the Late March Brown and the Large Brook spinner.

CHAPTER VI

UPWINGED FLIES—(Continued)

DISTRIBUTION — SEASON — FISHING

In the preceding chapters on the Upwinged flies the nymphs have not been discussed, and as these are in some cases important to the fisherman, a brief history on them is given prior to more detailed information on the adults.

All aquatic flies live the greater part of their lives under water, and in the course of time have adapted themselves to the environment most suited to each particular species. It will be appreciated therefore that the underwater forms of these Upwinged flies (nymphs) vary considerably, both in actual physical shape and characteristic features evolved to suit their aquatic mode of life. Some nymphs have adapted themselves to live in rough stony lakes such as some of those in the north, and live the best part of their lives clinging with their flat bodies to stones. Others inhabiting lowland waters live in little tunnels which they excavate in the bed of the lake. Other species of nymphs live largely in the weed beds which abound in many waters. Some of them have become accustomed to alkaline water, others to slightly acid water.

The study of insects in relation to their surroundings is known as the science of ecology, and from it we often can gather clues regarding the distribution of insects which can assist us to identify them when an element of doubt exists.

In general appearance the nymphs of these Upwinged flies are somewhat similar to the adult winged fly without its wings or long tails. They have a rather humped-back shape caused by the wing cases, although these are not apparent in the immature nymphs. When these wing cases first develop they are of a pale shade of brown, and as the nymphs advance in maturity they become noticeably darker. In fully mature nymphs which are at the point of emergence, the wing cases are prominent and dark brown. They are supposed to feed either on detritus algae or minute organisms present in the water, but whether this is in fact the case is uncertain.

The late Oliver Kite, in his standard work *Nymph Fishing in Practice*, sub-divided Ephemeropteran nymphs into various groups according to their habitat, and as this seems a very sensible and practical arrangement the same system will be followed in this book. The six main groups into which all the nymphs can be placed are as follows:

BOTTOM BURROWERS

SILT CRAWLERS

MOSS CREEPERS

STONE CLINGERS

LABOURED SWIMMERS

AGILE DARTERS

Before proceeding with the distribution and fishing information on the different species of these Upwinged flies I should like to mention several aspects applicable to the presentation of the artificial that is common to them all and, by so doing, obviate unnecessary duplication.

GENERAL FISHING INFORMATION

When fishing a floating pattern on stillwater, whether it is a dun or spinner pattern, the fly should be fished with little or no movement. The most effective method is to present the artificial either to the rise of a trout or the estimated position of its next rise. An alternative, particularly on days when the fish are only rising occasionally, is to impart a slight animation to your fly as it rests on the surface. This is most efficiently produced by giving an occasional twitch to your rod top. When fishing patterns to represent the duns on stillwater, my personal preference is for a winged pattern, as I feel that the slow moving trout in stillwater may notice their absence and regard the hackled only fly with suspicion. Also, the wind playing on these wings often produces pseudo-natural animation. Patterns to represent spinners should be fished in the surface film, and to achieve this the hackle of the artificial should be tied sparsely or clipped in the case of commercially tied patterns.

So far as nymphs· are concerned, there are many different ways of fishing these, but over the years I have found the following method consistently successful. It is best practised in open water in the vicinity of weed in depths between 5 and 10 ft. A weighted nymph pattern should be used on the point, and an unweighted one may be included on a dropper. The artificial is cast from the bank, or better still from an anchored boat, and allowed to sink to the bottom; it is then fished sink-and-draw being retrieved as slowly as possible, allowing a long pause of at least half a minute between each sink-and-draw. When fishing from a boat the last few retrieves are usually the most effective.

The Mayfly (*Ephemera danica or E. vulgata*)

This is the largest of the Upwinged flies, and is often referred to as the Greendrake. Probably more has been written on this particular fly than all the other Upwinged species put together, and therefore it is not necessary to expound at too great a length. Even the merest novice fly-fisherman must be familiar with this distinctive-looking insect. With its heavily veined wings, cream-coloured body, very large size and three tails, it can hardly be confused with any of the other Upwinged flies. The difference between the two species, *E. danica* and *E. vulgata*, is so slight that it is of little importance to the angler, although the latter is considerably darker in overall colouration. However, for the angler entomologist, *E. danica* is probably the more common of the two and occurs in the faster flowing rivers and lakes, whereas *E. vulgata* seems to favour sluggish rivers with muddy bottoms, but they may occasionally be encountered in small ponds or gravel pits. For the record, there is also a third species, *E. lineata*, but it is very rare in these islands.

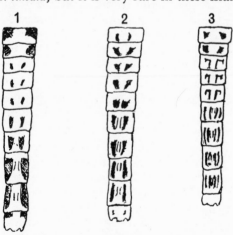

1. E. danica   2. E. vulgata   3. E. lineata

Fig. 19. Showing difference between constant black markings on segments of abdomens of Mayflies.

For positive identification of these three species the only certain way is to refer to the sketches (Fig. 19) of the markings of the body segments. Mayflies are abundant and common in many rivers of the British Isles and Ireland, but unfortunately only occur in comparatively few lakes in England and Scotland, although they are very prolific on many Irish loughs. They have a comparatively short season, usually lasting about two weeks, in either late May or early June. Hatches tend to build up to a crescendo during this period, culminating usually in two or three days of really prolific hatches at the end of the fourteen days, after which they rapidly thin out. During this time the emergence normally commences about midday, often continuing till early evening. However, on some occasions I have experienced a delay in the main hatch until four or five o'clock. Unfortunately, the colossal hatches of this fly that used to be prevalent seem to have diminished, perhaps due to a natural cycle tendency or the ever-increasing effects of pollution in many of our lakes.

The Spent Gnat

This is the popular name given to the female spinner of the Mayfly as she lies dying on the surface after laying her eggs. The body of this spinner is a pale cream colour, and the wings, although transparent, have a distinct bluish tint. While ovipositing, the female spinner will often alight on the water for short periods and at this stage she is referred to as a Grey Drake, the artificial pattern of which is particularly good at this period. The male spinners of the Mayfly are also worthy of mention as they often fall on to the water after mating. In appearance they have dark legs and thorax, with a creamy-white body, and the three rear segments of the body are brown. The transparent wings are tinged quite distinctly with dark patches. A fall of Mayfly spinners is always eagerly awaited by fly-fishermen, as the trout seem to prefer the spinner to the dun and take them readily. Also, of course, it is much easier to deceive the fish with an artificial pattern representing the spinner. A useful indication of whether or not there is likely to be a fall of spinners in the evening can often be determined by looking for swarms of the male spinners. These normally form in the vicinity of trees or bushes along the lake banks in the late afternoon or early evening, and if the swarms are absent or sparse by mid-evening it is doubtful whether any appreciable fall will occur. The nymphs of Mayflies (Plate 3, No. 30) are bottom burrowers, adult specimens being over an inch long, having specially shaped gill filaments along the body. They usually burrow into the silt or gravel of the lake bed and live in the tunnels so formed. The head is narrow and pointed, and is provided with a pair of large mandibles which are used for excavating. The gill plates, which are very active, provide a constant flow of water past the body of the nymph, thus supplying the necessary oxygen; perhaps this flow of water also carries minute particles of food to the nymph in its burrow.

Fishing Information: As far as the Mayfly is concerned, so much has been written about this, our most well-known species, that I feel there is little of value I can add. In England it is far more common in running water and of the host of patterns available for dun, spinner and nymph, the majority were perfected for use on this medium, and fortunately most of these patterns are just as effective for stillwater. I would add, however, that a hatching pattern such as the Grey Wulff will often prove most effective. A popular and singularly successful method, particularly on the Irish loughs, where these flies are very common, is to dap a live Mayfly.

The Blue Winged Olive (*Ephemerella ignita*) (Plate 2, No. 11)

Without a doubt this is the most common, widespread and well-known of all our Upwinged duns. With its bluish wings, three tails, olive-coloured body, it is probably the easiest of all our flies to recognize. The male is considerably darker than the female and often has a very brownish-olive body. In the late autumn the body colour of both is often more of a rusty-brown colour than olive. This species is found all over the British Isles in nearly all types of flowing water and in many big lakes. Although this is not generally recognized as a lake fly, I have decided to include it in the list as in latter years it has been positively identified by qualified observers on several bodies of stillwater. In the summer of 1965 I personally observed large hatches of this fly on two widely separated lochs in Scotland. I therefore suspect that it may be present on many waters where it has not been identified. It first appears in quantities in mid-June and continues right through to the end of the fishing season. In the early part of its season, hatches are frequently confined to the evenings only, often just as dusk approaches. Later on in August, when the days begin to shorten, hatches will often begin in the late afternoon or early evening, and on several occasions in recent years I have observed quite good hatches of this fly shortly after midday. It is a large and robust fly and with experience the angler can soon learn to identify it from a fair distance, as it hatches and floats on the surface. The reason for this is that the large forewings of this fly slope back slightly over the body, much more so than the wings of any other Upwinged flies.

The Sherry Spinner (Plate 3, No. 24)

Although the colour range of these spinners, even of the individuals within the same swarm, varies from olive-brown to sherry-red to a distinct lobster-red, the most common shade is the sherry colour, whence the popular name. The females are often to be seen in vast swarms in the late evening, preparatory to egg-laying. The nymph is one of the moss creepers and is more robust than the relatively slim nymphs of the Olives. It is rather lethargic and spends some of its aquatic existence creeping along the stones or debris of the lake bed, although it is sometimes found on weed. So far I have been unable to ascertain whether it has a preference for deep or shallow water.

Fishing Information: Being a very common species to the river fisher, several very good patterns are available to represent the dun. Although the Orange Quill is widely fished when the duns are on the water, it is fairly well established that this imitates the Sherry spinner. There are many other patterns which imitate the dun, notably those designed by J. W. Dunne, D. Jacques and G. E. M. Skues, although the latter is probably best fished wet to represent the emerging dun. As the dun is often rather lethargic when freshly hatched and remains on the water surface longer than most Upwinged species, a dry pattern is usually most effective. In addition to the Orange Quill there are two very well-known artificials to represent the spinner, and these should suffice for most occasions. They are the Sherry Spinner and the Pheasant Tail Spinner. Patterns to represent the nymph are not usually very successful, although a hatching nymph pattern fished in the surface can often be effective.

The Small Spurwing (*Centroptilum luteolum*) (Plate 2, No. 9)

This fly was originally classified as one of the Pale Wateries. With only a superficial examination it is very difficult to distinguish this dun from the small Olives of the *Baëtis* species found on rivers, as it can be similar in size and colour to either the Pale Watery or Small Dark Olive. With a good lens it can readily be identified by the small spur-shaped hindwing and the single marginal intercalary veins of the forewing. The eye of the male is also a brighter red than those of the males of the Olives. At one time this fly was called the Little Sky Blue Pale Watery from the reputed colour of the wings, but from my own personal observation the wing colour of most specimens is very pale grey. Occasionally, however, the lower part of the wing is faintly white, and one may say that by contrast the upper portion appears to have a bluish tinge. Although this is a common species on many rivers, it has not been generally recognized as a lake fly, but I have decided to include it in the list for the same reason as the preceding species, as it is found on stillwater and may well be more common than is generally supposed. They first appear in early May, continuing through to September. Hatches are fairly prolific over most of the day in the early months of the season, but later in the year are often confined to late afternoon or early evening. The peak flight period is June. A useful point for identification of the male fly is the rather square appearance of the tail end of the body when viewed from the side. This is undoubtedly due to the thick basal portions of the male claspers.

The Little Amber Spinner (Plate 3, No. 27)

The popular name given to this female spinner describes it extremely well. Once it has been seen and identified it is unlikely ever to be forgotten. The upper part of the body, which appears to be faintly ringed with cream due to the segments having a cream edging, varies from a yellow-brown to a lovely pale amber colour. The under part is creamy-yellow, and the last two segments are light amber. I have little personal experience of this nymph in stillwater, although I did positively identify a specimen that I captured in Two Lakes near Romsey. This nymph is one of the agile darters and certainly in rivers it shows a distinct preference for weed beds. It may be of interest to note that in several of the books written on loch fishing the authors mention hatches of a small, pale watery-coloured Olive that were observed on occasions, and it seems reasonable to assume that they may well have been this particular species.

Fishing Information: Again, a well-known fly to the river fisherman, and many well-known artificials are available to represent the dun should it be encountered. These include several tyings of the Pale Watery, Locks Fancy, Little Marryat and my own pattern, the Last Hope. For the spinner, Lunn's Yellow Boy, Lunn's Particular or the Pheasant Tail Spinner, all tied on small hooks, should suffice. The nymph can be satisfactorily represented by an Olive nymph or my own P.V.C. nymph pattern, also tied on a small hook. This can be fished in the vicinity of weed beds as a weighted pattern by the sink-and-draw method, or as an unweighted pattern fished in the surface film if trout appear near the surface.

The Pond Olive (*Cloëon dipterum*) (Plate 2, No. 47)

This species is probably the most important of the Upwinged

flies to the stillwater fisherman and is very common and abundant on stillwaters in most parts of the British Isles, apart from Ireland. It has a long emergence period and is seen during most of the summer, with a peak flight period between June and July. Hatches of the adult winged fly usually occur during the middle part of the day, and it will often be observed that the trout will take the emerging nymph in preference to the winged dun, as they become airborne very quickly after metamorphosis is completed. This is not necessarily always the case, however, as on wet days, or when there is a heavy surface film or scum on the water, their flight may be delayed and the trout will then feed on them readily enough.

Of all the Upwinged flies the Pond Olive seems to vary in size most of all. Although the average size of this fly is designated as medium, I have on numerous occasions come across specimens that can only be described as large. In some cases I have even doubted my initial identification and have had to re-check. These larger specimens are usually females and are encountered early in the summer. As the season progresses it will become apparent that the average size of specimens encountered decreases until, late in the summer, they are barely 6 mm. long in the body—little larger than an Iron Blue.

C. F. Walker mentions in his book that a noticeable feature of the *Cloëon* duns, particularly the Pond Olive, is their habit of spreading their wings slightly apart when at rest, instead of pressing them fairly closely together as do most other Ephemeropteran duns. This has also been my experience. He also mentions that this may account for their ability to become airborne so quickly as, due probably to the absence of hindwings, the forewings are very wide at the base and this may make it difficult for them to close over the thorax; this could, of course, facilitate drying after emergence. In confirmation of this theory I would mention that this feature also occurs in the Large Spurwing, *C. pennulatum*, found on rivers; this species too has exceedingly small hindwings with a correspondingly wide base to the forewings.

The Pond Olive is not likely to be confused with any other Upwinged fly on stillwater apart from the Lake Olive. Both these species belong to the large Family, *Baëtidae*, which includes except, for the B.W.O. all the Olives and Pale Wateries so dear to the heart of the river fly-fisher. It is relatively simple to identify these two species apart, as the Pond Olive has a black ringed tail, an olive-brown body often blotched reddish, and darkish grey wings, while the Lake Olive has wings of a smoky shade, a more drab-coloured body and greyish tails. A further useful point of identification so far as the female dun and spinners are concerned is that the underside of the body segments on the Pond Olive usually has two parallel red lines or streaks running along it. Positive identification can be achieved by referring to the venation of the wings described in Figs. 17 and 18. With practise it will rarely be necessary to refer to these, as it will be found that this particular area of the wing in both species of duns are different. In the Pond Olive it is almost clear and the veins stand out clearly, but in the Lake Olive it is opaque and the veins are not too easy to define.

Although both of these species are very common and are without doubt important to the stillwater fisherman so far as dry fly fishing is concerned, in my experience the Pond Olive seems to be the more common of the two. Probably this is due to the fact that it is more tolerant of temperatures and is consequently encountered on many types of still or even slow flowing waters, while the Lake Olive seems to be confined mainly to the larger or deeper lakes.

The Apricot Spinner (Plate 3, No. 19)

This seems to be the popular name now current for the female spinner of the Pond Olive, and this is no doubt due to its distinct over-all apricot coloration. Once seen and identified it is unlikely ever again to be confused with any other spinner, due to the fascinating colours of the body and wings, which have a broad band of yellow-olive running along the leading edges, while the apricot body is strongly marked with reddish blotches or patches. As previously mentioned, the male spinners are rarely found on the water, but in the late evening, when the spent females of this species fall exhausted on the surface after ovipositing, the trout will often eagerly accept them. On stillwater where both the Pond and Lake Olive are found the trout seem to show a distinct preference for the Apricot Spinner.

In an article written by the late Major O. W. A. Kite, published in *Angler's Annual* in 1963, he relates the following. "After mating, the Apricot Spinner does not necessarily lay her eggs immediately, as the female spinners of many other Upwinged species do. Instead, she flies off to shelter in bank-side trees or other vegetation for an unknown period. During that time her eggs begin to hatch in her oviducts into minute larvulae. Eventually, just before darkness and sometimes almost certainly during the night, she leaves her hide to seek the water and relief from her labour. As the Apricot Spinner flies across the water to fulfil her purpose, she dips now and then on to the surface, each time releasing a few of the tiny larvulae, as was first discovered by the German, von Siebold, as early as 1837. The suggestion that many females spend themselves on the water after dark calls for supporting evidence. The fact is that only in the mornings at first light are they sometimes seen on the surface in tremendous numbers. At Two Lakes, where this species abounds, the lake surfaces may be almost covered with the spent Apricots on a quiet summer morning. Very little wind is necessary to drive them towards the shore, and in the wanton airs the most gentle wave action rapidly demolishes their fragile remains. Even after a large fall during the night there is little or nothing to disclose what has taken place by the time the fisherman arrives after breakfast."

The nymphs of this species seem to colonize the weed beds mainly in the shallower margins of lakes, and it is therefore unlikely that they will be found in the steep-sided rocky lakes of higher altitudes. They are agile darters and can often be observed moving rapidly from weed stem to weed stem. Quite a small nymph, rather slim in appearance, they have, like all nymphs of the Order Ephemeroptera, three tails, the centre one being slightly shorter than the two outer. These tails are banded very dark brown and are fringed with fine hairs to assist rapid swimming. The colour varies so much that it is pointless to be specific in this respect, but the average body colour is olive and brown, giving a mottled appearance.

Fishing Information: As previously mentioned, due to the often quick emergence and flight of this dun, a pattern to simulate the emerging insect such as a wet Greenwell's Glory or a Gold Ribbed Hare's Ear, or my own Hatching Olive Nymph will usually be effective. At times, when it is apparent that the trout are actually taking the adult dun on the surface, the following patterns should prove adequate: the Large Dark Olive, the Rough Olive, Greenwell's Glory, or Olive Quill. The size of artificial chosen is important, as these particular duns vary so much in size throughout the season that the pattern decided upon should match the natural in this respect as closely as possible. When fishing a deep lake with shallow areas where this particular species is known to be present, it is useful to remember that hatches during the day are likely to occur in the shallower parts. The female spinner is usually accepted eagerly by the trout when it falls spent on the water but, infortunately, there are no commercially standard tied flies available to represent this spinner. The late Oliver Kite has published a pattern which he perfected called appropriately the Apricot Spinner. The dressing for this is given later in the book, together with a pattern of my own dressing which I call the Pond Olive Spinner. An Olive or my own P.V.C. nymph tied on a medium size hook, either weighted or unweighted as conditions determine, may be used to copy the nymph, which seems to prefer shallow water in the vicinity of weed beds, and therefore a single weighted pattern tied on the point and fished sink-and-draw along the edge of the weeds should pay dividends. When the adult winged fly is hatching one should use the unweighted pattern, allowing it to sink about twelve inches and then slowly working it to the surface by lifting the rod tip.

A particularly rewarding method of fishing the weighted pattern of this nymph or, in fact, any artificial to represent nymphs that are to be found in the locality of weed, is as follows. It is first necessary to find a fairly extensive weed bed breaking the surface. The artificial is then cast over it, ideally dropping into the clear water beyond the far edge of the weed by at least the length of the point. It is then allowed to sink down the edge of the weed with the fly line lying over the top, then slowly retrieved in small jerks until the nymph appears over the edge. The procedure is then repeated. In practice one would suspect that the nymph would continually snag in the surface weed when retrieved, but this seldom seems to happen providing the line and cast are smartly aerialized at this point. This method is best employed from the bank, but it can also be used from a stationary boat. Trout are very fond of patrolling the edge of weed beds on the look-out for any aquatic life that may have ventured away from the sanctuary of the weed. Where the water has been undisturbed I have had some excellent bags of trout using this method. It must be appreciated that the odd fish may be lost in the weed, but it has been my experience that they usually head into the open water when hooked, and this should give you sufficient time to walk along the bank to a clear area through which the trout can be netted.

The Lake Olive (*Cloëon simile*) (Plate 2, Nos. 2 and 5)

As the entomological name suggests, this is very similar indeed to the previous species which was identified first. It has a very wide range, and is found in all parts of the British Isles, and is exceedingly common in most of Ireland. I have encountered some very large hatches of this fly on some of the Scottish lochs, and in my limited experience of this part of the country it seems to be a fly more likely to be seen than the Pond Olive, although according to T. T. Macan (1961) both species are found in Scotland. The Lake

Olive is very similar in size to the previous species and has an average body length of about 8 mm. The adult insects emerge in May and June and again in late August and September, perhaps resulting from two separate generations. It should be mentioned, however, that odd specimens are encountered throughout all the summer months. Apart from its similarity in size to the previous species, it is also somewhat alike in coloration, although the angler should have little trouble in telling them apart with the naked eye. The Lake Olive is a much drabber fly with pale grey tails as opposed to the blackish ringed tails of the Pond Olive. These duns also tend to become airborne quickly, although this characteristic of their nature is not so noticeable as in the previous species. The main emergence period is usually between 10.00 and 16.00 hours, although this may extend to the early evening during very hot weather.

Lake Olive Spinner (Plate 3, Nos. 17 and 20)

The female spinner is easily distinguished from the spinner of the Pond Olive by its wings, which are more or less transparent and only very faintly yellowish along the leading edge and by the body which is a deep brownish red. During hot, still evenings in June, these spent females may often be observed in considerable numbers, when the trout will feed on them avidly. On some of the larger lakes, however, they are often confined to specific areas.

The appearance of the nymph is similar to the previous species, and for those anglers interested in a positive identification the only sure way is to examine the gill leafs under magnification. In the Pond Olive nymph it will be found that these are rounded, while in the Lake Olive they are pointed. These nymphs also come in the agile darter group and they too favour weed beds as their habitat. Most of them that I have captured have come from deeper water, so it would seem that they favour a lower water temperature than most other stillwater Ephemeropterans, and this could of course account for their absence in many shallow lakes or small ponds. Most authorities seem to agree that they seem to have a preference for deeper water, and T. T. Macan (1961) states that the nymphs are usually located in depths between 6 and 10 ft. No doubt, under favourable temperature conditions, they do occasionally move into shallower water, as I have taken odd specimens from marginal weed beds. On bodies of stillwater of variable depth the above information could be of some value.

Fishing Information: As this fly is very similar in appearance and habitat to the previous species, except for its preference for deeper water, fishing technique is more or less the same. Useful representations of the dun are any of the many Olive Dun patterns, including the one perfected by Mr. C. Henry which is, in my opinion, an exceptionally good one. The female spinner can be successfully represented by either the Pheasant Tail spinner or the Port spinner. Apart from the above, C. F. Walker and J. R. Harris suggest patterns for both the dun and spinner. The nymphs of this species are very elusive creatures and, as they are nearly always found in deeper water, are of little interest to the angler. An Olive Nymph fished just under the surface film may be tried during the period that the adults are hatching, particularly when hatches are on the sparse side, and the trout are not concentrating on the surface duns.

The Large Summer Dun (*Siphlonurus lacustris*) (Plate 12 No. 132–4 *S. Armatus*)

This dun belongs to the family *Siphlonuridae*, which also includes *S. armatus* and *Siphlurella linnaeana*, although these two species are of doubtful value to the fisherman, the former being quite rare, while the latter is rather localized, mainly confined to Northern Ireland and Scotland. As the vernacular name implies, *S. lacustris* is an exceedingly large dun, some specimens being almost as large as some of the smaller Mayflies. The average length of the body is between 14 and 15 mm.; they are a very handsome fly indeed and are somewhat similar in silhouette to the Large Brook dun, *E. torrentis*, found on small rivers and brooks. The angler should have no difficulty in recognizing this particular species as, apart from the Mayflies, they are the only very large Upwinged flies likely to be encountered on stillwater. They can be quickly distinguished from the Mayflies, which have three tails, as all species in the Family *Siphlonuridae* have only two.

The male and female duns of *S. lacustris* are somewhat similar in appearance, having large, rather narrow forewings, greyish in colour and heavily veined, and the hindwings, like all other members of the *Siphlonuridae* Family, are relatively large in comparison to other families. The predominant body colour is olive, heavily marked with brown, while the underpart or ventral segments are yellow with pale brown markings. This species is likely to be encountered in hilly country in parts of Wales, the North of England and Scotland, and so far as I am aware it has not been recorded recently in the Midlands or Southern England apart from Darwell

Reservoir where I have recently observed fair hatches of *S. Armatus*. The adults are on the wing throughout most of the summer, but the main hatches appear to be confined to July and August.

The female spinner has clear wings with light brown veins and, although the body colour is somewhat similar to that of the dun, it is darker in appearance, having an overall dull-green coloration.

The nymph of this species (Plate 12, No. 131) a robust creature and a very strong swimmer, is the largest of our agile darters; it is brownish-olive in colour, and apart from its size it can be readily identified by the slightly elongated rear edges of the body segments which are, in addition, drawn out into keel-like spines. These nymphs seem to prefer a slightly lower water temperature than many other species and are consequently confined mainly to lakes, lochs or tarns above 1,000 ft. It is said that they avoid exposed barren shores and, like most of the agile darters, prefer the shelter of weed, but nevertheless they are also found in stony lakes where weed is scarce, so it would appear that they are able to adapt themselves to this environment.

The various other species of this family, as previously mentioned, are of dubious value to the stillwater fisherman, but as it is possible that *S. linnaeana* may be encountered, a brief description may not come amiss. In fact, in Ireland it is more likely to be seen than *S. lacustris*. J. R. Harris states that the nymphs of *S. linnaeana* seem to show a preference for alkaline water, and are found in many of the Irish limestone lakes. They have a similar season to *S. lacustris* and are of a like appearance and size, although the body is of a more pronounced greenish shade, and the hindwings have a distinct whitish border along the trailing edges. For the record, there is also one other species in this Family by the name of *Ameletus inopinatus*, and this is very similar to the other members except for colour. It has a dark brown body and reddish-brown wings, but according to T. T. Macan it is only likely to be met at high altitudes in the far North of Scotland and is, therefore, not of interest to the bulk of fishermen.

Fishing Information: This dun is most likely to be encountered in the more sheltered areas in the vicinity of weed. A pattern to represent it will need to be fairly large, but unfortunately, to the best of my knowledge, there are no standard commercially made patterns available. It will therefore be necessary to have these tied specially, and C. F. Walker has evolved a pattern that should be effective. Apart from this many of the popular Mayfly patterns may be used.

For the female spinner, any of the darker-bodied Mayfly spinner or Spent Gnat patterns will suffice, or alternatively C. F. Walker gives a dressing for the spinner. In areas where the nymph is found, either a Mayfly nymph pattern can be used or a large tying of a standard Olive nymph. This can be fished in a similar manner to the *Cloëon* nymphs, but as this species is a strong and fast swimmer, a faster retrieve is advised.

The Yellow May Dun *(Heptagenia sulphurea)* (Plate 3, No. 28)

This is a medium large insect and it cannot be confused with any other species as it is the only common yellow-winged dun which has two tails. On rivers it is a very common fly, although it seldom hatches in quantities. I decided to include it in the list of stillwater flies as it is reputed to be common on many of the Irish limestone lakes, where it is said to hatch in considerable numbers during the day and on occasion on hot summer evenings. It may occur on certain lakes in England or Scotland, but I personally have not seen it. Although odd specimens may be seen throughout the summer, the main hatches occur during May and June. The dun is most striking in appearance, having a distinct yellow body and wings, and the eyes, particularly of the females, are often a bright blue. It is reputed to be disliked by the trout but, as I have observed on occasions on rivers the odd specimen being taken, I feel it is more likely they are neglected due to the relatively sparse hatches than their taste. Furthermore, on the Irish loughs, where they apparently hatch in large numbers, I understand they are accepted readily by the trout. The female spinner has clear wings with heavy brown veins and with a pale yellow area along the leading edge; the body is pale yellow. The male is similar but has a dark brown body (Plate 2, No. 13). The nymphs of this fly are of the flat-bodied type belonging to the stone clinger group.

Fishing Information: So far as I am aware, these duns and spinners only occur in sufficient quantities to interest the fish or angler on some of the Irish limestone lakes where the duns are referred to as the Yellow Hawk. I do not know of a specific dressing for these flies and I have had no occasion to evolve any for my own use. The nymph is unlikely to be of interest to the fisherman.

Dusky Yellowstreak *(Heptagenia lateralis)*

This fly is rather locally distributed. It occurs in many parts of the country, however, having a preference for higher altitudes and stony lakes, where it is often quite common. In localities where it is found, hatches are often abundant and prolonged. The medium-large dun is extremely dark, with a dark grey-brown body, two tails, very dark grey wings heavily veined, and fairly large upright hindwings. A useful point of identification is a distinct yellow streak on each side of the thorax just in front of the root of the forewings and it is from this feature that its modern angling name is derived. The spinners also have this characteristic feature and both male and female have dark olive-brown bodies. They are to be seen throughout most of the summer months. The nymphs are also stone clingers, and they will be found clinging to stones or rocks along the shores of lakes, prefering the colder water in hilly or mountainous country. It is a fly that until now has been rather neglected by the fisherman and only in recent years has been given a vernacular name. It may well be more common on stillwater than is generally supposed, although it should be noted that it is unlikely to be encountered in the lowland waters of the south.

Two closely related species are *Heptagenia longicauda* and *Heptagenia fuscogrisea*. The former is very similar to the Yellow May Dun but is exceedingly scarce and therefore of no interest to the angler. The latter has been given the name of the Brown May Dun by J. R. Harris and is reputed to be brown in colour, although I have never personally come across one. The nymph is also a stone clinger and is fairly common in some of the rocky limestone lakes of Ireland. It is local or scarce in England. An aid to identification of the adults are two sherry-coloured bands on the femur (thigh) of each leg. All of these members of the *genus Heptagenia* belong to the Family *Ecdyonuridae* and are recognizable by their large upright spurred hindwings and two tails.

Fishing Information: As the Dusky Yellowstreak often hatches in fairly large numbers in localities where it is found, it should be an advantage to have artificials to represent both dun and spinner. Unfortunately, there are no specific patterns known to represent any stages of their existence, but I would suggest that an Iron Blue Quill, tied on a medium sized hook about No. 14, should prove acceptable to imitate the dun and a Dark Watchet wet pattern of the same size for the emerging dun. One can do little better than a Pheasant Tail spinner to emulate the spent female drifting in the surface film. It is unlikely that the nymph in its natural habitat amongst the stones will be of interest to the angler. According to J. R. Harris and from other independent reports I have received, it would appear that the spinners are more likely to be seen on the water than the duns, due probably to the preference shown by the dun for hatching via emergent vegetation as do some other species of this Family.

Claret Dun (*Leptophlebia vespertina*) (Plate 2, No. 8)

This is a fairly common species which is widely distributed over most of these islands and is particularly common in Ireland. I first encountered these several years ago on a small lake, when they were hatching out in fair quantities, and I must admit that to start with I was a little puzzled as to their identity. On the wing they had the appearance of a Large Iron Blue, but as I realized these had never been reported from stillwater I was doubtful. The mystery was solved as soon as I had caught one, when I recognized it as a Claret from descriptions I had read of it. Despite its common name the colour of the dun can hardly be described as claret, for the body is a very dark brown, although in certain light conditions it does have a slight claret tinge.

Identification of this dun is fairly simple, as the combination of three tails and upright hindwings, without a costal projection (spur), only occurs in one other stillwater species—the Sepia dun. Apart from the above physical features the Claret dun can be recognized by its dark grey forewings and the contrasting colour of the hindwings which are of a much paler buff colour. Hatches of the adult winged fly are often spasmodic and usually take place during the middle part of the day. They are to be seen from mid-May until early July. It is known that they prefer water of an acid or peaty nature, which probably accounts for their abundance in Ireland. They are also to be found on many peaty tarns in the North. I have also encountered them on several waters in the Southern Counties and West Country. I was recently fortunate to visit a small water in the south-west where these duns are regularly observed, and on this occasion at least the trout seemed to prefer them to Pond Olive duns that were hatching at the same time.

The Claret Spinner (Plate 3, Nos. 23 and 26) and Nymph

The female spinners will often be in evidence in considerable numbers usually in the early evening. They have a reddish-brown body with a distinct claret tinge, their wings are transparent with light brown venation, and their three tails are pale brown lightly ringed with black. The nymph of this species belongs to the group known as laboured swimmers, and they are slightly flattened in appearance and a little larger than the nymphs of the pond or lake Olive. The nymph is reddish brown in colour, and J. R. Harris suggests that in Ireland, where this species is common, its colour may be influenced by its location, which is usually confined to the peaty areas of many of the limestone lakes. The nymph is nearly invisible against wet peat, whereas its dark body would show up clearly against the grey-green limestone and would be easy prey for any predator. They are most likely to be found in the silt, mud or stones on the bottom and usually in shallower water. A Pheasant Tail nymph, either weighed or unweighted, depending on whether it is fished near the bottom to copy the nymph in its natural environment or in the surface film to imitate the transformation from nymph to adult, is a good representation.

Fishing Information: As this dun is rather similar in appearance to an Iron Blue, a large tying of the artificial of the latter will usually be accepted by the trout. However, there are also specific artificials to represent both dun and spinner perfected by C. F. Walker, J. R. Harris and J. Henderson, and the dressings for these are given later in the book. Apart from the Pheasant Tail mentioned above, J. Henderson has also devised a pattern to represent the nymph and, although I have never used his pattern myself, the tying appears to be very good. As these particular nymphs are rather lethargic, an artificial should be fished slowly at all times.

The Sepia Dun (*Leptophlebia marginata*) (Plate 2, Nos. 3 and 6)

This is very similar in appearance though slightly larger than the previous species and is probably a little less common. It is an important fly to the stillwater fisherman in areas where it is found. This is mainly in the South of England, the middle North and parts of Scotland. So far as I am aware it has not been reported from Ireland. It is a most handsome fly and with its very dark sepia body and dark wings, is fairly easy to identify. In common with the Claret dun, the upright hindwings lack a costal projection, but in this species the hindwings are the same colour as the forewings. A further interesting feature of this species are the three tails which are spread very wide apart. As far as the stillwater angler is concerned they are the first of the Upwinged flies to appear, and the adults are on the wing from early April until mid-May. Hatches are usually confined to the middle of the day and are seldom on a large scale.

The Sepia Spinner (Plate 3, Nos. 18 and 21)

Both male and female spinners are very similar in appearance and also similar to the previous species. As with all spinners of interest to the lake angler, only the females are of importance as the males are seldom found on the water. The female spinner of this species can be distinguished from the Claret fairly easily as its tails are very dark brown and it has a distinct smoky black patch along the leading edge of its semi-transparent wings.

The Sepia Nymphs (Plate 3, No. 29)

Probably the easiest nymph of all to recognize. They are deep sepia brown, have very prominent gill filaments down either side of their bodies and three long tails and these like the tails of the adults are spread very wide apart. They are also included in the group designated laboured swimmers; they are heavily built and slightly flattened in appearance. As far as I have been able to ascertain they are seldom to be found in the shallower margins of lakes in any quantity until the first winged adults are seen in early April. As the period of peak emergence approaches, many of the nymphs move into very shallow water, and most of them change to the winged stage via emergent vegetation or in some cases by crawling up the bank. However, as I have also observed quite large hatches in open water, often in the deeper areas, it would seem that the location and method of emergence varies. They are very similar in shape and colour to the Claret nymph but a little larger and for those anglers who may be interested in identification, the leaf-shaped gill filaments along each size of their bodies are pointed in the Claret and rounded in the Sepia.

Fishing Information: The Sepia dun, being the earliest of the Upwinged flies to appear, is an important species to the fisherman on stillwaters where it is found, and in addition the main emergence is in April and early May when all forms of food are rather scarce. Due to the very dark colour of this dun it most assuredly requires a specific pattern to represent it, but despite it being known to the angler for a number of years, there are apparently no standard commercially tied patterns available. This situation, unfortunately, applies to many of these lake species, and it would therefore seem advisable for the keen stillwater fisherman to learn to tie his own flies, or alternatively to locate a professional or semi-prófessional fly-tyer to tie the suggested patterns to order. Both Oliver Kite and C. F. Walker provide a dressing to represent this dun. The spinner is generally of less importance, and it is only on odd occasions that I have seen these in sufficient numbers on the water to warrant the use of an artificial, and if one is required that wonderful all-rounder, the Pheasant Tail spinner, will usually suffice, but for those that require a closer imitation, one is given by C. F. Walker. The latter also gives a very good pattern to imitate the nymph, and I am surprised that other authors have neglected the nymph of this species. I have always found it an excellent artificial, particularly during the month of April, and by fishing it in the surface film I have had some excellent bags of trout. It can also be dressed weighted with a judicious amount of copper wire, but personally I have not experienced much success fishing it on the bottom, which is the habitat of the natural, although other anglers I know find it very effective fished in this manner.

The Autumn Dun (*Ecdyonurus dispar*) (Plate 2, No. 10)

In some areas this species is also referred to as the August dun; its season is from July to October, but it is most in evidence during August and September. Until quite recently it had not been realized by the fisherman that this species was sometimes found in stillwater and it was first mentioned in *An Angler's Entomology* by J. R. Harris. Since then they have been recorded from many bodies of stillwater and as it seems likely that they may be more common than is generally supposed, I have decided to include it. They are fairly common in areas they favour, such as the Middle North, Wales and the West Country and they are usually to be found in the larger rugged type of lakes. It is a large fly with darkly veined, fawn-coloured wings and large upright spurred hindwings. The body is pale olive-brown and it has two tails. The female spinner has transparent wings heavily veined dark brown, and a dark red body and very long tails. The large nymphs, which are very wide across the thorax, have the flattened body typical of all the Family *Ecdyonuridae*. They belong to the stone clinger group and spend most of their aquatic lives on stones or boulders on the bed of the lake.

Fishing Information: It is difficult to give very much information about this species as I have little personal experience of it on stillwater. It is, of course, well known on rivers, and Roger Woolley perfected a pattern many years ago which will doubtless be acceptable to the stillwater angler. He also gave a pattern called the Great Red Spinner which should be eminently suitable to represent the female spinner.

Caenis or Broadwing (*Brachycercus and Caenis Spp:*) (Plate 2, No. 14)

At a cursory glance the various species which comprise the Family *Caenidae* appear confusing. In all there are six species in this Family, and for the record they are as follows: *Brachycercus harrisella*, *Caenis rivulorum*, *Caenis macrura*, *Caenis moesta*, *Caenis horaria* and *Caenis robusta*. Of these, the first three species are believed to be confined to rivers, and therefore do not come within the scope of this book. The fourth species, *C. moesta*, is exceedingly small and consequently very difficult to match with an artificial. Fortunately, hatches of this particular species are mainly confined to the very early morning before most anglers are on the water and, apart from this, it is less common than its larger cousin, *C. horaria*. The latter is larger than any of the preceding, and is sometimes referred to as the Yellow Broadwing, and is the one most commonly encountered by anglers. Finally, *C. robusta* is the largest of the family but is not often met. C. F. Walker has given it the vernacular name The Dusky Broadwing.

From the above it will be apparent that, out of the six species mentioned, only three are of interest to the stillwater angler. Of these, one is of doubtful value due to its small size and, as far as the remaining two are concerned, they are so similar in size and appearance that they can be treated as one. I therefore propose for simplicity to refer to them all as Broadwings.

The Broadwings

These flies are very easy to identify as, apart from the fact that they are by far the smallest of our Upwinged duns, they are the only family to combine the absence of hindwings with the presence of three tails. The wings of the dun, which are exceptionally wide in comparison to their length (hence their vernacular name), are greyish-white, while the body colour varies from a very pale yellow to a greyish-cream. As previously mentioned, they are very small, the length of the body of an average specimen being about 4 mm., and in many localities they are referred to as the Angler's Curse, not without considerable justification.

Hatches of these duns, which usually occur in the early morning or late evening, are often on a massive scale and this, added to their diminutive size, results in considerable frustration when anglers attempt to deceive the trout which are feeding on them.

Fishing Information: In the first place it is difficult to imitate these tiny duns successfully, although there are several patterns available I have had most success with my own pattern, which I call the Last

Hope, tied on a ooo (No. 17) hook. Secondly, due to the density of these duns on the water at most times, it is often a question of luck whether the trout accepts your artificial or a natural, even when you estimate its next rise correctly. When they are about, the angler should have little difficulty in recognizing the characteristic rise of the trout, as this usually results in a quick head and tail rise, more often than not with subsequent rises in a straight line. The trout often become preoccupied when feeding on these Broadwings and will not look at any other form of food; however, on occasions they will accept a large dry Sedge pattern when so engaged, and this is always worth trying.

To add to the difficulties, when the fish are feeding on these flies they will often take the nymph in the act of changing to the winged adult. The rise form in this case is very similar indeed to the rise to the adult, but with experience it will be noticed that the trout do not rise quite so high out of the water. A very tiny Hare's Ear or a pale coloured nymph tied on a ooo hook fished in the surface film will often prove productive in this case. The natural will be seen from May until September, with peak hatches occurring during July and August.

The spinners are very similar in appearance to the duns, except that the over-all coloration is paler and their tails are considerably longer. It should be noted that this particular family of Upwinged flies is unique on two accounts. The wings of the spinners still retain the fringe of fine hairs along the trailing edge and the dun stage lasts only a few minutes before the insect changes to a spinner. It is no uncommon sight when fishing at the lake-side to observe this transformation when the duns settle on one's clothing. To further complicate the fishing when these flies are on the water, due to this rapid change from dun to spinner, it will often come about that both duns and spinners are on the water together and as the rise to the spinner is practically impossible to tell from that of the dun, the angler is faced with the difficult decision as to which artificial to use. Personally, I have found it best to use a dun or nymph pattern at the commencement of the hatch and switch to a spinner pattern when it is apparent that the main hatch is thinning. Apart from this the trout usually seem to prefer the spinner. There are a number of dressings available for these spinners, including one suggested by C. F. Walker, although a good alternative would be a Lunn's Yellow Boy tied on a very small hook.

The nymphs are of doubtful value to the angler except just prior to transformation, when they are in or near the surface. The two species, *C. horaria* and *C. robusta*, live the majority of their nymphal life on the bottom mud, stones or silt, while the third species, *C. moesta*, the smallest of the trio of lake species, prefers a substratum of gravel, or of large stones with finer material in between. As previously mentioned, this latter species is of less value to the stillwater angler as hatches are usually confined to the very early mornings. The nymphs of the Family *Caenidae* are fairly easy to identify and belong to the group called silt crawlers. They have two pairs of gills, the first so small they are difficult to see with the naked eye, and the second in the shape of two large oval plates covering the foremost dorsum of the body. Viewed from above these give the appearance of a long-skirted coat. These nymphs are adepts at the art of camouflage, and they will often be found covered with fine particles of silt (Plate 5, No. 56).

As both adults and nymphs are most difficult to imitate with an artificial, probably due to their small size, it is worth mentioning that I have recently achieved considerable success with one of my own patterns called the Last Hope. This was evolved several years ago to represent the Pale Watery Dun and other small light-coloured river naturals, and has proved to be one of my most successful patterns, killing many large trout. It is now apparent it is equally effective on stillwater when *Caenis* are on the water, and it may be fished as a dry fly to represent the dun or spinner, or sunk just below the surface film to imitate the nymph about to hatch.

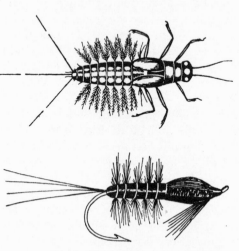

Typical stillwater nymph and matching, artificial
(*Drawings reproduced by permission of Richard Walker*)

CHAPTER VII

THE FLAT-WINGED FLIES (DIPTERA)

This Order of flies is far larger than all the other aquatic Orders put together, and in all contains several thousand species, although by far the greater number are terrestrial and of little interest to the angler. They are commonly known as the true flies and, as the name Diptera indicates, have only two wings, which lie flat along the top of the body, often overlapping. These wings are usually transparent and colourless, although in some species small areas of colour are to be seen. Some of the more common flies in this group are House-flies, Mosquitoes, Crane-flies (Daddy-long-legs), Dung-flies, Gnats, Horse-flies, Smuts and various species of Chironomidae or Midges. We are concerned with only a very few of the many land-bred species, because it is only on windy or gusty days that they may be blown on to the surface of the water in sufficient numbers to arouse the fish.

The Midges (Chironomidae spp.)

This family is a relatively large one containing over 380 different British species, and while a few of them are of terrestrial origin, most are aquatic in both larval and pupal stages. In size they vary tremendously, the adults of some of the largest species having a wing length of almost 8 mm. and the smallest having wings less than 1 mm. Without doubt these insects provide a source of food of the utmost importance for trout in most stillwaters. Throughout the season hardly a day goes by without hatches of at least some species occurring between dawn and dusk.

For these reasons it is considered that they are probably the most important group of all insects to the stillwater fly-fisher. Up to comparatively recent times their value to anglers seems to have been overlooked and consequently little information on their life history and behaviour is known to them. Nor has this lack of detailed information in angling literature been supplemented from other sources, as entomologists have not paid as much attention to fisherman's Chironomids as they have to many other Families. In an effort to rectify this situation I have over the last two or three years bred and studied under laboratory and field conditions many of these species, and I have consequently been able to fill in at least a few gaps. However, much work still remains. In view of the importance of these insects to the fisherman an endeavour will be made to provide as much detail as possible on all facets of their life and behaviour.

So far as I have been able to ascertain, that famous fisherman, Dr. Bell of Blagdon, was the first angler to foster a pattern to represent the pupa of one of the more common species. He called it the Black Buzzer, or Buzzer Nymph, and even today the pattern is still popular and widely used. Although their importance may not have been apparent before Dr. Bell's research, individual anglers, long before, were probably aware of these insects, and I am indebted to Conrad Voss Bark for the following interesting snippet of information. In the early days of Blagdon, between 1904 and 1913, his grandfather, one William J. Cox, was a well-known local angler who used to tie many of his own flies. A pattern that he used to dress and thought very highly of, and probably devised himself, he referred to as a Midge pattern. I have personally handled one of his original tyings that has survived the years, and unquestionably it is meant to represent a Midge pupa.

The following detailed descriptions and behaviour of the larva and pupa are actually based on observations of different specimens over long periods and therefore do not refer to any one particular species. Most of the artificially reared specimens, however, were of the more common types, and so should be reasonably representative of the various species that anglers are likely to encounter.

The Eggs

These are deposited by the adult females on the surface in a gelatinous mass, sometimes being laid in the shape of a string or rope, and at other times in the shape of a raft. The mass floats on the surface and within a matter of days the larvae that have developed within the eggs burst out and descend to the bottom.

The Larvae

These form a staple diet of many trout and will often be found among the stomach contents in considerable numbers.

In size they vary greatly, according to species, in a similar manner

to the adults, with some of the larger species being in excess of
1 inch in length. The larvae, which generally feed on organic
detritus, are most likely to be found in depths between 3 and
18 ft.; they are not confined to the deeper water as many anglers
have been led to believe. They also vary their habitat a great
deal, some living in tubes of mud which they build and locate
in the bottom silt or which they attach to stones, shells or the
leaves of plants. Others build tubes of sand, or make tunnels in
the mud, while a few isolated species make cases, which they
carry around similar to those made by caddis larvae. Many species
are free swimming and will be found among the leaves of aquatic
plants. The Tanypodinae, which is a sub-family of the Chironomidae,
belong to this latter group, and a fuller description of these particular
insects will be found at the end of this chapter under the heading
"Other Diptera".

The larvae vary in colour, brown, green or red being predominant,
although some are almost colourless. The red larvae are probably
the best known and are often referred to as blood worms. Most of
these belong to the Genus *Chironomus*, and this startling red coloration
is due to the presence of haemoglobin. This substance, which is
also found in the human body, is present in the blood of these
particular larvae, and this substance assists the blood by storing
oxygen and providing it when required, thus enabling them to live in
water or situations of a low oxygen content. In many of the specimens
that I have studied it has appeared that the more mature the larva,
the brighter the red coloration, and therefore suspect that the
density of the haemoglobin may increase as pupation approaches.
Many of the red larvae in this group build a "U"-shaped tube of
mud and spin a net over one end to collect food, while others
emerge from it to feed. As previously stated, some species are free
swimming, but at times even those that live in fixed abodes leave
them and move about. On numerous occasions I have found the
red larvae in quantities amongst silkweed, presumably feeding.
When swimming they all follow the same routine, and this vigorous
means of locomotion can best be described as a figure-of-eight
lashing movement (Plate 5, No. 48).

In appearance these larvae are very worm-like, but under a low
power magnifier the head section and body segments can clearly be
defined. As pupation approaches the thorax or section behind the
head becomes swollen and the legs and wings of the coming adult
may be faintly seen through the skin. So far as I have been able to
ascertain the larva goes through four moults or instars (Ford 1959)

when it completely sheds its old skin or cuticle (see Plate 9. p. 108).

The Pupae

In the latter stages of its larval life the developing insect undergoes a complete change within its case, and in a comparatively short time it is ready to cast the final larval cuticle or skin and emerge in its new pupal shape (see Plate 9, No. 109). I understand that it often takes several hours to shed its old skin, and as a matter of interest I have observed quite a high mortality rate among pupae I have raised in captivity due to their inability at times to free themselves completely. Thus, when pupal maturity is reached, partly trapped in their old larval skin, they are unable to swim to the surface to transform into the adult insect. The new pupa develops very rapidly, and although in the early stages the wing cases and filaments on the head are not fully formed (see Plate 9, No. 107), these take up the typical pupal appearance, as shown in many of the photographs, within a matter of hours.

So far as I have been able to observe, the pupal stage in captivity lasts between 36 and 72 hours, although this probably varies with different species. During much of this period they remain in their burrows, but as the time approaches for the final ecdysis the now mature pupae emerge partially from their burrows and commence a rythmic swaying movement. This presumably creates a constant circulation of water, which assists the whitish bunches of filaments (tracheal gills) on their heads to abstract the maximum amount of oxygen. During this period they are particularly vulnerable to predators such as trout, who feed on them when the opportunity arises. In the final stages of pupation the body darkens considerably, or in some species changes colour completely, and the thorax and wing cases turn to light or dark brown.

When conditions are suitable for emergence, they swim slowly to the surface, where the final transformation takes place and the adult winged insect becomes airborne. This last stage in the life of the midge is of utmost importance to the fishermen, so it will be described in detail. Up to now observations in my aquaria and in the field lead me to believe that the pupae ascend directly to the surface and spend little time in midwater, as do pupae of many other insects. The majority of species in this family hatch into the adult in the surface film. On the other hand I have read reports in the angling press that many of these Chironomids hatch on the way to the surface and emerge very rapidly in a similar manner to Simulium or reed smuts. While I do not doubt the authenticity of these observations,

I am somewhat dubious about them being identified as Chironomidae.

The Chironomid, or Midge pupae, as they are commonly called by anglers, vary greatly in size and colour, and as a general rule the resulting adults fairly closely follow the pupae in both respects. Most of the species in this Family that are of particular interest to the fisherman belong to the Genus *Chironomus*. They have a strongly segmented body, and caudal fins or appendages at the tail which facilitate swimming, and while these are mainly transparent they often have a distinct whitish tinge around the edge which under water gives the pupae the appearance of having white tails. The dark wing cases and thorax are very distinct, and on top of the head are four tufts of very white tracheal gills (respiratory filaments). After arrival in the surface film some species seem to transform immediately, but I have observed others that remain suspended in the film for as long as two or three hours. The density of the film on the surface may account for this delay, as under these conditions they appear to have great difficulty in breaking through. Consequently, the heaviest rise of trout are most likely to be encountered on hot, calm evenings when these conditions are most likely to apply, and large numbers of the pupae are hanging in the surface film. Midges appear to favour reasonably calm water for emergence, for they certainly do not like cold windy weather with consequently rough water, and at such times hatches are likely to be sparse or absent.

The movement of the pupae in the surface prior to emergence is particularly interesting and is subject to considerable variation. Some remain hanging stationary with the head filaments just touching the film, and some swim spasmodically for short distances towards the bottom. Others spend most of the time swimming along horizontally just under the surface with a strong wriggling action, only occasionally stopping to take up the more typical vertical position. When the time for emergence arrives, the pupa, hanging vertically, slowly adopts a completely rigid posture and then floats upwards until it is horizontal in the surface, with the thorax just breaking the surface film. Finally, the thorax splits down the centre (see Plate 9) and the fully adult winged insect emerges on the surface, resting briefly near its now empty pupal case (Plate 5, No. 47) before flying away. The time taken for this transformation varies a little according to conditions, but an average time would be about ten seconds. If a specimen in the surface film is observed closely just before the cuticle splits, it will be noticed that the pupa apparently contains air or gas, and the head and thorax can be seen to swell as pressure, which probably splits the skin, is built up. It is also interesting to note that in those species which possess it, the red haemoglobin seems to gather at the tail end *en masse* and slowly travels up the body as the thorax expands. Specks of this red pigment will often be found on freshly hatched adults. Also at least one of the very common species emerges with distinctly orange wings, but this colour disappears very rapidly and no trace of it remains by the time the insect is airborne. Whether this is due to the haemoglobin, or to some other reason peculiar to an individual species, I have been unable to ascertain.

It is generally accepted by many anglers that these pupae emerge only from the deeper water, and this up to a point is a fallacy, as some species actually prefer shallow areas, although many are found in deep water only. The heaviest hatches of the larger species nearly always take place in the late evening, after the sun has set, but quite often good hatches occur in the early morning shortly after dawn.

Some of these larger buzzers also hatch during the day, but they usually emerge rather sparsely and seldom in sufficient quantities to bring about a general rise. On the other hand some of the medium sized or smaller species do emerge in large numbers during the day or early evening, and this quite often results in a good rise. Apart from these, there are also some species which hatch out after dark, but they will not be dealt with as they are of no interest to the angler. Most species have an emergence period extending from two to three weeks, and some of these appear to have two or three generations during the summer. A few species appear to have a much longer emergence period. As far as the fly-fisher is concerned, the first Midges appear in late March or early April, and different species are to be seen throughout the whole season until late October.

The Adult Midge

Despite the fact that there are many species in this family, they are all of a somewhat similar appearance but, as previously stated, they vary tremendously in size. The females have stout, strongly segmented cylindrical bodies, and the wings, which are usually colourless and strongly veined are almost always considerably shorter than the body. These are mounted well forward, giving the insects a rather humped-back appearance in profile. They have six long legs and two rather short antennae protruding from the head.

When at rest the wings are folded down the body and barely overlap, and an interesting characteristic of these Midges is their habit of often holding their front legs clear of the ground. The males are similar to the females except that their bodies are usually slimmer and a little longer, *pro rata*, and their antennae are also longer and heavily plumose. With a low power glass the male claspers can clearly be seen at the tail end of the body. The colours of these Midges are very diverse and the more common species and colours are listed at the end of this section.

The male adult Midges usually form large swarms early in the evenings, and while many of the smaller species may be found adjacent to the water, most of the larger seem to favour localities inland. Swarms are often on a very large scale, and can sometimes be observed in the vicinity of trees or buildings, while at other times they form high in the air, even on occasions over the tops of very high trees. In this latter case, from a distance they give the appearance of a column of smoke. The females, after mating, return to the water to deposit their eggs, and in the case of the larger species this is usually in the very early morning, after sunset, as dusk approaches or possibly during the night. Most anglers will be familiar with the hook-shaped silhouette of these egg-bearing females flying around one's head while fishing; indeed, their colloquial name arises from the buzzing sound they emit. The appearance of these females is often the prelude to a buzzer rise and many fishermen seem to be under the mistaken impression that they are in fact the freshly emerging adults. I must again emphasize, however, that they are the returning females of a previous emergence, bearing at the tail end of their bodies the egg mass which appears to be held in position by the long trailing rear legs.

Up to now no one has attempted to provide even a partial list of the more common Midges for the angler, and in an effort to remedy this situation I would suggest the following. A few species have already been given vernacular names by various authors and therefore, to save unnecessary confusion, I have retained them.

It must be pointed out that the following list of Midges is only a rough one, as due to the very large number of species within this Family many are similar in size, colour and appearance. It should also be noted that the vernacular names suggested in the above list are related to the colour of the natural as seen by the fisherman on the water surface, and not necessarily the specific colour as viewed under magnification out of water. I am deeply indebted to

Mr. A. M. Hutson, of the British Museum of Natural History who was largely responsible for identifying most of the species that appear below.

THE ADULT MIDGES (CHIRONOMIDS)

ANGLER'S NAME	ENTOMOMOGICAL NAME	WING LENGTH
The Large Green Midge	*Chironomus plumosus*-group	6·5 to 8 mm.
The Large Red Midge	,, ,,	,,
The Orange Silver Midge	,, ,,	,,
The Golden Dun Midge	,, ,,	,,
The Ribbed Midge	,, ,,	6·5 to 7 mm.
The Black Midge	*Chironomus anthracinus*	5 to 7·5 mm.
The Blagdon Green Midge	*Endochironomus albipennis*	4 to 6 mm.
The Small Brown Midge	*Glyptotendipes paripes*	4 to 6 mm.
The Small Red Midge	*Microtendipes pedellus*	4 to 4·5 mm.
The Small Black Midge	*Polypedilum nubeculosus*	3·5 to 4 mm.

It will doubtless be noticed that out of the three species of Midges mentioned in most angling literature covering this particular subject only *C. plumosus* appears. The remaining two, namely *C. tentans* and *C. viridis*, do not appear in this list, as during my fairly extensive research on this group I found them to be less common than the species chosen for final inclusion. All the more common specimens of the larger Midges collected were found to be of the *C. Plumosus* group despite differences in size and colour, and it therefore seems possible that this species may one day be sub-divided into a number of different sub-species.

The Large Green Midge
(See Plate 4, No. 32)

The dark green body of the adult has a pale brown thorax with darker patches and yellow-olive legs. These seem to be the largest of all the Midges. The pupae have a similar body colour with a dark thorax and brown wing cases and as they are so large I would suggest an artificial tied on a size 10 hook to represent them. The adults hatch in the late evening, often in large numbers, usually during late July or August.

The Large Red Midge
(See Plate 4, No. 35)

Very nearly as large as the species mentioned above, they are in my opinion the most handsome of all the Chironomids, having beautiful reddish-orange coloured bodies and legs. The pupae are dark red and some specimens have dark blotches on their bodies, and a hook size 10 or 12 is suggested for the corresponding artificial. These seem to be a mid- to late-summer species and hatches are usually rather sparse, often occurring in the late afternoon or early evening.

The Orange-Silver Midge
(See Plate 4, Nos. 36 and 33)

This would seem to be one of the most common and widespread species of all and I have personally encountered numbers of them on practically every stillwater that I have fished. The adult has a silver-grey body with reddish-orange ringing, and a greyish thorax with touches of bright orange; the legs are orange-brown. Hatches are usually prolific, and the insects have a very long season from April to early June, probably consisting of more than one generation, while odd localized hatches are likely to be encountered throughout the season. The main emergence period is in the late evening, although later in the season hatches may also occur in the early mornings at sunrise. The colour of this particular pupa is quite fascinating (see Plate 5, No. 50). It has a dark thorax, orange wing cases, and the body segments are bright silver ringed with dark red. A hook size 10 or 12 should be used for the artificial. I have also observed quite good hatches of a medium-sized species in the late morning or early afternoon during May and June. Whether or not they are a different species I have been unable to ascertain, but apart from size the colours of both adults and pupae are exactly the same.

The Golden Dun Midge
(See Plate 4, Nos. 34 and 37)

This is also a medium to large species, the adults having bodies of a distinct golden-olive colour with dark patches along the top of some of the body segments. Their legs are a similar colour to their bodies but often have touches of black at the joints. They are common and widely distributed and are likely to be encountered from time to time during most of the summer months. The main emergence is usually confined to the late evenings. The pupa has a pale buff thorax and wing cases and the body varies from olive to olive-brown; again a hook size 10 to 12 is recommended (Plate 5, No. 51).

The Ribbed Midge
(See Plate 4, Nos. 38 and 41)

The adults of this species are of medium size and, as the name suggests, their bodies are olive-brown ribbed very distinctly with thick ivory coloured bands. They too are an extremely common and widespread species having quite a long season. They emerge during May and June and again in August and early September, the gap possibly dividing two distinct generations. The pupa has a body of a similar colour to the adult, with the bands of ivory still apparent although thinner, while its thorax and wing cases are often dark brown. The adults hatch either in the late evening or very early morning, and on occasions odd specimens will be found emerging during the day. A hook size 12 is suggested for the artificial to represent the pupa.

The Black Midge
(See Plate 4, No. 39)

There are many species of Midges with dark or almost black bodies, but of all these *Chironomus anthracinus* seems to be the one most frequently encountered, and for this reason it was the species I decided to include in the list. *C. tentans*, which is so often classified as the Black Midge or Buzzer in fishing literature, is in fact quite dissimilar as this is a large and pale coloured species.

The former has a grey-black body with black legs, and in some cases the transparent wings have a whitish tinge; they are of a medium size and the bodies of the males seem to be very much slimmer than the females, and although this difference between the sexes is apparent with all the species in this group, it seems to be particularly noticeable in this one. Unfortunately, I have been unable to discover much information on the life cycle of this Midge, as they proliferate in parts of the country which I seldom visit. I think the pupae may be brownish-grey in colour but I am by no means certain. It seems likely that it is this species that is referred to in parts of Wales and Scotland as the Duck Fly or Harlequin Fly. They hatch out in the middle of the day and although they are seen throughout the summer the main emergence occurs during late March and early April; a well-known artificial tied to represent them is the Blae and Black.

The Blagdon Green Midge
(See Plate 4, No. 42)

This is a medium to small species, the adult having a vivid green body, a brownish thorax and faintly white wings. A closely allied but smaller species similar in colour with a wing length of 3.5 mm. is *Chironomus viridis*. Up to now it is this particular species that has been classified in angling literature under the above vernacular name. However, of the two, *Endochironomus albipennis* appears to be the more common and is therefore the species I have decided to include in the list. Although it is a very common and widespread species it tends to emerge in relatively small numbers. Hatches are usually spread over a period of two or three hours often during the middle part of the day, although on occasions a larger emergence over a shorter period sometimes takes place in the very early mornings. I have seen these Midges during most of the summer months, and the trout seem inordinately fond of the pupae, which have pale green bodies with buff-coloured wing cases. These pupae are small, and on many occasions I have spooned out trout to find literally hundreds of the little creatures among the stomach contents. Despite this, when trout are feeding on them they seem to be very difficult to tempt with an artificial, which should be tied on a hook size 14.

The Small Brown Midge
(See Plate 4, No. 44)

This is a day-hatching species and is very common and occurs in most areas. The adults are medium to small with dark to chestnut-brown bodies and dark brown legs. The main emergence period seems to be between 11 a.m. and 5 p.m. and they are most likely to be seen during mid-summer. Hatches are often on a large scale, and trout seem extremely fond of them, feeding on the pupae or emerging adults in the surface film. The rise form of such trout is unmistakable, being quick and often repeated, usually in a circular direction during a flat calm, or in a straight line upwind in a ripple. Unfortunately, the fish are notoriously difficult to catch when so occupied. The very dark brown pupae which often have a distinct orange tinge are small and for the artificial a hook size 14 or even 16 is recommended.

The Small Red Midge
(See Plate 4, Nos. 40 and 43)

This is also a predominantly day-hatching species, the adults being small with dark legs and port wine red bodies. They are not quite as common as the species mentioned above, nor is the emergence always on a large scale. Apart from the above, the remarks applying to the Small Brown Midge also apply to these and other even smaller species, although the Small Red are often in evidence a little later in the season. The pupae are so similar to the Small Brown that it is virtually impossible to tell them apart.

The Small Black Midge
(See Plate 4, No. 45)

The adult is very small and has a black body and thorax and dark brown or black legs, with distinctly whitish wings. It is common and widespread, and hatches are often on an exceptionally large scale in the early evenings or occassionally mornings during the spring or late summer. During this period the winged adults form large swarms along the banks of lakes and reservoirs. When the trout commence feeding on these or other even smaller species (usually too small to imitate) they often become preoccupied and very selective, and are extremely difficult to catch. In some cases they seem to feed on the ascending pupae, while on other occasions they will only take them in the surface film or when the pupae are transforming into adults. The pupae are very small and dark in colour, and it is essential to use a very small hook to represent them, a 16 or even smaller. The rise form is similar to that described for the Small Brown Midge.

In conclusion, I should like to make it quite clear that there is still considerable scope left for further research on this particular Family of insects. Up to now little has been known by fishermen about their life cycle or behaviour, and although I have during the past three seasons been engaged in an extensive study of them, and I hope, resolved some of the problems, I feel I have barely scratched the surface. It is therefore possible that in the course of time my descriptions of the life cycles of some of the species mentioned may have to be modified and the numbers of species covered considerably extended as more information becomes available.

FISHING INFORMATION

The Adults

Due to the fact that, to the fisherman, the winged form of the adult fly is probably the least important of the three stages of its life, I propose describing it first. Undoubtedly trout do occasionally accept them, but out of the hundreds of autopsies I have performed only in a few cases were the winged flies present. During the preparation of this book I have also received autopsy reports from other anglers in different parts of the country and, broadly speaking, these appear to confirm my own findings. It therefore seems a little strange that an artificial to represent the newly hatched adult resting on the surface after hatching should prove effective. On the other hand it is, of course, possible that on some waters or on certain occasions, the trout do show a preference for the winged adult rather than for the pupa.

Since this volume was first published reports on trout feeding on the adults particularly during some of the heavier early morning or evening rises have been escalating. In some cases the trout even seem to prefer the adults to the hatching pupae. I have recently observed trout feeding heavily on the adults on more than one water for several successive evenings, on each occasion the trout appear to have been taking the females as they have been flying low along the surface. If one watches carefully it is possible to see a faint V shaped wake caused by their trailing legs.

I do not think that there are any commercially tied patterns to represent the winged adults, but there are several dressings available for those anglers keen enough to tie their own flies. When the naturals are in evidence on the surface, the artificial should be fished as a dry fly on a floating line with a lightly greased leader. Little or no movement should be imparted, but every now and then the fly may be given a slight tweak to provide sufficient animation to draw the attention of any trout in the vicinity.

The Larvae (Plate 5, No. 49)

As previously stated, these form a staple diet for the trout and are often to be found in the stomach contents. Unfortunately, due to their appearance and mode of life, they are exceedingly difficult to imitate. The larvae spend most of their life in the mud, silt, weed or silkweed on the bottom, but they do move freely along the bed of the lake sometimes. It is therefore possible to impersonate them at this stage reasonably successfully with a special pattern. I believe there are several dressings available, but the pattern with which I have experienced most satisfactory results is one I have devised myself (red and green larvae) and which is given in the appropriate section at the end of the book.

This pattern should be fished where possible in the deeper water on a sinking line mounted singly on the point. It is essential to let it sink to the bottom, and it is then retrieved very slowly indeed in a series of tiny jerks. This movement animates the soft curly tail on the pattern which loosely simulates the lashing movement of the natural. I tie it in either of the two most common colours of the natural larvae, red and green.

The Pupae (Plate 5, No. 51)

It is at this stage of their existence that the Midges are most accessible to the trout, thereby providing the angler with excellent opportunities to imitate them. When trout are feeding on these medium to large hatching Chironomid pupae the rise form is most distinctive and is best described as a slow head and, tail rise, with the tip of the dorsal and tail fins just breaking the surface. As a general rule the only other time that trout rise in this manner is when they are feeding on rarer occasions, Caenis or on floating snails. As mentioned previously, a pattern to represent the pupa as it hangs in the surface film preparatory to transposing into the adult is the Black Buzzer. This, and several other lesser-known artificials dressed in a similar manner have, over the years, been very successful, and the most popular method of fishing them is as follows. The leader should be lightly greased to within an inch of the two or more artificials being fished to keep them as near the surface as possible. They should be retrieved very slowly with a long steady pull or, alternatively, very slowly with brief pauses. As with all pupa patterns a floating line should be used. Buzzer rises, which usually take place either early in the morning or late in the evening on most summer days under calm, warm conditions, are often heavy, and there is corsiderable difference of opinion as to whether it is better to cast in the path of a rising trout or whether to fish the water. Personally, I prefer to fish the water during a heavy rise and only cover individual fish during a sparse rise.

So far as I am aware the above method, until very recently, has been the only one generally recognized, and I feel sure most anglers will agree that although it is successful on occasions it often proves of little avail. During the last two or three seasons I have carried out many experiments to try and find a more effective method of fishing these pupa patterns. If reference is made to the section dealing with the life cycle of the natural pupa it will be evident that there are several other possible methods open to the fisherman. Although I have evolved several new styles of fishing these patterns with a certain amount of success, none in particular has proved to be the complete answer, and it therefore seems apparent that the trout vary in the way in which they feed on the natural. Consequently, it would seem that there is still considerable scope for further experimenting in this direction. Before proceeding with details of these new methods, I should like to point out that I feel that close imitation of the artificial is of utmost importance, more so than with any other stillwater pattern. The reason for this should be apparent. The natural pupa is a relatively slow-moving creature, and consequently an artificial representing it must be fished in a like manner with little or, on some occasions, no movement at all. The trout therefore have every opportunity of a close appraisal of the artificial. Following this line of thought I have dressed a series of patterns which I have called the Hatching Midges. They are based on a close study of the naturals, and I believe that they are sufficiently lifelike to fool the trout. It should be noted that I dress my patterns with a bunch of white hackle fibres tied in sloping forward over the eye of the hook to represent the head filaments of the natural and a tag of the same material to represent the whitish tail or caudal fins of the natural. I feel that these features are particularly important and are certainly not incorporated in commercially tied or older standard patterns which are tied with white floss sloping back over the body to, I quote, "represent wing cases", which is of course a fallacy. My tying has certainly proved very effective during the last few seasons and the dressings are given at the end of the book.

Although trout sometimes sift the pupae from the bottom silt, the first real opportunity they have of feeding upon them is during their ascent to the surface. Of the following methods the first two are intended to simulate the natural at this particular stage.

Method 1. This can be used satisfactorily only from a boat. When all the signs indicate that a buzzer rise is about to commence, two or three Hatching Midge patterns should be mounted on the leader, one on the point and one on each dropper, each about 2 ft. apart. The leader is left ungreased and as long a rod as possible is used, only enough fly line being pulled off the reel to sink the leader as far as the top dropper. It will be appreciated that a short length of line and leader will now be hanging straight from the rod tip into the water. If the angler is fishing on his own from a boat in a flat calm it will be necessary to slowly raise and lower the rod tip about 2 ft. at a time. If there is a slight wave or another angler is in the boat casting, it will only be necessary to hold the rod perfectly still, as the rocking of the boat will provide all the movement necessary to animate the artificials.

On the face of it this method may appear to be a little revolutionary, but it certainly seems to be very effective on occasion providing the angler has sufficient patience to persist and ignore the temptation to cast to any trout that may rise within casting distance. Fishing a team of three Hatching Midges in this style, the artificial on the top dropper, which will be moving slightly up and down just below the surface, is likely to be taken by any trout feeding on or just under the surface. The other two artificials being fished deeper and moving in a like manner simulate the natural pupae on their journey to the surface and will account for trout feeding on them at a deeper level. It may be thought that fishing directly under the rod top in this manner will put fish down, but this does not seem to be so, probably due to the fact that this method is usually practised during failing light.

Method 2. This presents the artificials in a similar manner but enables a larger area of water to be fished, and is equally suited to both boat and bank fishermen. In this case the Hatching Midge on the top dropper is replaced with a large Sedge pattern which is heavily greased to float. The team of artificials is then cast as far as is necessary, and the floating Sedge carefully watched; at the slightest sign of any movement it is usually necessary only to tighten and any trout that has taken the artificial pupa below the surface will be hooked. On several occasions when fishing in this manner I have had trout literally hook themselves, as they seem to accept the artificial fished in this way very confidently. It is best to use this technique when there is a ripple or wave on the water, as the bobbing sedge will provide the necessary animation to the artificials below. In a flat calm a slow sink and draw retrieve is suggested to provide the desired animation.

Method 3. Both this and the following method require the Hatching Midge or similar patterns to be tied on straight-eyed hooks. The first artificial is threaded direct on to the leader, and a 2-ft. length of about 5 lb. breaking strain monofil is then tied into the leader with a treble blood knot; the second artificial is then threaded on to this and a 2-ft. point of the same monofil is then tied in with a further blood knot. The third artificial is then tied direct on to the point. The two artificials tied direct into the cast are held in the requisite position by the blood knots. The leader should then be lightly greased along its complete length. This team of artificial pupae may be cast either in the path of a rising trout or the water may be fished. They can be fished without movement to represent the natural pupae hanging vertically in the surface film, or retrieved very slowly with short pulls and frequent pauses to simulate the swimming and resting action of the naturals. In practice it will be found that the artificial on the point tends to sink a little below the surface, thereby allowing the angler to represent the natural insect rising to the surface also. When I first thought of this idea of threading the artificial directly on to the leader in an effort to present the artificial in a natural manner hanging vertically with the head just breaking the surface where the natural is found, I was a little dubious as to the hooking qualities, but I am happy to relate that so far this has presented no problem.

Method 4. Basically this is very similar to the above method, and the straight-eyed pupae artificials again are mounted on the leader in the same manner and the leader lightly greased. The pattern on the point, however, is now replaced by a large heavily greased artificial Sedge. When fishing this team it will be found it will float almost indefinitely, allowing the fisherman to cast and to leave the artificials hanging motionless in the film until taken by a trout. As in Method 3, the team may also be retrieved slowly if desired. Later in the summer, when the natural Sedges are found on the water, the angler will often be presented with a bonus when the artificial Sedge on the point is taken in no uncertain manner. I have found during a heavy buzzer rise that it is best to cast the artificials in the vicinity of rising trout and allow them to lay there until one is accepted. I usually adopt the alternative of a little movement when the rise is less heavy, but the angler in time will be able to judge this best in the light of experience.

I would add that Methods 1 and 2 are best practised during the early part of the rise before the trout have settled to feeding on the surface. When the pupae first start ascending the trout tend to feed on them at this stage gradually working nearer to the surface. On warm, calm evenings, when there is a heavy surface film, the emerging pupae often have difficulty in breaking through and therefore hang in the film for longer than normal. This, of course, nearly always results in a heavy and extended rise of trout, as the pupae are then in large concentrations and provide rich pickings for the fish. During this period Method 3 or 4 is the best proposition. Cold and breezy evenings during summer are never conducive to a large emergence, and the rise on these occasions is seldom on a worth-while scale, and under these conditions Methods 1 and 2 are well worth trying.

Method for Small Pupa

The information given up to now applies to the large and medium size pupae. For the smaller pupae a different technique is required, although as yet I have been unable to discover a really satisfactory one. These small Midges, of which the predominant colours are green, red, brown or black, usually hatch during the day or early evening. They often emerge in large numbers, and the trout usually become preoccupied in feeding upon them on the surface. For some reason the trout in calm conditions usually move in a circular direction, or in a straight line upwind in a ripple and sip down the hatching pupae extremely rapidly. My observations to date lead me to believe that the trout are in fact feeding on the pupae as they lie horizontally in the surface film in the act of emergence. When the trout are so engaged they are most difficult to tempt. Up to now I have enjoyed most success with my small Hatching Midge pattern tied on a very tiny hook on a fine point. The leader and fly should be lightly greased, and cast accurately in the path of a rising fish; the retrieve should be as slow as possible.

The Hawthorn Fly (*Bibio marci*) (Plate 7, No. 90), also known as St. Mark's Fly

This latter name is probably due to the fact that hatches usually start about St. Mark's Day (25th April). It is quite a large black fly with a hairy body, about 12 mm. long, an obvious characteristic of which is a pair of long, drooping hind legs. When this fly is on the wing it can usually be identified immediately by these long, trailing hind legs. It is normally found some distance from water, often over open meadowland, flying in swarms about 6 ft. or higher above ground level. In a strong wind, numbers of insects from these large swarms are often blown on to the water. When this happens the trout take them greedily and the fly-fisherman usually has a day to remember. Unfortunately for the trout-fisher, these days are all too rare, as in most localities the season for this fly is comparatively short, lasting only about two or three weeks. Although this species is more frequently encountered on rivers during late April or May, it is still sufficiently common on many stillwaters to be of considerable value to the fly-fisherman. On rivers it usually requires a fairly heavy fall before the trout will start feeding on them, but this is not always so on stillwater. Therefore, at this time of the year, even when only a few specimens may be observed on the water, an artificial pattern is usually worth a try and will often succeed. There are many artificial dressings available to represent this species, and while some are dressed to be fished wet or dry, others are essentially dry flies. My own preference is for a dry pattern fished on a floating line with a greased leader and, as with so many floating patterns for stillwater fishing, I find that a slight twitch to the rod top every now and again to provide a little animation to the fly is most effective. For some reason a little difficult to understand, wet dressings are quite popular and will often kill when fished slowly a little below the surface, but this seems strange, as the natural fly will rarely, if ever, be encountered beneath the surface. Another effective artificial is a pattern I call the Mating Hawthorn, which represents the mating pair locked together, and during prolific hatches these will sometimes land on the water still joined. These pairs naturally make a very juicy mouthful and the trout will often become selective, feeding on these in preference to single flies, hence the value of this particular pattern.

The Heather Fly (*Bibio pomonae*) (Plate 7, No. 89)

This is also a terrestrial species of the same family as the Hawthorn-fly, and is in fact very similar in size and appearance. The Heather-Fly, however, can be readily identified as the tops of the legs or tibiae are a distinct reddish colour. As the name suggests, this fly is found in the vicinity of heather and is therefore most likely to be met in parts of Wales or the North, including Scotland. It is a very prolific species, and in areas where it abounds it is undoubtedly of considerable value to the fly-fisherman, being often blown on to the water in large numbers, where the trout accept them readily. It is in season longer than the Hawthorn, and is on the wing during July, August and September. The local Scottish name for this fly is the Bloody Doctor. I do not know of any particular dressing for it, but any of the many dressings to represent the Hawthorn-fly should suffice, the black hackle being replaced with a reddish one.

The Black Gnats (*Bibionidae* Family) (Plate 7, No. 91)

This is another similar but much smaller land-bred fly of importance to the fly-fisher. The scientific name is often given as *Bibio johannis*, but the name Black Gnat is in fact given to a number of different species, and *B. johannis* is but one of them. In some parts of the country *Dilophus febrilis* is the Black Gnat, in others it is *Hilara maura* or *Ocydromia glabricula*. *Bibio* spp. can be positively identified by the venation of the wings and the curious long-pointed spur on the knee joints of the two front legs (see Fig. 21). In a similar manner *D. febrilis* can be recognized by the many-spurred projections on the knee joints of the two front legs (see Fig. 20). The males of *Hilara* can be similarly recognized by the enlarged "Popeye" joints of the tibiae on the forelegs. These latter flies are a more important fly to the fisherman than is generally realized in areas where they abound. Dr. Michael Wade has made a study of this particular insect, and I am indebted to him for the following extract from one of his letters.

FIG. 20. Showing spurs on the knee joint on forelegs of *D. febrilis.*

FIG. 21. Showing long spur on knee joint on forelegs of *Bibio* Spp.

At Monkswood on the Usk in Wales, *Hilara* are the most important types of Black Gnats from the fisherman's point of view, and in May they are accepted eagerly by the trout. It should be pointed out however that they are not true Black Gnats because they belong to the very large Family of Empididae which contains over 300 species. Apart from *Hilara* mentioned here there are probably many other members of this family that are similar in size and appearance that are found on stillwater. They can be seen flying in all directions in swarms very close to the water; these swarms I believe are associated with mating, during which the males often secure small midges or seeds or even bits of grit and wrap them up in a silk web for presentation to the female. Mating takes place while she unwraps the parcel. These mating couples often fall on the water and the trout do not hesitate to bring this hasty marriage to a speedy and tragic end.

Apart from the above, there are many other flies which could equally come under the general heading "Black Gnats", including, of course, many of the Simulium spp. found in running water. Some of these species are seen only in spring, others only in the summer or autumn, so from the angler's point of view "Black Gnats" are about at any time during the fishing season. Again, as with the Hawthorn-flies, they are usually on the water during windy conditions but, owing to their longer season, they are likely to be seen more frequently.

As far as artificial patterns are concerned there is a wealth of dressings from which to choose, and one of the most successful is the Knotted Midge, which is meant to copy the paired gnats as they fall on the water during mating, and it certainly seems to be good medicine during a heavy fall. Apart from dry patterns there are also wet patterns, but whether any of these are suitable for the stillwater angler I have been unable to discover. The floating patterns should be fished as a normal dry fly on a lightly greased leader.

The Crane flies—(*Tipulidae* etc.)

The larger species of this family are a familiar sight at home or in the garden as well as by the waterside, and they are generally referred to as Daddy-long-legs. This is a very large Family and anglers may be surprised to learn there are nearly 300 different British species, which vary greatly in size, a large number being no larger than some of the mosquitos. The largest species is *Tipula maxima*, and with a body length of about 32 mm. has the distinction of being one of the largest of all the British flies, exceeded only by some of the Dragonflies. This is the species most likely to be seen on the water by the fly-fisherman as the larva is semi-aquatic, frequenting the damp margins of lakes or reservoirs, or in some cases actually living underwater. Pupation takes place ashore, the larva seeking a drier location in which to bury itself. Apart from this species there are many belonging to other genera of a similar appearance but smaller in size that are likely to be on or near water. One of the more common of them is a handsome yellow and black species, *Nephrotoma crocata*, usually found in bodies of water adjacent to woodland. Another very common species, *Ptychoptera contaminata* and other species of the Family Ptychopteridae, have larvae of a purely aquatic nature, which live in the mud or debris on the bottom in the shallow margins and these larvae are usually referred to as rat-tailed maggots in common with the larvae of some of the Drone flies. The long tail of this larva is in reality a breathing tube which reaches to the surface, thereby allowing the larva to breathe air. This tube or tail, consisting of three sections, is telescopic and this enables the tube to be adjusted to a water depth of up to about three inches.

From the above it will be apparent that there are very many species that are likely to be found in the vicinity of water. As they are all very similar in appearance although varying in size, they can all be classified by the angler as Crane-flies and it is therefore only necessary to have two or three patterns in different sizes.

They are all poor fliers and if they fly or are blown out over the water they soon descend on to the surface, where their struggles soon attract any trout in the vicinity. The fish seem inordinately fond of these large ungainly insects and seem to accept them eagerly and, furthermore, they are reputed to attract the attentions of the larger fish, although I have not personally found this to be so.

They are probably better known on some of the Irish loughs, where the live insect is a great favourite for dapping. This is usually throughout the month of August when the naturals are at their maximum. However, they are likely to be effective throughout the summer, although July, August and September seem to be the best months to fish the artificials. During this period, when one is often faced with hot, bright windless days of flat calm, they can often provide the chance of a fish when all else has failed. Under these conditions providing a few of these flies are on the water a correctly tied and presented artificial will sometimes succeed in enticing an otherwise lethargic trout to the surface.

Generally these Crane-flies seem to have been rather ignored by both fisherman and fly-tiers and this seems a pity as, during periods when reasonable quantities of these flies are on the water, it can be a very killing pattern. In the southern parts of the country, anglers seem to treat them with even less interest than elsewhere except for a few notable exceptions such as Weir Wood reservoir in Sussex. Their popularity on this water justifies my belief that their use elsewhere in the south would be well repaid. There are not many dressings to imitate these Crane-flies but two that are reputed to be excellent patterns are given in the appropriate chapter later in the book.

The artificial should be fished on a floating line, as a dry fly, with a lightly greased leader. Due to the long, thin shape of the natural, artificial patterns, unless tied with a cork body, are not good floaters and therefore they will have to be retrieved and re-cast regularly. It should be fished in jerks to simulate the struggle of the natural insect as closely as possible.

Drone Flies—*Syrphidae*

This family includes the Hover-flies, and as far as the angler is concerned they can all be classified as Drone-flies, for only an expert on entomology could classify the species correctly. In appearance and size they are somewhat similar to honey bees or common wasps, except of course they have only two wings like all Diptera. The larvae and in some cases the pupae of many species of this family are aquatic or semi-aquatic in origin and may therefore be of some interest though of little value to the fisherman.

One species of Drone-fly in particular is quite common in stillwater and this is *Eristalis*, the larvae of which are colloquially known as Rat-tailed Maggots (Plate 12, No. 136). These curious creatures are usually found in the black mud or silt in shallow water of small ponds or possibly larger bodies of stillwater rich in decaying matter. Their bodies are about half-an-inch long, greyish in colour, and their tails are extended into long breathing tubes which reach the surface of the water. It is supposed that these tubes, which are telescopic, can extend up to a length of nearly three inches, allowing the larvae to live and move freely about the bottom in water up to this depth, although they are also known to occur in water that is deep as they are fairly active and can swim. The pupae are very similar to the larvae except that near the heads they have two small breathing tubes which are used by those species that remain in the water to take in air while they are suspended passively near the surface. Usually they are located in shallower water, but at times they may be found in deeper water, where I have no doubt trout would take them, although I have not personally observed it.

The adults vary tremendously but the predominant body colours being dark brown or blackish sometimes combined with orange patches. When the females return to the water to deposit their eggs in small clusters on the surface, as they sometimes do, they may at this period be of interest to both fish and fisherman. Although I would not normally expect to find them on large lakes or reservoirs I am given to understand that they are native to Grafham Water and also Hanningfield reservoir in Essex, and that at this period an orange and black artificial often does well, but as yet I have been unable to substantiate it.

It should be noted that one of the Crane-flies results from aquatic larvae of a very similar appearance to some of the species just mentioned and which is also referred to as a Rat-tailed Maggot.

The Phantom Midges—*Chaoborus* spp. (Plate 8, No. 95)

There are a number of species in this family and one of the more common is *Chaoborus flavicans*, and it is this species that I have reared and studied. The adults hatch out during the warmer weather of summer, but as the emergence period seems to be between midnight and dawn they are of little interest at this stage to anglers. In appearance the winged fly is very similar to a medium sized Chirono-mid or midge. They average a little over a quarter of an inch in length and the body colour of the female is a very pale green, while that of the male is a dirty white on the underside turning greyish on top. The adult females return to the shallower margins of lakes in the late evenings in considerable numbers to oviposit, and at this period it may well prove worth while to fish a representative artificial floating pattern.

This particular family of insects, up to now largely ignored by the fisherman, is undoubtedly most prolific and many stillwaters support extremely large numbers. The phantom larvae and pupae are taken occasionally by the trout and therefore should be of interest to the fisherman. Unfortunately, the larvae which when fully grown are about 16 mm. long and for the most part lie horizontally in the water completely motionless, are quite transparent apart from two black eyes and four blackish air bladders, two in the thorax and two in the rear end of the abdomen. It will, therefore, be appreciated that it is virtually impossible to dress or fish an artificial to represent them in this stage of life. They do, of course, move at quite frequent intervals but this movement is very rapid and difficult to follow with the naked eye.

The pupae, on the other hand, have a little colour (Plate 5, No. 60) and although they remain stationary for short periods, they frequently wriggle and occasionally move position. They are a little over quarter-of-an-inch long and have a creamy semi-transparent body with a large bulbous thorax. This turns a pale brown or orange colour as pupation progresses, and they hang in a vertical position resembling a comma in outline, similar to a Chironomid pupae but not quite so curved.

The pupae have a pair of appendages on top of the thorax shaped rather like a pair of donkey's ears, and many authorities state that the pupae regularly ascend to the surface to absorb air through them. As a result of the observations and experiments of David Jacques and myself, we are reasonably certain that these appendages play no part in respiratory action, but probably assist to maintain the pupae in an upright position and to control their depth in the water.

We have reared many dozens of these creatures to maturity and the average time in the pupal stage is approximately four days. During this period they hang in the water at various depths between the bed and the surface of the lake, and it is only immediately before transformation to the winged adult takes place that they actually ascend into the surface film. It will therefore be realized that as countless numbers of these pupae are present in many of our stillwaters at varying depths, mostly in the shallower areas, it may be possible to present an artificial in a manner to deceive a trout.

The main difficulty is to present the artificial in a natural manner.

and although I have developed a pattern which closely resembles the natural I have not yet succeeded consistently with the presentation, but feel there should be considerable scope for experiment in this direction.

Reed Smuts or Black-flies (*Simulium* spp.)

These very tiny flies often hatch out in countless numbers and in many old angling books are referred to as the Black Curse. They are extremely small, the average size being less than an eighth of an inch. There are little more than a dozen species in this family, and some of the larger types closely resemble the terrestrial Black Gnats and are possibly mistaken for them by many anglers. The body is short and stout with the segments hard to discern. The wings are short, broad and transparent and are carried flat on top of the body when at rest. Resembling House-flies in miniature and varying in colour from dark brown to black, they are found only in a reasonable current for the very good reason that the larvae require water with a fair amount of movement. Therefore, they will live only in bodies of stillwater that are fed by constant inflow and then only in the area immediately adjacent to it. Despite the small size of these insects, trout will often feed on them avidly to the exclusion of all else, and fish so engaged are extremely hard to catch, due partly to our difficulty in dressing an artificial small enough to deceive them. The larvae are often found at autopsy by anglers on rivers, the trout having browsed them off the weeds.

Other Diptera

As previously mentioned, Diptera is an extremely large Order of flies and, apart from individual species of particular interest already discussed in some detail, there are many others that are sometimes found in, on or near water, and some may be of interest to fishermen. Most of them are only encountered occasionally and are consequently of dubious value.

Culicidae

Of those that could be included in this category, the one of most interest to anglers is the Common Gnat, *Culex pipiens*, a Mosquito (Plate 10, No. 118). They are very prolific insects and both larvae and pupae (Plate 12, No. 137) are aquatic, being found in all types of stagnant water such as wells, tanks, water butts and ponds. They are also on occasion to be found in numbers in larger bodies of water, and in fact those that I have reared were collected from Grafham Water.

The larvae are long and slender and spend most of their lives hanging head downwards from the surface film. They are more or less colourless and when disturbed sink slowly to the bottom. In the pupal form they seem to be short lived, as I have observed the pupae hanging in the surface film for only a matter of hours. They are considerably smaller than the common large species of Midge pupae, while in shape they look like an inverted question mark with a large head equipped with two trumpet-like appendages or ears, which protruding through the surface film are apparently used for respiratory purposes. They spend most of their brief lives in the surface film, but at frequent intervals they make short journeys to the bottom, particularly when disturbed. This is accomplished by powerful strokes from their tail fins, and while they can move quite rapidly their movements are rather jerky.

The transformation from pupa to adult winged insect (see Plate 10) takes place on the surface, in a manner similar to a Midge, usually as dusk approaches. Although it seems generally accepted that these Gnats prefer a habitat of stagnant water, I wonder to what extent this is true, as I have found the larvae in quantities in at least two large bodies of stillwater. If, in fact, they are more common on lakes and reservoirs than is believed, these or other similar species dealt with next could account on at least some evenings for the late and widespread rise of trout that are apparently rising to nothing visible and are notoriously difficult to hook. Although I must make it clear, in my personal experience this typical rise is usually due to hatches of Midges. However, in either case in the poor light of dusk it is almost impossible to see any of these adult insects actually emerging or even if one does, to identify them.

I think it would be possible to dress an artificial to represent these smaller species, but it would have to be on a very tiny hook, and the artificial would have to be fished actually in the surface film in a manner similar to the new method described for fishing the Midge pupa. In any case I feel that there is considerable scope for further research and experiment in this direction.

There are many other similar species of Diptera worthy of further study and some of the more common types are as follows.

Tanypodinae

These are common in stillwater and while the larvae, which are almost colourless, are similar in appearance to the larvae of the Midges although generally smaller, the brownish coloured pupae resemble in shape, size and habitat the Gnat pupae described above.

It is therefore likely that research in this direction may also one day prove to be of considerable value to the fisherman. The adults of Tanypus are very similar indeed to some of the smaller Midges, the predominant colour being brown, while the wings of some species are also faintly mottled brown; they average 6 to 7 mm. in length (see Plate 4, No. 46). It is interesting to note that the pupae of this species prior to transformation into the adult are usually found in midwater, and when disturbed descends rapidly to the bottom or nearest cover.

Ceratopogonidae

These are extremely small biting midges and the adults are barely one-tenth of an inch in length. They are most commonly encountered during May or June and they are quite widespread on many bodies of stillwater. The larvae are slender worm-like creatures usually found on the surface in the shallow margins among floating or decaying vegetation, and are therefore unlikely to be readily available to the trout. The pupae which have slender segmented bodies with a large bulbous head may be found near the surface in open water and could be worthy of further investigation by the angler.

The Dixinae

This small sub-family contains several species, all somewhat similar in appearance and in the light of recent research they would now appear to be more widely distributed than was previously supposed, particularly in many small stillwaters in the Home Counties. They belong to the same family as the Chaoborus (Phantom Flies), and while the pupae are similar in size and shape, with a slender strongly segmented body and a very large elongated head on top of which are a pair of ear-like appendages (respiratory horns), the larvae are dissimilar. The larvae usually found in the shallow margins on rocks or weed are inactive creatures and when at rest usually adopt a U-shape. They are smaller and stouter than the larvae of the chironomidae. Many of the adults in this sub-family have dark brown or even black bodies, and they have two or three distinct thoracic stripes or patches on the head. The wings, some of which have a brownish tinge and vary in length according to species between 4 to 6 mm, are similar in appearance to a medium sized chironomid but the males do not have the strongly plumose antennae which are characteristic of this family. Both the pupae and the adults of these Dixa-Midges could be important to the angler where they occur. There are about a dozen species and one of these, *Dixa Aestivalis*, is a particularly handsome insect, the adult having a stout black cylindrical body, contrasting strongly with its bright yellow legs and head on top of which are three distinct black stripes. I am indebted to Alec Pearlman who provided the specimens probably of this species from the stomach content of a trout he caught. (See Plate 13, No. 145).

Finally, two other species of Diptera should be mentioned, and these are the Dung-flies and the Oak-flies, which seem to be popular with many authors of fishing books. Both are terrestrial, but as their habitat is sometimes in the vicinity of water it is, of course, possible that occasionally they may be observed by anglers, but why some authorities suggest they are of value to the fisherman I find a little difficult to understand, as it is seldom that one sees more than an occasional specimen blown on to the water. Certainly, so far as my own experience of these insects is concerned, their interest is strictly limited.

CHAPTER VIII

THE SEDGE-FLIES (TRICHOPTERA)

FLIES WITH ROOF-SHAPED WINGS

The Sedge, or Caddis-flies, as they are known in some areas, make up a fairly large group containing nearly 200 different species. They are related to certain families of moths, but differ mainly in the structure of the wings. Each has four wings, but those of the moth are covered with tiny flattened scales, while those of the Sedge-flies are covered with tiny hairs. A brief account of the life cycle of the latter is given in Chapter IV.

Like moths, many of the Sedges are nocturnal, hatching out either after dark or just as the light is beginning to fade. Fortunately for the angler, some species do hatch out during the day or late afternoon. To generalize, the nocturnal species of Trichoptera seem to be larger, paler and less hairy than the diurnal species. Several are well known to fly-fishermen, and while the most distinctive of all of the day-time Sedges is the Grouse Wing, the Sedges which are probably the most common of all seen at the waterside are the Silverhorns. These small to medium sized flies can be seen on most days in the late afternoon right through the summer, and are generally found flying in clouds just above the surface of the water. Unfortunately, although they are so prolific they seldom seem to interest the trout, and in hundreds of autopsies on trout I have seldom come across one.

The Larvae

Most species of Sedge-flies make cases in which they live, but there are a few families that are free swimming and do not make cases. It is not proposed to discuss in this book these latter types which, require running water to survive, as they are rarely encountered in stillwater, and therefore the conditions that suit them are generally found only in bodies of stillwater that have fast-flowing inlets and outlets, and these are in the minority. The larvae are often referred

116

to as caddis grubs and they are somewhat similar in appearance to a caterpillar, except that they have a clearly defined head and six legs. The body colour varies and the head is usually of a darker colour, often brown, although in many species this is marked with dark patterning on a lighter ground.

Shortly after hatching the young larvae commence to build their future home or caddis case, and although this may appear far from luxurious, it is in fact a masterpiece of insect ingenuity. Apart from being roomy and comfortable, being lined on the interior with a smooth secretion provided by the larva to seal the gaps between the sections of material holding the case together, the outside is well camouflaged as a protection against predators, and the whole complex structure can be increased in size when required. Most caddis cases are tapered from front to back, and when the larvae grows it builds on to the front or wider end. The cases are formed from a wide variety of materials, and although most species have their particular preferences, not only in this respect but also for the actual shape of their dwelling, it would be a mistake to rely on these characteristics alone for identification of the species. Among the materials used are small discarded shells, gravel, sand, pieces of stick, vegetable matter or cut sections of leaves. Whatever the substances, the artistry with which they are applied is quite incredible. As far as is known all larvae live in their cases for up to a year, and during this period they are in constant danger from predators. When on the move in search of food, their heads and legs are extended from the case, which is held in position by small hooks on their bodies, but when danger threatens they quickly retreat into the comparative safety of their cases. Most species are omnivorous, while a few are herbivorous, feeding on vegetable matter only, while many are carnivorous, feeding on other small aquatic creatures or at times even on their own kind. In the following descriptions of the more common species of adults, I have, where possible, also given a description of the larval case which can sometimes be helpful in identifying the species. This method is far from infallible, as previously mentioned, and is well illustrated by the following.

Some time ago I procured from Two Lakes, for rearing in my tanks, some specimens of caddis that had formed their purse-shaped cases from several large sections of fallen beech leaves. Apparently this particular species, apart from building its case from these leaves, also feeds on them, and before I became aware of it several of them had partially eaten their own homes. At the time I was unable to procure a further supply of these leaves, and, anticipating incorrectly that they would fail to survive in their incomplete cases, I left them to their fate. To my surprise, a few days later I discovered they had made completely new domains for themselves from various small shells, and they now bore little resemblance to their former appearance.

The larvae in their cases are usually to be found in the shallower water in the vicinity of weeds or stones, although certain species that enjoy a measure of immunity from predators will often be found in profusion on the bed of the lake in full view. Trout will feed on some species avidly when available, but as far as I am aware few fly-fishermen attempt to imitate them at this stage of their existence. In any case, even if this could be accomplished, it may appear to many anglers to be far removed from fly-fishing in the accepted sense. On the other hand, the very essence of fly-fishing is to deceive a trout with an imitation of fur, feather or silk to represent some particular form of food on which it may be feeding, so apart from the fact that here we are dealing largely with an inanimate object, as opposed to an animate one such as a nymph or a fly, there is basically little difference. While I am sure it would be relatively easy to tie a lifelike artificial to represent some of these larvae in their cases, and indeed I give one in the appendix—developed by Geoffrey Bucknall—I feel it may prove rather difficult to present it to the trout in an attractive or successful manner. Undoubtedly there is considerable scope for experiment in this direction for those fishermen who feel inclined to do so.

The Pupae

When the time for pupation arrives, the larva anchors its case to weed, stones, etc., and then seals or plugs it at each end. This is accomplished in diverse ways, using tufts of algae or moss, cut pieces of weed, small stones or gravel or, in some cases, it is sealed with a web of its own chitinous substance. Whatever the material used, minute gaps are left to allow the passage of water, presumably for respiratory purposes, and the pupa constantly undulates its body within the case to assist the flow.

In the early stages of pupation certain changes take place until, shortly before pupation is complete, the main characteristics of the adult are noticeable. The wing cases are fully formed and the legs developed, and while these are bunched under the body, at least two of those enveloped in the pupal integument are capable of independent movement to help its final journey to the surface. The antennae, which are a characteristic of the adult, can also be observed lying down either side of the body, and with species that have antennae longer than their bodies the excess length is either folded at the tail end or, in some instances, actually wound spirally round the rear segments of the body. The pupa is also equipped with a powerful pair of mandibles well adapted to their function of sawing through the sealed end of the case, to release the pupa for its journey to the surface, where transformation into the winged adult takes place (Plate 10, No. 116). The duration of pupation varies from days to weeks, according to species or condition.

As previously mentioned, at least one pair of legs, although still enveloped in the pupal skin, are functional. These, as far as I have been able to ascertain, are always the median legs and generally are fringed with extensive hairs on each side, and so, well adapted for their purpose of providing the pupa with a pair of paddle-like instruments to enable it to swim to the surface.

Certain species transform into the adult as soon as the surface is reached, while others apparently swim considerable distances until they find, projecting above the surface, some object or weed up which they climb, and where metamorphosis is completed. At this stage the pupal skin loosely enveloping the formed imago expands as internal pressure which eventually bursts it is built up. The skin usually splits at the top of the head behind the mandibles, and except that the wings are not yet fully inflated the fully developed adult emerges.

It is during their final journey to the surface that the pupae are most vulnerable to predators such as trout, thereby providing the angler with an excellent opportunity of imitating them at this stage.

Further Information on the Sedge Pupa (reproduced from an article provided for *The Fly Fisher's Journal* by the author, Plate 13, No. 142).

In recent years it has been established that on both rivers and particularly on lakes the pupa of the sedge, next to the pupa of the midge, provides the main diet of trout throughout the latter half of the season. Until comparatively recently apart from my own sedge pupa patterns and the longhorn patterns of Dick Walker, little progress has been made in this direction to develop specific pupa patterns to represent the many different species. To some extent this is now being rectified, as during the past two years several excellent new tyings have appeared from the United States where sedge pupa patterns are used extensively on rivers.

As a result of this I have been taking an increasing interest in this particular stage of the insect, and I have subsequently come to realize that there are many misconceptions about the anatomy of the average pupa. I am sure most amateur fly dressers will appreciate that it is essential to have a clear picture in one's mind of the precise appearance of the anatomical structure of an insect before one can attempt to dress a lifelike pattern. Despite a diligent search I have been unable to find full and accurate information in this respect as, unlike the larva and the adult, most books seem to skate over specific details on the pupa. The following information on the pupa has been gleaned from various statements in scientific papers and books, plus a certain amount of information which I have collected from my own research, which I hope will in the course of time prove to be accurate.

As the behaviour of the pupa prior to and after hatching into the adult is of direct interest to the fisherman, I will commence by giving some brief information on its life cycle. When the larvae are ready to pupate, case making species construct a cocoon by partially sealing the ends of their cases, while most non-case making species construct their cocoon from various materials such as tiny stones or gravel fastened together with silk on the side of a stone which is then sealed upon completion. Pupation can take from several days to two or three weeks according to conditions and species. When pupation is complete they cut their way out of their cocoon utilizing powerful mandibles with which the pupa is equipped. They then swim either to the surface or towards the shore, depending whether they are species that hatch out on the surface or via emergent vegetation along the shoreline, where ecdysis into the adult takes place. I would add that some authorities suggest they may swim around for some time before emerging. The pupa is quite a powerful swimmer as the middle pair of legs are fringed with dense hairs and are used like paddles for propulsion. Those species which transform into the adult on emergent vegetation seem to be provided with extra strong tarsal claws on their front legs probably as an aid to climbing, and once they have attained a safe position well clear of the water appear to take their time before the transformation into the adult is completed. On the other hand those species that hatch on the surface in open water usually do so quickly, which is probably nature's way of ensuring survival of at least a percentage. On most of the occasions when I have been able to observe closely the pupa hatching on the surface, it would appear that the emerging adult is able to inflate the pupal case from within until it bursts along the top of the thorax, whence the adult emerges (Plate 10, No. 116). This is usually within seconds rather than minutes. Whether the inflation of the case is peculiar to certain species or not I have been unable to ascertain. It should also be noted that certain structural features of the pupa such as the fringe of hairs along the legs, the powerful biting mandibles and abdominal hooks, are part of the pupal envelope which is eventually discarded.

I am indebted to my very good friend the Danish angling entomologist Preben Torp Jacobsen for the following description of the actual transformation, as he observed it many times recently during very dense hatches on a Norwegian river. "We saw at close range how the caddis pupae swim up to the surface, using their middle legs like paddles, many hatched out on the surface which was the most usual way, but others—probably different species—upon reaching the surface moved rapidly over it like skaters using both middle and also the front legs as paddles creating a V-shaped wake, many being taken by the trout with a savage sort of rise. Those that reached emergent vegetation or in many cases our waders, crawled quickly out of the water, and within a short period ecdysis commenced. They appeared to arch their backs, then the front of the thorax would split and out would come the head followed by the thorax and then the wings. The antennae appear to lie alongside the body under the wing cases, as do the rear legs which seem to lie in such a position that they are used to actually withdraw the wings from the pupal envelope. Many trout, whitefish and grayling we caught were crammed full of sedge pupae, many of them still alive."

The Pupa The pupal integument is transparent and loosely envelops the fully formed imago lying underneath. The general shape and colour of the pupa therefore closely follows the shape and colour of the adult sedge. The abdomen of the pupa, composed of nine segments, is generally rather larger than the body of the adult, and in many species a pronounced fringe of dark hairs may be observed on each side along the lateral line. The dorsal or upper surface of the pupa also has a series of dark coloured plates surmounted by hooks. These vary in size and shape according to species, and are used for gripping the sides of the cocoon when emerging. The pupal envelope at the end of the body covering the genitalia is darker and in some species is elongated and equipped with distinct bristles. The antennae covered by the pupal skin closely follow the colour and shape of the underlying adult and lie along the body but under the wing cases. With those species that have exceptionally long antennae they are wrapped spirally around the body many times, and it is worth noting that these often become unwrapped and trail behind the pupa as it swims along, while the spiral shape at the end often persists. Each of the four wings are separately housed in the integument, but as they are folded within these wing cases their length is considerably reduced and they only extend about half- to two-thirds along the length of the body. The larger fore wing cases are positioned over the shorter anterior ones so that they both cling closely along the sides of the body with the tips projecting slightly downwards. The colour of the wing cases of the pupa closely follow the colour of the wings of the adult. The legs, six in all, are free although they are covered closely by pouches of the pupal envelope. The middle legs used for swimming and lined with dense hairs are entirely free, while the fore and rear legs are partly adherent to the body. Finally, the eyes of the mature pupa are usually black and very prominent.

It will, I hope, be appreciated that the above is a general description of an average pupa. There are of course minor features besides the size that differ according to the specific species. I have also excluded many taxonomical features as these are only of importance to the entomologist.

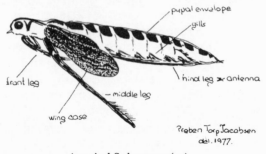

A typical Sedge pupa (4x)

Fishing Information: Although pupae artificials are often successful when used indiscriminately throughout the fishing season, the most productive period is usually from late June onwards. Apart from this it will be apparent that maximum success will be assured during the actual emergence period of the natural. Unfortunately, the natural swimming to the surface is rarely observed, so one has to look for other clues to the event. Of these, undoubtedly the most reliable are the sudden appearance of adult winged sedges over open water, the appearance of empty pupal shucks floating in the surface film where previously none had been observed, or finally, the discovery of live pupae in the stomach content of a freshly caught trout.

The artificial pupa should, of course, imitate as closely as possible the natural in both size and colour. The size of the natural varies greatly according to species, and while the colour of the hatching pupa is usually the same as the subsequent adult, the colour range is rather limited, and therefore artificials dressed with bodies of cream, green, orange or very dark brown will cover most eventualities. At times I feel the colour aspect is of considerable importance and it should be noted that, as the pupal case of the natural is virtually transparent, the colour of the developed imago underneath is always apparent. Although the artificial pupae may be successfully fished from either boat or bank it is undoubtedly most effective from the latter. It is suggested that a floating line be used with, depending on personal preference, either a single artificial on the point or additional artificials on each dropper. There are two methods of retrieve which are, sink-and-draw to represent the natural swimming from the bottom to the surface, or a slow, steady retrieve in the subsurface to simulate the natural swimming along under the surface. The latter is, of course, the more suitable method of the two for the boat fisherman. To the best of my knowledge there are only a few patterns available to represent the pupae, and of them the best known is probably the Amber nymph perfected by Dr. Bell of Blagdon to represent, I believe, these particular creatures. While it is an excellent pattern when naturals of a brown or orange coloration are in evidence, it has its limitations. I have, therefore, recently developed a series of patterns which I tie in different colours and sizes and which have now proved to be most effective, under most conditions. The dressing of my new pattern called a Sedge Pupa will be found in the appendix.

The Adult or Imago

Most Sedges are confined to shades ranging from a pale yellow-fawn to a dark red-brown through to a dark grey-brown or almost black. The life cycle is similar to the previous Dipteran group, the insects passing through three stages before emerging as adult winged flies: egg, larva and pupa. The adult fly has four wings, the front wings being slightly longer than the hindwings, and when at rest these wings cover the abdomen rather like a roof. In general structure they are similar to the Ephemeroptera, though certainly not in appearance. The abdomen, or body, which is tailless, is composed of nine segments, and the thorax of the usual three. They have a fairly large pair of compound eyes and a pair of antennae of varying length. It is interesting to note that while all species of Sedge-flies are equipped with a pair of these large, many-faceted compound eyes called oculi, some species are also equipped with very small simple eyes mounted on top of the head, and these are called ocelli (see Plate 11, No. 130). Protruding from the mouth parts are two pairs of palps called the maxillary and labial respectively (these were mentioned in Chapter IV). The legs are long, slender and many jointed. The middle joints often carry several slender spurs, and the number of these spurs on each leg can often assist the entomologist to identify the species. The Sedge in the adult winged form is unable to partake of solid food but is able to consume liquid. It is rather difficult to distinguish between the sexes, and from the angler's point of view, unnecessary.

To generalize, adult Sedge-flies may be divided into two groups as follows: day-hatching species and night-hatching species; each may be further sub-divided into those that hatch from open water and those that hatch via emergent vegetation, etc. The species that hatch out during the daylight hours are generally smaller, darker and more hairy than the night-hatchers, and although the former are very much in the minority there are several species in this category classified amongst the fisherman's Sedges. Fortunately for the angler, many of the night-hatching species hatch in the late evening as dusk approaches, so coming within the scope of the fly-fisherman. Several of the species that hatch from open water are of particular value to the fly-fisherman due to the disturbance they create while endeavouring to become airborne after emerging on the surface from the pupal case. Depending on species and conditions, some become airborne comparatively quickly, while others remain on the surface for a considerable length of time drying their wings preparatory to flight. Some species travel along the surface for comparatively long distances, flapping their wings occasionally in their efforts to take off, and this behaviour attracts the trout to them in no uncertain manner. At least one species, notably the Large Cinnamon Sedge, *Potamophylax latipennis*, usually after hatching, proceeds rapidly along the surface towards the shore, creating a V-shaped wake like a small speedboat. This usually occurs in the late afternoon or early evening, and on calm days they can be spotted from a long distance. If the hatch is a good one it is surprising how few escape the depredations of the trout on their shoreward journey. Those species that hatch via emergent vegetation are of little interest to the fly-fisherman except for the females that return eventually to the water to lay their eggs.

As previously mentioned, there are nearly 200 different species of Sedge-flies, and of these a large percentage are found in stillwater. With such a large number of species, anglers may well be excused for thinking that identification of any would be virtually impossible except by a trained entomologist. Nevertheless, while positive identification is often difficult, it is usually possible with practice to classify the Family or Genus of a specimen, and this will usually suffice. In any case, the problem is minimized to a certain extent as, despite the number of species involved, many are scarce and only occasionally encountered, whereas most of the fisherman's Sedges listed are extremely common and widely distributed.

To illustrate this point my colleague, Mr. David Jacques, the noted angler/entomologist, recently carried out a survey of the Trichoptera population of Two Lakes in Hampshire. This extended over four seasons, and during this period over 56 different species were identified. During the course of this research literally hundreds of specimens were caught and classified, but out of the resulting number that were identified over 30 were restricted to less than half a dozen specimens each over the period. Furthermore, of the remaining 15 species only eight could really be considered common. However, it must be pointed out that this research was not necessarily conclusive, due to restrictions of time. Many fly-fishermen may rightly query the need for identification of any of the Sedge-flies, and in defence I can only state that on occasions it can be of value in anticipating hatches of particular species in locations or at expected times, according to their known behaviour. Also, correct identification of the adult can in most cases give a clue to the colour and behaviour of the corresponding pupae, although much research is still required in this direction.

Fishing Information: Fishing the artificial Sedge to represent the winged adult on stillwater is essentially dry fly fishing, and as such is probably one of the most exciting experiences of all. There are several methods of presenting the floating artificial and, broadly speaking, most of these may be practised equally well from boat or bank. These varying methods should be related to the particular type of species of Sedge-fly that may be on the water at the time and that one is endeavouring to copy. A floating line should be used and it is the normal practice to fish only one artificial on the point, and this should be lightly greased with a floatant in calm conditions, but on rough, windy days I find a light application of a heavy grease such as mucillin most helpful.

The first method to be discussed is meant to represent the action of those species of Sedge-flies which, hatching out in open water, run or flutter along the surface in their efforts to become airborne; it also proves effective in imitating those naturals blown on to the water which are endeavouring to take off. For this fishing I prefer an artificial with a hackle tied along the body Palmer fashion but in reverse, so that the hackle points face forward. This seems to provide the maximum animation and disturbance, and this is highly desirable. The artificial should be cast as far as possible and recovered at speed with frequent pauses along the surface. In some situations a medium fast recovery will prove effective, while at others it is impossible to retrieve too fast. An effective technique seems to be to retrieve the line in one hand with a long fast pull and at the same time accelerating the action by lifting the rod from the horizontal to the vertical. With this method the artificial moves so fast that on a rough day it will literally skip along the tops of the waves, and from the way the trout jump out of the water in their eagerness to intercept it, it seems they love it fished in this manner. Another successful plan is to loop the point of the leader in a half-hitch round the eye of the hook of the artificial; this has the effect of keeping the artificials head elevated so that it skips along when retrieved in a most attractive manner. Although the open water may be fished, this method seems particularly productive when practised in the vicinity of trees, reeds or other vegetation either in the water or lining the banks. When fishing in this way it is not always necessary to strike, as the trout invariably hook themselves, and for this reason it is prudent to use fairly heavy monofilament on the point, as the "take" is often quite savage. Fished from a boat it is surprising how often a trout that has probably been following the artificial for some distance will suddenly decide to rise to the fly close to the boat just as the artificial is being lifted in preparation for the next cast. On some days this happens time and time again, and I find it is always a good plan to anticipate a rise to the artificial at this juncture. Another very similar and well-known technique from a boat that can be practised when Sedge-flies are about is to fish a hackled Palmer or Sedge artificial on the top dropper. This is also most effective when fished fast so that it is dribbled along the surface, and again the trout will often take extremely close to the boat.

It will doubtless be appreciated that there are several ways in which an artificial may be fished to represent the natural adult in its various phases before it dies. The first stage of the adult life of those species that hatch out in open water, when the insect is struggling on the surface to free itself from its pupal case, is particularly vulnerable to the attentions of the trout. At this period the most successful method seems to be to use a normal standard Sedge pattern on a floating line and to fish it ungreased so that it sinks into or even slightly below the surface film. The artificial should then be retrieved either very slowly or in small jerks. It is interesting to note that two well-known general patterns, namely the Invicta and the Silver March Brown, often prove effective when the natural Sedges are on the water, and it therefore seems quite probable that these are taken by the trout for hatching Sedges. Apart from these patterns there is also a special dressing called the Hatching Sedge, named and perfected by Cmdr. C. F. Walker, to represent the insect at this time; the tying instructions are given in the appropriate section at the end of this book.

The final method to be discussed is probably the best known and is the normally accepted dry fly method of fishing the artificial. This to my mind is undoubtedly the most exciting and satisfactory of all forms of stillwater fishing; the joy of covering a rising fish and see it turn and sip down your fly makes most other fishing pleasures pale into insignificance. Unfortunately, opportunities to practise this style do not occur every day, but it is often one of the best methods to adopt during July and August, although there are probably many stillwater anglers who have never considered trying it.

Many species of Sedge-flies return to the water to oviposit by dipping or releasing their eggs on to the surface, and at least a proportion of these eventually finish up lying spent and struggling on the water surface. Apart from this many are accidentally, in windy conditions, blown on to the water. It is at this time when the naturals are observed that dry fly fishing should be most effective. Although this method may be practised either from boat or bank, under windy conditions, owing to the fast drift of a boat in the wind it is better from the bank. A floating line should be used, and the artificial should be well greased to give maximum floatibility, particularly if one is fishing the water rather than to rising fish. When trout are rising, the artificial can be placed either in the estimated path of the fish or, alternatively, if one can cast quickly and accurately, within the actual rise ring. But either method will often be successful. The artificial can be retrieved either very slowly, or it can be left motionless but for an occasional twitch to imitate the struggle of the natural trapped in the surface film. This is best achieved with a sharp jerk or lift of the rod top. This latter method is my personal favourite and will often bring a slashing rise to the fly.

Some lakes have heavy screens of rushes or similar aquatic vegetation extending from the shore, usually at the shallower end, forming interesting little bays and points. Most fishermen tend to ignore these areas due to this very shallow water, but with a stealthy approach from either boat or bank they often prove to be most productive. Providing they are not alarmed, trout during the warmer weather frequently lie close to these reeds or rushes, in spite of the shallow water, waiting for any unwary insects that may venture forth or be blown off the vegetation. An artificial Sedge presented therefore in the manner described above will often take a heavy toll.

Finally, it should be pointed out that when choosing the colour of the artificial to match the colour of the natural on the wing, the following fact should be taken into consideration. The coloration of the freshly hatched Sedge-fly is usually a lot weaker or paler than specimens that have been hatched out for several hours. This applies in particular to the wings. As most authorities seem to indicate that trout can discern the difference between colours, this is a point worthy of consideration. Both those eminent authors, Col. Jocelyn Lane and Courtney Williams, mention this factor. The former also emphasizes the desirability of using a sparse amount of hackle on artificial Sedge patterns, and while I am inclined to agree when using these patterns as a dry fly, I cannot agree with the assertion he makes in his book that over-hackling is also a mistake on patterns to represent the adult Sedge moving rapidly over the surface. In this case I am of the opinion that the more disturbance one can create the better, and a heavy hackle is a definite advantage.

Despite the large numbers of species in this group, only relatively few have been identified by the angler with vernacular names, and of these many are common to both lake and river. In Chapter V, which deals fairly extensively with the Ephemeroptera, it was possible to give considerable detail for positive identification of the various species and Families for the angler with an entomological leaning. Due to the fact that there are many more species of Sedge-flies, in a book of this nature it is just not possible to do this and, in any case, identification is so much more complex that it is not certain that even the keenest angler would want to identify precisely all the Sedges in view of the doubtful value of such knowledge.

Unfortunately, much less detailed study has been made of the Sedges than of the Ephemeroptera, possibly because nearly all the great fly-fishing writers of the past have been habitues of the chalk streams. Consequently most of the species of significance to the angler are lumped together under the headings of "Large",

"Medium", or "Small" permutated with "Red", "Brown", "Grey", etc., and artificial patterns are dressed accordingly. The fact that these general patterns are usually effective leaves the average fly-fisher disinclined to investigate the natural insect any further. This is a great pity as, to the stillwater angler, the Sedge-flies are a very important group.

It is possible to pick out certain species that are fairly regularly seen, and without too much technical detail to describe them.

N.B. When fishing the Sedge as a dry fly, do *not* strike too quickly. Many trout, when rising to a Sedge, first slash at it with their tail before turning to take it. Therefore, do not strike until you see the leader draw. Alternatively, count to three then strike.

LIST OF FISHERMAN'S SEDGE-FLIES (Trichoptera)

(In order of size)

Great Red Sedge (Murragh or Northern Bustard)	*Phryganea grandis or P. striata*	20 to 27 mm.
The Caperer	*Halesus radiatus or H. digitatus*	20/23 mm.
Large Cinnamon Sedge	*Potamophylax latipennis*	18 to 19 mm.
Mottled Sedge	*Glyphotaelius pellucidus*	17 mm.
Brown Sedge	*Anabolia nervosa*	11 to 16 mm.
Cinnamon Sedge	*Limnephilus lunatus*	14 to 15 mm.
The Welshman's Button	*Sericostoma personatum*	12 to 15 mm.
Black Sedge	*Athripsodes nigronervosus or Silo nigricornis*	11 to 13 mm.
Medium Sedge	*Goera pilosa*	10 to 12 mm.
Small Silver Sedge (Vide J R. Harris)	*Lepidostoma hirtum*	9 mm.
Brown Silverhorns	*Athripsodes cinereus*	8 to 10 mm.
The Longhorns	*Oecetis lacustris O. Ochracea or Trianodes Bicolour*	7 to 13 mm.
Black Silverhorns	*Mystacides azurea or M. Nigra or Athripsodes atterimus*	8 to 9 mm.
Grouse Wing or Grouse and Green	*Mystacides Longicornis*	8 to 9 mm.
Small Red Sedge	*Tinodes waeneri*	8 mm.

In the above list angler's common names have been attributed to specific species which are identified by their scientific names. It is more than likely, however, that fishermen have used, and still use, these common names not only for those identified in the list, but for any other species (and there are many) that superficially resemble them.

The Sedge-flies are particularly subject to variations in colour and size. Therefore the following detailed descriptions should be used only as a rough guide. The only sure way to achieve positive identification of any particular species is by a close study of the anatomical structure. This is the method used by trained ento-mologists, but it is unfortunately beyond the capacity of the average angler. In view of the importance of the pupa to the stillwater angler, where possible brief details of colour and other features have also been included. It is interesting to note that the colour of the body of the hatching pupa is invariably similar to that of the subsequent emerging adult.

As an aid to identification of the common species listed I have included in the margins two factors which can assist to a positive identification. These are as follows: *The Ocelli* or simple eyes, present in some families and absent in others: positioned on top of the head they are small, little larger than a pinhead, and usually of a whitish shade. *The Spurs* occur on all adult sedge flies and are to be found behind the two main joints on their legs. They can be easily observed with a low-power magnifying glass and the number of spurs on each leg varies according to families and species. As an example, the Great Red Sedge has two spurs side by side on each front leg, four spurs (two pairs side by side) on each middle leg and four again on each rear leg. The spur formula is therefore 2,4,4.

INFORMATION ON THE VARIOUS SPECIES

The Great Red Sedge (*Phryganea grandis and P. striata*)
(See Plate 6, No. 62)

Ocelli present
Spur formula
2, 4, 4;

These two species are the largest of the British Trichoptera, the length of their anterior wings varying between 20 and 27 mm. The female is generally larger than the male, as is usual with most of the Caddis-flies. The wings are mostly brown to reddish-brown, and broad, and the female of *P. grandis* has a longitudinal black bar running along the centre of the anterior wings, while *P. striata* has two shorter bars, interrupted in the middle but more or less in line. The antennae are stout, strongly annulated and about the same length as the wings; the legs are yellowish, with light brown rings, and the eyes are brown. The insects are fairly common and widely distributed in lowland lakes and reservoirs throughout the British Isles, but *P. striata* is also found in tarns and lochs at higher altitudes. The females often deposit their eggs on surface or sub-surface vegetation, and the egg mass can easily be recognized as it is usually in the shape of a ring. They are to be observed on the wing between late May and the end of July, hatching out in open water probably in the late evening. The caddis case is large (see Plate 5, No. 55) and made from fragments of leaf uniformly cut, and arranged in a spiral whorl tapering down to the tail end. The emerging pupae, like the adults, are large and also have a body of a greyish colour with a darker head.

The Caperer
(*Halesus radiatus or H. digitatus*)
(See Plate 6, No. 65)

Ocelli present
Spur formula
1, 3, 3;

Without a doubt this is one of the best-known species, probably due to the fact that it has an artificial of the same name developed by that great river-keeper and fly-tier, William Lunn of River Test fame. The common name apparently results from the habit of the female dancing and fluttering over the water in the early evening, rising and dipping as she lays her eggs. It is also a large species with a broad anterior wing, mottled yellowish brown. A useful point of identification that is noticeable when the insect is at rest is the black striate marking near the centre top edge of the anterior wings. The legs are orange brown, the eyes are black to brown and the body is often orange brown, but in some cases may be greenish. A common and widely distributed species, it is usually seen on the wing during late August, September and October. Hatches often commence in the late afternoon or early evening and, although often sparse, are continuous over a long period, and due to this reason and their large size the trout often accept them readily. The larval case is fairly large, up to 32 mm. long, and is formed from small pieces of bark, stems, cut pieces of leaf and vegetable matter. Attached to its case will often be found one or more short pieces of slender twig. The adults hatch out in open water, quickly scuttling for the shore leaving a distinct vee-shaped wake in a similar manner to that of the Cinnamon Sedge.

**The Large
Cinnamon
Sedge**
(*Potamophylax
latipennis*)
(See Plate 6, No. 66)

Ocelli present
Spur formula
1, 3, 4;

This is so similar in appearance to the Caperer that from the fisherman's point of view they can be treated as one. However, in place of the dark striate marking in the centre of the wings, they have an equally distinctive pale area. This species is fairly common and found in most areas, and although hatches are never on a large scale, it is probably more widely distributed than the previous species. They hatch out in open water and scuttle towards shore or any handy emergent vegetation on to which they crawl, flying off as soon as their wings are completely dry. The peak flight period is late June to early September, although odd specimens may be observed later in the season. The larval case is composed of gravel or coarse sand, is slightly curved, and about 20 to 23 mm. in length.

The Mottled Sedge
(*Glyphotaelus
pellucidus*)
(See Plate 6, No. 67)

Ocelli present
Spur formula
1, 3, 4;

During the past few seasons I have come across this particular species on many waters, and as it is a fairly large and particularly handsome Sedge-fly I felt it worthy of inclusion in the fisherman's list. It is of a similar size to the Large Cinnamon Sedge and the colour of the wings varies from cream to pale yellow-brown with large dark brown patches, somewhat paler in the female, giving the wings a distinct mottled effect, hence the common name I have ventured to suggest and which I hope will be considered appropriate. The antennae are fairly stout and a little shorter than the wing length, and the body is occasionally a dull green. A useful point of identification is the strongly excised margins of the anterior wings; when the insect is at rest these are clearly visible at the top rear edge. So far as I have been able to ascertain, the adults usually hatch out in the open in the shallower areas of stillwater, and although they may be observed from May through to October, the peak flight periods seem to be late May, June and again in August. When the adults first hatch they are a very pale colour indeed, and therefore a very light coloured artificial is to be recommended. The larvae are easily recognized as they make a most distinctive case, which is formed from three large cut discs of beech or other leaf on top, and three similar but smaller discs underneath, and the central case between the discs is formed from very tiny cut leaf sections. If smaller fallen leaves are available, such as those from hawthorn trees, the larvae will often use them in preference (see Plate 8, No. 94). The finished case is quite fascinating and in appearance resembles a small purse. The fat, juicy-looking emerging pupa has a creamy-greenish body with a brown thorax and wing cases.

The Brown Sedge
(*Anabolia nervosa*)
(Plate 6, No. 68)

Ocelli present
Spur formula
1, 3, 4;

This is a medium-sized species which varies considerably in size. The anterior wings, vary between 11 and 16 mm., and are of an overall mid-brown shade with two small light-coloured areas, one in the centre and one in the middle of the leading edge; these two areas often join. Their legs are a chestnut-brown colour, the bodies dark brown and the eyes blackish. It is very widely distributed, and on some stillwaters it appears in considerable quantities during the evening, when both small and large specimens often appear in the same swarm or locality. During the day, however, it shelters in the bank-side vegetation. The adult fly usually emerges via convenient weed beds and seldom in open water. It is an autumn species, although odd specimens will be seen as early as July. The caddis case, about 26 mm. in length, is constructed of small grains of sand and small sticks, and it usually includes one or more twigs two or three times as long as itself. It seems quite likely that the purpose of these twigs is to prevent predators such as fish or birds from swallowing the case, and it is noticeable that while most other caddis larvae seek protection from their enemies by camouflage, or by sheltering among stones or vegetation, the Brown Sedge, in common with some other species, seeks salvation by attaching an inedible twig to the case.

The Cinnamon Sedge
(*Limnephilus lunatus*)
(Plate 6, No. 69)

Ocelli present
Spur formula
1, 3, 4;

This is a distinguished-looking species, slimly built with long, narrow anterior wings 14 to 15 mm., varying from a deep rich yellow to a cinnamon-brown with blackish markings. The name, however, is derived from the supposed similarity of their scent to that of cinnamon. The wings also have several pale areas in the centre and a distinct pale patch along the trailing edge. The abdomen is usually greenish but in some cases may be orange-brown. The eyes are orange and the legs usually match the colour of the wings. It is a very widely distributed species which first appears in June and is with us right through the summer until the early autumn. Hatches are usually rather sparse, but to the fisherman this is a useful Sedge-fly, being very common and often hatching throughout the day close to emergent vegetation in deeper water. The larvae frequently construct their cases of sand grains, small pieces of plant, rush stems, or cut leaves, and the average length is about 20 to 23 mm. The eggs are deposited on bankside vegetation.

A recent paper by Novak and Sehnal, of the Czechoslovak Academy of Sciences, describes how some species of the Genus *Limnephilus*, and perhaps of other Genera, emerge from the pupa into the winged state in April, May or June, and live throughout the summer in a sexually immature state. During this period of diapause they live in obscurity some distance from the water, and when sometime later they attain sexual maturity, usually in the late summer, they return to it to lay their eggs. Consequently, they are not often seen in mid-summer, and because of this it was assumed that there were two generations each year, the first when they were observed hatching from the pupae, and the second when some months later the females were seen ovipositing. It is now known that they are of the same generation. This destroys the popular belief that all Sedge-flies live only a short time after attaining their winged state. It is interesting to note that the above also applies to *L. lunatus* in this country according to a paper written by A. M. Gower in 1967.

In addition to the above, it should be pointed out that there are several other species of the Limnephilidae so similar in appearance that they can also be included under the vernacular name of Cinnamon Sedges. One of these, *L. marmoratus*, has been chosen by Col. Jocelyn Lane, and in his book *Lake and Loch Fishing* he suggests it should be given a popular name, the "Mottled Sedge". I do not propose to follow his suggestion as, frankly, the differences between at least six species (including the above mentioned) within this family are so slight that only a microscope will enable positive identification to be made. Most of these Cinnamon Sedges appear to hatch during the hours of daylight and many of them have greenish bodies. The emerging pupae of these Sedges tends to vary in body colour, in a similar manner to those of the adults, while the thorax and wing cases vary between brown and orange.

The Welshman's Button
(*Sericostoma personatum*)
(Plate 6, No. 70)

Few fly-fishermen can have failed to have heard of this well-known Sedge-fly. There seems little doubt that originally this was the common name for a small beetle, but for some inexplicable reason that great fly-fisherman/entomologist, Frederic Maurice Halford, chose to apply the name to this species of

Ocelli absent
Spur formula
2, 2, 4;

* in some cases almost black

Sedge-fly, and since his day this has been generally accepted. Although a common and widespread species on rivers, it may not be so common on stillwater as is generally supposed, and certainly on the waters I fish I seldom come across it, but as it may be common in other localities I have decided to include it in the list. It has a dark grey-black body, sometimes tinged green. The length of the anterior wing varies between 12 and 15 mm. and is of a dark or golden chestnut-brown colour*, clothed with dense golden hairs, sometimes with small pale patches in the rear centres of the anterior wings. The antennae are dark brown, stout and a little shorter than the wings, and the legs and eyes are golden brown. The adults often hatch in open water, possibly in fair numbers during the day or early evening, and the female in flight is generally to be observed carrying her large, dark brown egg ball. They are usually seen in early June through to the middle of August. The larva constructs a slightly curved case of sand grains or fine gravel, with a smooth finish. It is similar to the case of the Silverhorns, although a little larger.

The Black Sedge
(*Athripsodes nigronervosus*)

Ocelli absent
Spur formula
2, 2, 2;

This Sedge-fly is an all-black insect, and although similar to the Black Silverhorns it is a little larger and can quickly be distinguished from the latter which has antennae that are black and scarcely annulated. The antennae of the Silverhorn are black but annulated with white. In both species they are long and slender and about twice the length of the wings. The anterior wings of the Black Sedge are slim, between 11 and 13 mm., and the veining is very conspicuous. They are widely distributed, but as far as I can tell not particularly common on stillwater. The female is smaller than the male, with shorter antennae and wings. It is a day-flying insect emerging from shelter

in the afternoon, and it can be observed flying in little swarms close to the banks. Their season is late May to July. The caddis case is usually constructed of fine grains of sand and is often slightly curved. Another species of Black Sedge is *Silo nigricornis* (Plate 6, No. 71), which is so similar in appearance to *A. nigronervosus* that from the fisherman's point of view they can be grouped together. In general appearance the former is a little wider in the wing and also a little smaller, between 9 and 10 mm. Also, the female of this species is often brown rather than black, while both sexes have pale brown legs.

The Medium Sedge (*Goëra pilosa*)

Ocelli absent
Spur formula
2, 4, 4;

A medium-sized robust species with the anterior wing, which is very broad, between 10 and 12 mm. long. The colour varies between dark yellow and greyish-yellow. It is very widely distributed, reputed to be abundant, and is most common during the early summer in May and June. It may be a very useful Sedge to the trout fisherman where it occurs, as it is also one of the day-flying species. A useful point of recognition is a small roughly circular patch free of hairs in the lower middle half of the anterior wing. The larvae construct a case with a central tube of sand or small stones, reinforced with larger pieces of stone at the sides. It is a species that I have not personally encountered on stillwater, but as it is reputed to be common by many authorities I felt it should be included. The pupa is not known to me, but Col. Jocelyn Lane describes it as having a golden yellow under abdomen, while the upper part is pale brown, with wing cases of a darker shade.

The Small Silver Sedge (*Lepidostoma hirtum*)

This fisherman's name has been given to *L. hirtum* by J. R. Harris, although it is generally applied to *Odontocerum albicorne*. It is quite a small species of Sedge-fly and for

(Plate 6, No. 72)

Ocelli absent
Spur formula
2, 4, 4;

this reason I felt it prudent to include the prefix "Small" in the vernacular name given in my list to avoid confusion in future with the much larger Silver Sedge found in running water. The wing length is about 9 mm., varying in colour from grey to grey-brown, with ginger-brown legs and red-brown eyes. The antennae are slightly longer than the wings and the basal joint is longer than the head, and is covered with long erect hairs. The body is usually pale creamy brown with a tinge of green, although I have seen complete hatches both male and female with a distinctly green body. The female is often to be seen carrying a bright green egg ball in a similar manner to the Grannom. It usually hatches out in open water early in the evening, often in large numbers. Although widely distributed, it tends to be rather localized, and is certainly more common on rivers than on lakes; it is most in evidence from May to August. The shape of the wings, viewed from the side when the insect is at rest, is somewhat distinctive, being wide at the centre with a pronounced curve. The larva builds a square sectioned tapered case of vegetable debris, and is usually about 17 mm. in length. Unfortunately, I have no knowledge of the pupa.

The Brown Silverhorns
(*Athripsodes cinereus*)
(Plate 6, No. 73)

Ocelli absent
Spur formula
2, 2, 2;

The Silverhorns are the most common of all the Sedges. They can be observed on most warm summer days, flying very rapidly and strongly in swarms close to the water, usually in the shelter of the banks or overhanging trees or bushes. Their extremely long antennae, often over twice the length of the wings, are a help to identification, as in flight they curve back over the body and look like a pair of long horns. These antennae have white annulations, which give them a distinctly speckled appearance. The anterior wings, which vary between 8 and 10 mm. in length, are narrow and very variable in

colour, although most specimens are brown with faint blackish markings. They have brownish bodies and legs and dull brown eyes. It is noticeable, and useful for identification, that when the insect is at rest and viewed from the side, there is a slight hump protruding from the top of the anterior wing at the rear end. This is formed by a widening of the rather narrow wings at this point, but this feature is by no means exclusive to this species. It is significant that Silverhorns are only occasionally found in trout during autopsies, and it may therefore safely be assumed that they rarely alight on the water for a long enough period to interest the trout. Consequently, imitations of the adults are of doubtful value to the fly-fisher. However, this does not apply to the hatching pupae, which are eagerly sought by the trout and form a useful addition to their diet. These have bodies of a creamy brown colour, with thorax and wing cases of an orange-brown. The success of the Amber nymph artificial could be due to its resemblance to these prolific pupae, and it seems likely that this was designed to imitate them and similar species. The larval cases, which are usually curved, are constructed from fine grains of sand. They generally inhabit the shallower areas of stillwater.

The Longhorns
(*Oecetis lacustris—
O. ochracea*)
(Plate 6, No. 76)
and (Trianodes
Bicolour)

Ocelli absent
Spur formula
O. lacustris
0, 2, 2;
O. ochracea and
T. Bicolour
1, 2, 2;

Although I was not too keen on introducing further species to the fisherman's list of Sedges, I felt that these particular insects should be included, as they seem extremely common and widespread. I have encountered these Sedges in fair numbers on practically every water I have visited, and although I have seldom found a large swarm, they seem to hatch out over long periods during the day and should therefore prove to be a very useful Sedge to the fisherman. It should be noted they are very variable in size, usually with a wing length between 7 and 8 mm. on

O. *lacustris* and 11 to 13 mm. on O. *ochracea*. However, I have on several occasions recorded specimens well in excess of the normal upper limits on both species. The common name that I would suggest for these species is, I hope, applicable, as they seem to have the longest antennae of all the common Sedge-flies, being in some cases nearly three times as long as their wings. These antennae are very pale in colour, and the anterior wings are extremely narrow, giving the insect a very slim appearance when at rest. The colour of the wings varies from a grey-yellow, with faint darker markings, to an overall pale fawn shade, and the body is generally greyish-green or in many cases distinctly green. The larval case is strongly curved and tapering, and is usually composed of fine sand grains with the wider end sometimes furnished with larger sand grains or pieces of vegetable material. The emerging pupa appears to have a pale green body with a dark brown thorax and wing cases. (See Plate 6). I would also include under this common name *Trianodes Bicolour*. Very similar in appearance except that they have conspicuously annulated antennae with reddish brown anterior wings 7 to 10 mm in length. The adults are on the wing from June to mid-September, and the trout seem to accept them readily, usually when the females return to the water to oviposit.

**The Black
Silverhorns**
(*Mystacides
azurea, M. nigra,
Athripsodes
aterrimus*)
(Plate 6, No. 74)

Ocelli absent
Spur formula
M. Azurea and
Nigra 0, 2, 2;

These three species are all very similar in appearance and therefore a general description should suffice. They are usually all black, but in some cases have brownish legs with dark reddish eyes and in silhouette, apart from colour, could be mistaken for a Brown Silverhorns, having also very long dark antennae with white annulations, which curve back over the body in flight. Common and widely distributed, they are likely to be seen hatching during the hours of daylight between June and August, often

A. aterrimus
2, 2, 2;

in the company of other similar species. They are occasionally found in the same localities as the Brown Silverhorns, although seldom in such large concentrations, and they are also of doubtful value to the angler. The larvae construct their cases from sand grains mixed with a certain amount of vegetable matter and small sticks; they are slightly curved and about 15 mm. in length.

The Grouse Wing
(*Mysticides longicornis*)
(Plate 6, No. 75)

Ocelli absent
Spur formula
0, 2, 2;

Although these Sedge-flies are a little smaller than the Silverhorns, they also have very long antennae, white with brown annulations. Slim in appearance, they are a most distinctive species, having greyish-yellow anterior wings generally with three broad transverse bands of a darker shade, giving the wing a slight resemblance to a grouse feather. However, this is not a constant feature and cannot be relied upon for identification purposes. Their bodies are grey-brown and the eyes are blackish-brown, but in some specimens appear distinctly reddish-brown. They are very common and found on most stillwaters, and are seen on the wing from June to September often in large concentrations. They emerge from the shallower areas of stillwater usually during the late afternoon or early evening, and on occasion may be taken by the trout. Like many other Sedge-flies they mate in flight, the female supporting the male which hangs head down with its wings closed, and while coupled tail to tail in this way the female flies to a considerable height. As the mating pairs ascend they appear in silhouette more like an elongated beetle than a pair of Sedge-flies. The caddis case is made of fine sand grains and is only slightly curved. So far, I have not been able to identify the pupa, although the empty pupal cases, which probably belong to this species, may often be found in quantities floating in the surface film, adjacent to the swarms.

**The Small
Red Sedge**
(*Tinodes waeneri*)

Ocelli absent
Spur formula
2, 4, 4;

These, the smallest of the Sedge-flies of any value to the fisherman, are reputed to be readily accepted by the trout. The adult is quite small, having a wing length of 8 mm. or less, and the body is dark brown; the antennae are stout and a little shorter than the wings, which are densely covered in hair and in colour vary from golden-grey to yellow-brown, although some specimens I have caught have had wings of a distinct red-brown shade. They are very widespread and I have found them on most stillwaters that I have visited. Emergence of the adults often commences in the afternoons, but the larger hatches are usually encountered in the evenings, generally over open water. They have a very long season and may be observed on the wing from May to October, and it is suspected that they may be one of the species of Sedge-flies that produce more than one brood a year. Two artificials that are particularly suited to represent them are the Little Red Sedge and the Little Brown Sedge. The larvae construct tunnels of mud, sand grains and vegetable matter, and the large amount of silk (chitin) that goes to construct the case gives it a distinct greyish colour. These tubes or cases, which are firmly fixed to stones or rocks, are often sinuously curved and very long, and in many localities reach a length of 35 mm. The emerging pupae are quite small and appear to have a brownish body and darker thorax and wing cases.

CHAPTER IX

THE STONEFLIES (PLECOPTERA)

THE HARDWING FLIES

The flies in this group are of doubtful value to the stillwater fisherman, but I have decided to include them as they may be of importance in areas where they occur in sufficient numbers. Unlike flies in other groups, the various families in this group as a general rule favour colder water for their habitat. Most of them prefer water with a predominantly stony bottom, hence their name. It is a fairly small group of flies and, according to Dr. Hynes, contains in Britain a little over thirty species. In the North Country the larger species are often referred to as "Mayflies" in the absence of a true Ephemerid Mayfly.

The Stoneflies vary a great deal in size, the larger specimens having a wing span of nearly two inches, and the smaller barely three-quarters of an inch. The anatomical structure is similar to that of the Sedge and other flies, with the usual three-segmented thorax and the ten-segmented abdomen. The legs are of fairly uniform length but somewhat stouter than those of the Sedges. On top of the head there are two prominant antennae which are usually about half the length of the body and thus relatively shorter than those of most Sedges. Unlike the latter, which are tailless, all Stoneflies have two tails which vary considerably in length. Some are as long as or slightly longer than the body, while others have tails which are reduced to mere stumps and are difficult to see. When the fly is at rest the wings, which are hard and shiny, lie flat along the top of the body. They are often slightly convex and, particularly in some of the smaller species, appear to mould around the body. There are four wings, the hindwings always being broader than the forewings. In many cases, particularly in the larger species, the wings of the male fly are foreshortened and so atrophied as to be merely vestigial, and flight is impossible. A brief account of the life cycle of this group is given in Chapter IV.

Stonefly nymphs or creepers, as the larger ones are called in angling circles, are somewhat similar in appearance to the nymphs of many of the Upwinged flies, but are in most cases considerably larger. The latter, however, have three tails and the former only two. This is a point worth remembering. They are a very active and robust crawling type of nymph, and some of the larger species are carnivorous. As maturity approaches, the nymph crawls (or possibly in the case of some of the smaller species, swims) to dry land, usually after dark, and seeks shelter before transforming into the winged adult fly. Mating is said to take place on the ground, and usually two or three days later the female extrudes her eggs, which adhere to the underside of her abdomen prior to oviposition. Favourite resting-places for the adult Stoneflies are the bark and foliage of trees and shrubs, stones, rocks, posts and the walls of sheds and huts. It is believed that the Stonefly nymph, which during its aquatic existence crawls along the bed of the lake, is of doubtful interest to the fly-fisher because of the difficulty of simulating the crawling action of the natural, on which trout are by no means averse to feeding. The life-span of these nymphs is about twelve months, but species of at least two genera, namely Perla and Dinocras, I believe to have a life-span of three years. However, I strongly suspect that one other species, *Perlodes microcephala*, has a span also of three years, as I personally have obtained specimen nymphs in one locality on the same day, each in a different stage of growth. The largest was about 23 mm., the next about 13 mm. and the smallest barely 7 mm., and as on this particular river hatches are limited to a maximum period of three weeks, I suspect that the two smaller specimens (of which there were many) would not be sufficiently mature for metamorphosis within the given period. Therefore, it appears to me likely that their change into the winged state must await the following year and perhaps, in the case of the smallest one, the year after that. The natural nymph or creeper is a very popular bait on many of the North County lakes and rivers. Stonefly imitation really comes into its own when the female returns to the water to lay its eggs, and what a tempting target it makes for a hungry trout as it flutters and flops about on the surface!

Stoneflies—*Fishing Information*

In the following detailed description of the Stoneflies I do not propose to give fishing information on each particular species as I have with other Orders and groups of insects. In the first place, as far as the stillwater fisherman and his actual fishing is concerned, little is known about this Order of insects. Secondly, apart from two distinctly yellowish species, the adults are all of very similar colour and shape and vary only in size. From this it will be apparent that a small, medium and large pattern in a brown dressing and similar sizes in yellow-green should suffice. The main period for fishing the artificial pattern is during the time when the adult Stoneflies are blown on to the water under windy conditions or when the females are to be seen on the surface during egg laying. By studying the detailed descriptions the angler should be able to ascertain in what localities and at what time of the season the various species are likely to be encountered.

To the fly-fisher the nymphs are usually of value only as a means of forecasting the presence of the adults at a later date because, as I explained earlier, due to their habitat and mode of life under water they are extremely difficult to imitate.

The majority of flies in this Order are found in running water only, but a few of the more common species are found both in running and stillwater. The only types likely to be of interest to the stillwater fisherman are listed below:

LIST OF STILLWATER STONEFLIES (Plecoptera)
(In order of size)

ANGLER'S NAME	ENTOMOLOGIST'S NAME	LENGTH OF FEMALE
Large Stonefly	*Perlodes microcephala*	18 to 28 mm.
Medium Stonefly	*Diura bicaudata*	12 to 14 mm.
Yellow Sally	*Isoperla grammatica*	9 to 13 mm.
Willow-fly	*Leuctra geniculata*	8 to 11 mm.
	Nemoura avicularis	
Small Brown	*Nemoura cinerea*	6 to 9 mm.
	Nemurella picteti	
Small Yellow Sally	*Chloroperla torrentium*	6 to 8 mm.
Needle-fly	*Leuctra fusca*	5 to 9 mm.
	Leuctra hippopus	

In this list, anglers' common names have been attributed to specific species which are identified by their scientific names. As with the Sedge-flies, it is more likely, however, that fishermen have used and still use these common names not only for those identified in the list, but for any other species (and there are several) that superficially resemble them.

The Large Stonefly (*Perlodes microcephala*) (Plate 7, Nos. 79 and 80)

It is widely believed that this is the only large stonefly found in stillwater and it seems to be confined mainly to parts of Scotland.

The wings of the adult fly are mottled brown; the underbody varies from cream to yellow, and the legs are frequently tinged with yellow. It is often a bright yellow overall colour when first hatched, but quickly darkens with age. It is usually found resting in the shelter of posts, large stones or on the bark of trees or fences several yards back from the banks. The wings of the male are often atrophied or mere stubs, and the insects are incapable of flight, although active on their feet. Like many of the Stoneflies, the female is a poor flier and, even when disturbed, seems reluctant to take to the air. The male is 13 to 18 mm. and the female 16 to 23 mm. Like most of the other large species, it is unable to partake of solid food, but it can and does take liquid. The adults are seen from March to July, being most common in April and early May. The nymphs are very large varying between 18 and 28 mm., and their basic colour is yellow with a dark brown pattern along the head, the thorax, and the dorsal segments. They are usually encountered in large lakes or tarns on high ground, but rarely above 1,200 ft.; they prefer an exposed shore composed. of large boulders or loose stones, the underside of which they inhabit. When the fully grown nymph is ready to transform to the winged adult it migrates to the lake edge and crawls out, and with this particular species this usually occurs at night. These larger Stonefly nymphs will often crawl several yards from the water's edge until they find a suitable rock or tree on which to transform. They will then fix themselves firmly to the substrate with their claws, and their skin splits down the thorax and the fully adult winged fly emerges. (Plate 7, No. 78).

The adult winged females when ready for ovipositing either crawl or fly to the water's edge and then swim along the surface to the deeper water. The three or four hundred eggs which have been previously extruded are then washed off as they swim. The eggs fall away a few at a time until finally the whole mass becomes detached and sinks to the bottom. It is supposed that the eggs take about 90 days to hatch out, and that the nymphs mature in one or possibly three years.

The Medium Stonefly (*Diura bicaudata*) (Plate 7, No. 81)

On lakes this is more common than the previous species, but even so, although it is often abundant in areas where it occurs, which is mainly on high ground above 700 ft. in parts of Scotland, Ireland, the Lake District and Western Wales, it is not widespread. The adult winged flies are of a similar colour and appearance to the previous species but they are smaller, the males being 10 to 13 mm., and the females 12 to 14 mm. They are to be seen from April to July, and peak hatches occur during April and early May. According to Dr. Hynes the adults, both male and female of this particular species, are incapable of flight, and consequently the female is forced to crawl to the water's edge, where it swims out to release its eggs in a manner similar to the Large Stonefly. The nymphs, as in most cases in this Order, are larger than their corresponding adults, the males varying between 9 to 17 mm. and the females 19 to 24 mm.; their general colour is grey-brown with yellow markings above, yellow below. They are also found in similar localities to the Large Stonefly, under large boulders or stones on exposed shores of lakes, but at higher altitudes. They have a life cycle of approximately twelve months.

The Yellow Sally (*Isoperla grammatica*) (Plate 7, No. 82)

Of all the Stoneflies this is probably the easiest to recognize, due to its conspicuous yellowish-green wings, yellow-brown legs and yellow body. It is a medium-sized species and its name is often confused with one of the large yellow Upwinged flies known as the Yellow May dun, which is also referred to in some areas as a Yellow Sally. The male varies between 8 and 11 mm. and the female 9 and 13 mm.

Although this is a very common species on rivers in most parts of the British Isles, specimens found in stillwater seem to be confined to the northern parts of the country. The adults are to be seen on the wing during most of the summer from April to August, but are probably most common in June and July. They seem to be stronger fliers than any other Stonefly species of their size, and the adult females are often to be observed ovipositing while on the wing by dipping on to the water surface. The nymphs vary greatly in colour, but average specimens seem to be a uniform dark grey-green to yellow with dark markings on the head, thorax and dorsal segments. They vary between 11 and 16 mm. and are seldom found at altitudes above 1,000 ft. They seem to favour a sandy or gravelly bottom, interspersed with small stones, under which they can usually be found.

The Willow-fly (*Leuctra geniculata*)

This is a medium to small species, fairly slim and dark brown in colour. It is a late season species and the winged adults are most common during August and September. Hatches of this particular species are often quite heavy on rivers, but I have never personally observed them on lakes. However, I have decided to include it in the list, as both J. L. Henderson and Courtney Williams state they have encountered them on stillwater often in considerable numbers.

The Small Brown (*Nemoura cinerea*, *N. avicularis* and *Nemourella picteti*) (Plate 7, No. 84)

These three species are so similar in appearance that they may be grouped together under the above anglers' vernacular name, and for the sake of brevity I intend to describe them as one species, as they can only be separately identified by microscopic examination which is, of course, of little consequence to the angler. Without doubt, these are the most prolific and widespread of all the Stone-flies found in stillwater. The adults are fairly small, the male being 6 to 7 mm. and the female 6 to 9 mm. They are slim in appearance and of an overall brownish colour, and are to be observed on the wing throughout the fishing season. The active flying females oviposit in a similar manner to the previous species. The nymphs have very long tails and antennae and their general colours are either olive-grey, or light reddish-brown, with a paler under-abdomen. They vary in size between 5 and 9 mm. and they prefer stillwater where the bottom is composed of small stones, well silted and interspersed with weed. They are common and found in many parts of the British Isles (Plate 7, No. 85).

The Small Yellow Sally (*Chloroperla torrentium*) (Plate 7, No. 86)

This is also a very common and widespread species and is found in most areas of these Islands, except perhaps East Anglia and parts of the Home Counties. The adults are quite small, the males between 5 and 7 mm. and the females 6 and 8 mm.; of a rather slim appearance; the general coloration is yellow to yellow-brown. They are on the wing from April to August, being most common in May. The females lay their eggs in a manner similar to some of the previously mentioned species, and the egg mass, which contains between 15 to 40 eggs, is carried under the abdomen near the tails. They usually fly out over the water slowly, losing height, until the egg mass comes into contact with the water, where it becomes detached from the abdomen. The members of this species, in common with several others of the smaller species, are fairly active fliers and will often be observed on the wing prior to ovipositing. All Stoneflies can be readily identified in flight as they always fly in a more or less straight line, and their four large wings make them appear far larger than they actually are.

The nymphs are 7 to 9 mm. long, grey-brown with constant darker markings on top and yellow below. The tails and antennae are much shorter than in the previous species, and they are most likely to be found amongst the small stones or gravel on the lake bed. In some localities they will also be found on sandy shores, where they tend to burrow into the sand.

The Needle-Fly (*Leuctra fusca and L. hippopus*) (Plate 7, No. 87)

This is the smallest fly of this Order in this country and, as the name implies, it is extremely slim in appearance when at rest. Dark brown in colour and faintly mottled, it is occasionally found on bodies of stillwater. The two species mentioned above are so similar in appearance it is impossible to tell them apart with the naked eye. However, *L. hippopus* is an early season species, on the wing from March to June; being most common in March and April, whereas *L. fusca* is seen from June to November, with main hatches occurring during July and August. They are exceptionally common flies on rivers in all parts of the country, but as far as the stillwater fisherman is concerned they seem to be rather localized. The adult males are between 5 and 7 mm. and the females 6 and 8 mm. The nymphs seem to have a preference for small stones and gravel among decaying leaves. The general colour is grey-brown on top with pale wing pads and dark head, and underneath they vary from yellow to pale rose. They vary between 6 and 9 mm. in length, are very slim, with fairly short antennae about a third the length of their bodies, and their tails are of a similar length but densely clothed with bands of bristles.

CHAPTER X

SUNDRY INSECTS AND OTHER FAUNA

All the flies that have so far been mentioned may be classified into definite Orders, all families in each Order having a similar life cycle. However, in various other Orders there are a number of miscellaneous flies so diversified that it is impossible to deal with them in this manner. In addition, anglers are concerned with small creatures such as spiders and shrimps, which are not insects at all, but which, with the indulgence of the reader, I will refer to as flies or insects for the sake of simplicity. Each of these flies will therefore be dealt with separately, and where necessary a brief account of their life histories will be given. Under this heading there are many terrestrial insects whose life cycle is, to anglers, of little consequence, and it is only when they find their way on to or into the water that they become of significance to the fly-fisher.

It is remarkable that many of the insects in this category are largely ignored by fly-fishermen, and it is probable that the chance of an exceptional fish is sometimes missed because of it. A trout that has been born and bred in a lake, or a stock fish that time has made wild and wary, and which has learned from sad experience of the dangers to be met from painful encounters with a seemingly innocuous floating or aquatic insect, may live for many years and grow big and lusty. A fish of this type is usually very cautious and experienced in recognizing the difference between the natural and the artificial of the more common flies. However, it is surprising how often, in an unguarded moment, it can be deceived with an artificial pattern, which, although of an unfamiliar nature, nevertheless represents some kind of natural insect of an unusual variety.

Most bodies of stillwater harbour a far larger variety of insects and other fauna than do rivers and consequently the trout have a greater choice of food, much of which is of an aquatic nature, present, in some cases, throughout the fishing season, while in other cases present only for comparatively short periods. They also, have a wide variety of surface food, much of it of a terrestrial nature. It has been shown that trout in certain circumstances become selective feeders, and will concentrate on one particular species to the exclusion of all others. This is particularly apparent with some species, notably fauna that often appear in large quantities for a short period, such as the Flying Ant or the Hawthorn-fly. It will therefore be to the angler's advantage to take careful note of many of the species which are described in this chapter as many of them come in this category.

The Alder-fly (*Sialis* spp.) (Plate 7, No. 88)

There are two species, *Sialis lutaria* and *S. fuliginosa*, and so far as the angler is concerned they can be treated as one as they are so similar in appearance. However, only the former is found in still-water. The Alder has been known to the river angler for many many years and it has always had an extraordinary capacity for attracting antipathy or affection among fly-fishers. Despite the fact that Halford made a detailed and complete study of the life history of this species, he finally denounced it as valueless to fly-fishermen. On the other hand, Kingsley and other leading anglers of their day spoke very highly of it, and looked upon the artificial as a very killing pattern, as do many anglers of this day. So far as the stillwater fisherman is concerned, it is only in recent years that it has been recognized as a useful lake fly mainly in its larval form. It is very common and widely distributed and is to be found near all types of water, mostly in the early part of the season, about May and June. It is similar in appearance to some dark, medium-size Sedge-flies, having the same roof-shaped wings when at rest. The head and legs are very dark, being almost black, and the wings are hard and shiny like those of the Stoneflies. Like other members of the Megalopteran sub-Order, its life cycle is partly aquatic and partly terrestrial. The adult winged female lays its eggs in masses of between 500 and 800 on the leaves of plants or on reeds overhanging the water. After about ten or twelve days the young larvae emerge and fall to the bed of the river or lake, where they live in the silt and mud on the bottom. The larvae, when fully grown, reach a length of approximately one inch and are of a dark, sepia-brown colour. They have six stout legs, seven prominent tracheal gills down either side of the body, a single tail, and are equipped with a powerful pair of mandibles. During their early life in this form they spend most of the daylight hours in a tunnel that they dig quite rapidly in the mud or silt on the bed of the lake. It can be observed, however, that they nearly always leave the tip of their tails protruding above the surface of the mud; the tail is periodically waved, no doubt to provide a fresh current of water over the tracheal gills.

The larvae (Plate 5, No. 58) are carnivorous, and at night they leave their burrows and roam the bed of the lake in search of prey, which they seize with their powerful mandibles. Any small, slow-moving form of aquatic life is acceptable and they seem particularly partial to the various species of caddis grubs. During the latter part of their larval lives they become increasingly active and will often emerge from their retreat during the hours of daylight as well as at night. When they are ready to pupate they crawl ashore and burrow into the damp ground or debris along the margins, the pupae emerging within a few days, when transformation into the adult winged flies takes place. Although most authorities accept that the larvae crawl ashore to pupate, there appears to be considerable doubt about it, but so far as my experiments in artificial conditions to date are concerned, in all cases pupation occurred out of water.

From the above it would seem to be quite likely that an artificial tied to represent the larva and fished very slowly along the bottom during the early part of the season would prove effective. I have already had some success in this direction and I know of other anglers who find this is a killing method at the right time. Also, I now suspect that the success at times of the well-known Worm-fly, when fished slowly and deep, could be attributed to the similarity of this pattern to the natural. C. F. Walker, in his book *Lake Flies and Their Imitation*, gives an effective dressing to represent the Alder larva.

When the adult flies emerge from their pupal cases they appear on the soil surface as fully winged flies. The adults seem to swarm mostly in the shelter of trees or bushes in the vicinity of water, and thus often over the water itself. Sometimes they may be blown on to the water by accident, but even when this happens trout only occasionally accept them, and on this evidence it would seem doubtful that a specific pattern to represent the adult would be of value, but strange to relate, the artificial alder, which is a fairly popular general pattern, does take trout fished during the season of the natural.

The Ant (Order Hymenoptera)

There are many creatures of a terrestrial origin which, when they fall or are blown on to the water in sufficient quantities, will often bring trout up to the surface to feed. The fish are sometimes a little slow on the uptake, but once they get the taste of whatever particular species it may be, they probably look upon them as manna from heaven and commence feeding on them avidly, usually to the exclusion of anything else. Among these, to mention just a few, are several fauna of a seasonal nature such as the June Bug and several other beetles, the Hawthorn-fly, the Black Gnat and the Heather-fly. However, the particular insect I am about to mention is certainly not seasonal in the accepted sense so far as the fisherman is concerned, as some years it may not be observed at all, while in others it may be encountered on several widely separated occasions in different localities, of course, in the one season. This is the ant, or rather I should say, the ant in its winged form. As most people are aware, at certain times of the year, usually on hot sultry or thundery days during July, August or early September, many species of ants develop wings for their annual nuptial flight. It seems that they are often attracted by water in this winged state, and should there be a breeze blowing to take them out over the lake because they are probably poor fliers they invariably finish up struggling in the surface film, thereby making a tempting target for any hungry trout. There are, of course, many species of ants, but the two most common and likely to be encountered are the small Black Ant (*Acanthomyops niger*) and the common Yellow Ant (*A. flavus*). The former is black and the latter usually brownish varying between red-brown and yellow-brown. An artificial pattern is fairly easy to tie and should be fished in the surface film with an occasional twitch to animate and represent the struggle of the natural as closely as possible. An angler is indeed fortunate to find himself at the waterside during a fall of ants, but when it does occur the fortunate angler present is likely to have a day to remember all his life, providing he is able to offer the requisite artificial in either brown or black, as the trout are unlikely to accept a substitute.

Beetles (Order Coleoptera)

This is a very large Order, and it is therefore impossible to pick out many individual species of particular value to the fisherman. All sorts of different beetles find their way accidentally on to the water, and as they come in all sizes, shapes and colours, it is important to note whether any particular species is seen regularly on a water one fishes, and then endeavour either to buy or tie an artificial for future use. There are, however, several types that are known and recognized generally by anglers in certain areas; these are as follows. The Coch-y-bonddu (*Phyllopertha horticola*) (Plate 8, No 100). This is a beetle that appears in very large swarms in June, and is often blown on to the water. In some areas it is known as the June Bug or Bracken Clock, and is most common in certain localities in Wales and Scotland. It is a small beetle about half-an-inch long with a metallic bluish green head, thorax, and legs, and reddish-brown wings. Falls are most likely to be encountered during the middle part of warm days.

The Soldier-beetle (*Cantharis rustica*) (Plate 8, No. 97) is a very prolific species, seen in thousands during June, July and August. It is about half-an-inch long, quite slim, with orange-red wings which have a distinct bluish colour at the tips, and a dull yellow body. Another closely allied beetle is the Sailor-beetle (*Cantharis livida*) (Plate 8, No. 98), very similar in appearance but with dull blue wings and a more reddish body. Both are sometimes blown on to the water in sufficient quantities to merit the fly-fisher's attention.

The Cockchafer (*Melolontha melolontha*) (Plate 8, No. 96). This species belongs to the same family as the Coch-y-bonddu and is very similar in appearance, having a black head and thorax and wing cases of reddish-brown, while the underpart of its body is banded with black and grey. It is, however, larger and is in fact one of our largest terrestrial beetles, being well over an inch long. It is common in May and June and fairly widespread in habitat, although it is seldom encountered by anglers in the southern parts of the country. It is a dusk-flying species and is therefore only likely to be encountered on the water on windy evenings. The only dressing that I know to represent this particular species is one given by Henderson (see appendix) in his booklet *Fly-fishing on Lakes and Reservoirs*.

Common Ground-beetles (*Harpalus* and *Carabus* spp.) rarely fly but will often fall into the lake from the banks. They are of medium size, about three-quarters of an inch long and shiny black in colour. Also, of course, there are many other similar terrestrial beetles found in the bankside vegetation that will find their way on to the water by crawling rather than flying.

Apart from the terrestrial species mentioned above, there are very many other species which may be blown on to the water from time to time; of these probably the most likely to be encountered are many of the relatively small beetles from the Staphylinidae family commonly referred to as Staphs. These beetles have long and slender bodies with rather short wing cases, and some of the smallest members of this extremely large family are barely 3 mm. long. They may be seen on the water in May and June and again in September, and many are shiny black in colour.

Apart from beetles of a strictly terrestrial habitat there are also many of an aquatic nature, and in their underwater larval forms are readily accepted by the fish. Most of these fresh-water beetles spend both the larval and adult stages under water although, strangely enough, in most cases the pupal stage is passed in the earth There are two main groups, the Adephaga and the Polyphaga. The former, carnivorous by nature, breathe by pushing the tip of their abdomen at intervals through the surface film, while the latter, mainly vegetarian, breathe by regularly ascending to the surface and absorbing a bubble of air which they hold on the underside of the thorax.

They vary in size, shape and coloration tremendously, and some species, including the Great Diving Beetle (*Dytiscus marginalis*), attain a length of over 30 mm. In most cases the larvae (Plate 11, No. 128) are very much larger than the subsequent adults. Some of these larger species of larvae are vicious creatures and should be handled carefully. Apart from certain species such as the common Whirligig beetle, which tends to congregate in colonies, the majority are encountered in small numbers.

Occasionally adult aquatic beetles are found in the stomach contents of trout, but in my experience they are not of great importance. The larvae (Plate 8, No. 99) on the other hand are more commonly found in trout, particularly those of medium size. It is impossible, however, to quote specific species of larvae that are acceptable to trout, as a large number are involved and these vary on different waters and at different times of the year. It therefore behoves the angler to note those most common on the waters he fishes or those most commonly found in autopsies and then endeavour to dress matching artificials, which should be fished slowly on or near the bottom in the vicinity of weed beds or large stones. Patterns to represent the adult terrestrial beetles should of course always be fished on the surface, and it is often surprising how effective they are, particularly on hot and sunny days when the trout are dour and reluctant to rise. These floating patterns should be fished very slowly; a particularly effective method is to present a well-greased fly on a greased leader and to fish dry, occasionally tweaking the line to provide animation. To illustrate the importance of beetles on some occasions, I should like to recount the following incident.

Some time ago I was discussing trout fishing with Brian Harris the editor of *Angling* and he mentioned that he had recently spent a successful day on Darwell reservoir when most other rods had drawn a blank. The reason for his success on this occasion was due mainly to his power of observation. He described how most other anglers were fishing the deeper water at one end of the reservoir, which early in the year usually offers the best chances, when he observed what appeared to be a rise at the shallower far end of the water.

Deciding to investigate he walked towards it and settled down to watch. Within a few moments he noticed several more trout moving and so he proceeded to the water's edge in order to discover to what the trout were rising. At first he was unable to see any life in the water in sufficient quantities to account for the activity, but soon he noticed several small black beetles crawling in the marginal weeds. A light breeze was blowing offshore and numbers of these beetles were being blown out into the body of the reservoir on the surface film. Suspecting that it was these little creatures that the trout were feeding on, he followed one with his eye as it drifted out into the reservoir, and sure enough about twenty yards from the shore it disappeared in a swirl as a hungry trout rose to it. Mounting a small Black and Peacock Spider, heavily greased, so as to float high in the surface film, he commenced fishing. He subsequently netted several nice trout.

Finally, I should mention that there are quite a few well-known artificials that are obviously intended as general beetle patterns, and these are sometimes effective fished just under the surface. Why this should be is a little difficult to understand as those beetles found floating in or on the surface film are usually terrestrial, the aquatic types spending most of their time near the bottom among the stones or weeds. It is assumed therefore that this style of general pattern is accepted by the trout as an aquatic type rising to the surface to replenish its oxygen, an operation usually carried out in the shallower water which is its natural habitat. As these artificials mentioned below are more often than not successfully fished in deep open water, which it is believed the aquatic types usually avoid, it seems odd that the trout are prepared to accept them. These general patterns include Eric's Beetle perfected by Eric Horsfall Turner, the Bracken Clock, Little Chap, Black Palmer, etc., to mention just a few.

Dragonflies and Damselflies (Order Odonata)

Without a doubt the different species which make up these two groups of flies contain some of the best known of all insects frequenting fresh water. Their brilliantly coloured bodies, large size, and shining transparent wings makes it impossible to confuse them with any other Order of insects. Although both groups are very similar in appearance they can easily be distinguished, as the Dragonflies (sub-Order: Anisoptera) have unequal wings held open when the insect is at rest, while the Damselflies (sub-Order: Zygoptera) have equal wings which are held closed or nearly closed when at rest. Unfortunately, the adult flies are of little interest to the fisherman as they seem unattractive to the trout. On many occasions I have seen the spent flies fluttering and struggling on the surface where they have fallen spent after mating, but I have never seen one actually taken by a trout. This seems a little strange as in America, where these insects are very common, they are eagerly accepted by fish, the bass in particular.

The difference between Dragonfly and Damselfly nymphs, both of which, unlike the adults, are attractive to trout, seem to be as pronounced as the differences between the winged flies. The former are large, robust creatures with plump bodies, attaining a length in some cases of almost 50 mm. They are generally sluggish creatures and spend much of their lives among the stones or mud on the lake bed, although at times they are to be found in the weed, particularly when pursuing their prey, which are often small fish. When disturbed they, as do other dragonfly nymphs, escape by shooting water from the rectum—moving in fast jerky leaps. Their coloration blending with their environment provides the camouflage which helps to protect them from predators. The latter, with their long slender pale green bodies equipped with three large flat, leaf-shaped tracheal gills which look like tails at the extremity of their bodies, are quite dissimilar. They appear to prefer weed and can often be found clinging to the stems where their stick-like bodies and olive coloration blend into their background and make them very difficult to locate. The nymphs of both these sub-Orders are equipped with a so-called mask, formed from a fused third pair of jaws or labium, which is equipped with a powerful pair of strong claws and which can be rapidly extended from the head to grasp any unfortunate prey that comes within reach. Most species have an annual life cycle of a year, but it seems possible that some of the larger species may spend two years or more in the aquatic stage (Plate 13, No. 142).

Most of the larger Dragonfly nymphs emerge at night to transform into the adult. This is accomplished by either crawling ashore or to the surface via emergent vegetation (Plate 5, No. 59), and therefore at this stage they are of little interest to the fly-fisherman, unlike the nymphs of the Damselfly which are of interest, as when the time for emergence arrives, usually during the hours of daylight, many of them ascend to the surface and swim ashore on to any handy emergent vegetation. They swim with a most distinctive wriggle, creating quite a disturbance which seems to attract the trout. At certain periods during the summer, between May and August, these Damsel nymphs (Plate 8, No. 93) hatch out in fair quantities usually between 8 a.m. and 2 p.m., and when their shoreward migration commences they attract the trout in no uncertain manner. The trout, when taking the nymphs, generally do so in a typical way, slashing at them in a manner similar to a rise to a Mayfly, sometimes leaping right out of the water as a result of their eagerness. A pattern to represent this Damselfly nymph is given later in the book, and although it is impossible to fish it in the exact manner of the natural, it nevertheless seems to be effective if fished with a lightly greased cast, in the surface film, and retrieved at a moderate speed. An artificial to represent these nymphs should always be fished towards the bank, and this is best accomplished by the bank angler. Although as previously mentioned, many of these nymphs swim ashore on the surface, some of them do swim along near the bottom or even crawl ashore, so therefore on occasions a sunk artificial fished slowly along the bottom will prove effective.

Two of the most common Damsels, very similar in appearance, are *Enallagma cyathigerum* (Plate 11, No. 126) and *Agrion splendens* (Plate 13, No. 141). The adult males have a bright blue body, while the females are a grey-green colour. At certain periods during the summer they may be observed in considerable quantities and at this time it is always worth while fishing the Damsel nymph pattern, even though the main emergence period of the natural nymph may have already taken place.

In an article I provided for the *Trout & Salmon* magazine some time ago I described how the adult egg laying female damsel climbs down emergent vegetation or other projections sticking out of the water, such as decaying tree branches or posts, in order to oviposit her eggs. She will sometimes remain underwater for upwards of half an hour existing on the oxygen trapped under her wings. During this time she will often travel along the bottom or over weed for a considerable distance to find suitable egg laying sites. When oviposition is completed she swims to the surface where the attendant male who has been quartering the surface all the time literally plucks her out of the water. I am satisfied that trout do feed on the female as she returns to the surface, as I have on several occasions found partly digested adults in the stomach contents of trout. I have since fished a pattern to represent these female adults with some success. It should be fished in the sink and draw style in areas where the copulating flies are observed.

The Freshwater Louse (*Asellus aquaticus* or *A. meridianus*) (Plate 8, No. 101)

This small crustacean is also known in some parts of the country as the Water Slater or Water Hog-Louse. Extremely common, it is found in nearly all types of stillwater and seems able to exist in water of a lower oxygen content than can the closely related shrimp. The fully grown adults average 15 mm. in length and in appearance they closely resemble the well-known terrestrial Wood Louse. Although sometimes found in the company of the shrimp and of a similar colour, unlike the latter they seem to prefer a habitat of detritus or decaying vegetable matter rather than weed itself. Usually found in shallow water in vast numbers, they crawl in a slow or deliberate manner.

The two species of this Family mentioned above are the most common and likely to be encountered. Of the two, *A. aquaticus* is the larger and darker, and it is interesting to note that during the winter the male of this species has a habit of carrying the female under him. So far as the angler is concerned these crustaceans are rather difficult to imitate as they tend to remain on or near the bottom, and their movements are rather sluggish compared to many other fauna, but as they are often found in autopsies they are undoubtedly worth consideration. There are several dressings available to represent this creature, and the best of these seems to be C. F. Walker's pattern tied to represent the natural as closely as possible, which with these particular species is of prime importance. The natural is usually found in fairly shallow water, and therefore the artificial is best fished individually on the ungreased point on a floating line. It should be allowed to sink and retrieved in short jerks along the bottom as slowly as possible.

The Freshwater Shrimp (*Gammarus* spp.) (Plate 8, No. 92)

There are several species of these small freshwater crustaceans and probably the most common of them is *G. pulex* or *G. Lacustris*. The adults vary in size from about 12 mm. to a little over 18 mm. In appearance they are arched from head to tail, and have many legs. The colour varies from a translucent grey to a distinct brownish orange during the mating season in mid-summer. Fairly strong swimmers when they are disturbed, most species do so on their sides. However, at least one species imported from Canada a number of years ago does swim on an even keel. The males are generally larger than the females, and they will often be found swimming together, the male carrying the female under his body.

This species of fauna is one of the most common found in fresh water and few bodies of stillwater are without large colonies, although it is believed that they dislike waters of an acid type, and it is certainly most unusual to find them in small ponds of a stagnant nature where the oxygen content is too low to enable them to survive.

Despite their abundance in most waters they are of doubtful value to the stillwater angler. Although these shrimps form a major part of the diet of trout, unfortunately for the fisherman this is mainly during the winter months when other forms of food are often in short supply. During the summer months the trout rarely seem to bother with them and it is only occasionally that I have come across them in autopsies. Nevertheless, a good artificial representation will often take trout, even though they may not be feeding on the naturals at the time. The artificial is best fished in the vicinity of weed beds or large stones where the naturals abound, and I have recorded most success fishing it along the bottom, using a fairly slow retrieve with frequent pauses. I have developed my own weighted pattern for this style of fishing, to be used in conjunction with a floating line, (preferable for shallow water to avoid weed), or alternatively, J. R. Harris has also perfected a very lifelike pattern which seems to be successful. The dressing for both these patterns is given in the appropriate chapter.

Grasshoppers

Despite the fact that there are quite a few artificial patterns available to imitate these creatures, I have personally never had cause to require one. According to tradition it is a useful pattern to fish and is reputed to have a particular appeal to really large trout. Certainly the meadows or grass land which form the banks of many of our lakes and reservoirs abound in these active insects, and under conditions of high wind one would expect to see many of these blown out on to the water. This, however, in my personal experience seldom seems to happen, although the natural dapped on the Irish loughs is a proven killer.

The Lesser Water Boatman (Corixa spp.) (Plate 8, No. 102)

The Corixidae Family is quite a large one, containing in all thirty-one different species. Many of them are scarce and rarely encountered, while others are very small and difficult for the angler to imitate. However, several of the more common species are quite large, many being in excess of 10 mm. and are encountered in nearly all types of stillwater. In appearance they are somewhat beetle-like with a hard and shiny keeled back with long oar-like hind legs heavily fringed with hairs, and as the popular name implies, they do have a resemblance to a tiny boat, the legs looking like a pair of oars. The colour of their backs varies from yellow-brown greenish-brown to dark brown with darker patterning, and in contrast their abdomens are distinctly whitish. Their backs are in fact wing cases, although in immature forms (nymphs) these wing cases are not fully developed and the abdomen shows through. It would seem that these wings are used only during the mating period, during which time the adults leave the water and are capable of flying a fair distance. This is usually during late June or July. It is a sight I look forward to every year and it is one that never fails to fascinate. The flight is very rapid and when the Corixae re-enter the water they immediately disappear from sight, rather like a cormorant diving from a height.

Although they are to be observed throughout the summer in varying densities, when odd trout will be found to be taking them, the best period to fish the artificial is during August and early September, a period when the trout seem to accept the natural most readily. This is probably due to the fact that at this particular time they are usually in their thickest concentrations, and this often coincides with a shortage of other forms of aquatic food. I would once again emphasize the large variation in size of these insects, depending on species and time of year. However, to generalize it would seem that concentrations of the larger varieties are usually to be observed throughout August.

Specimens are usually to be found in the weeds in water less than three feet deep. It is interesting to notice their frequent journeys to the surface to replenish their oxygen supply, which is absorbed as a bubble of air and held near the tail between the wings and body; this glistens a bright silver when they are under water. The supply of oxygen lasts only for a limited period and it is therefore necessary for them to return to the surface at regular intervals, and it is at this period they are most vulnerable to any patrolling trout.

Many artificial dressings are available, but my favourite method is to fish a well-weighted pattern on the point by the sink and draw style to simulate the naturals swimming to and from the surface. It should be cast in the vicinity of weed beds, where concentrations of Corixae are seen, and then allowed to sink to the bottom and retrieved in a series of quick jerks. Sometimes a non-weighted pattern fished on the dropper and retrieved fairly fast just under the surface proves to be very killing, particularly early mornings or late evenings.

As a matter of interest, a closely related species of the Family Notonectidae, referred to as the Greater Water Boatman (see Plate

11, No. 124 and Plate 12, No. 135), are often to be seen. In appearance they are very similar indeed to the Lesser Water Boatman but should not be confused as, apart from being very much larger, they swim upside down with their abdomens uppermost. These are of little interest to the fisherman as they are seldom taken by the trout.

Leeches (*Hirundinae*)

There are many different species of Leeches found in stillwater, and as they are often found in the stomach contents of trout, may be worthy of attention by the angler. Several of the more common species are quite large and as some are of a dark brown or almost black in coloration could be represented with a black lure. This should be fished very slowly along the bottom.

Moths, Aquatic (Order Lepidoptera)

It may not generally be realized that there are in fact several species of Moths that are aquatic by nature. They nearly all belong to one Family Pyralidae (Plate 8, No. 104), and most of them spend their larval and, in some cases, pupal life under water. It will no doubt seem strange to find caterpillars under water, but this is, indeed, a fact. One of the most common is the Brown China Mark Moth (Plate 8, No. 103); as the name suggests the adults are dark brown in colour with a whitish patterning; they are quite large, being about 16 mm. in length, while the larvae or caterpillars are as much as 20 mm. long (Plate 12, No. 138). During the early spring the larva bites oval sections out of leaves and from these forms its case, which will then often be found floating in the surface where there is floating vegetation in abundance. I also understand that in some localities the larvae cut these oval sections from the floating leaves of water lillies, and seal the resulting case to the underside of the lilly leaves. Other smaller species make their cases in a similar fashion from duckweed fronds, and they look rather like the caddis cases of some Sedge-flies.

So far as the fisherman is concerned, Moths in their aquatic mode of life are of little interest, but the adults may be of some value, particularly during the evening, when they will often be found on or near the water. Apart from these aquatic species there are also several other species of moths, not strictly aquatic, often to be found in the vicinity of water. Among them are the Ghost and Swift Moths, Family Hepialidae, and some of the Wainscott Moths. The male Ghost Moth, incidentally, is fairly large with narrow wings and has a distinctly white appearance, and it may possibly account for the White and Ermine Moth artificials. In all probability the well-known Windermere Moth pattern, called the Hoolet, represents the aquatic China Mark Moth. This latter pattern is a favourite of Geoffrey Bucknall, the well-known professional fly-tyer, and he informs me it is a very popular and apparently successful pattern. The Wainscott Moths, Genus *Leucania* and *Nonagria*, previously mentioned, are often seen in the vicinity of water. They are variable in size, very thickset and drab-coloured creatures usually a dull yellow-brown in colour. Both caterpillar and adult inhabit the reeds in the margins, and the former bores into the reed stems and feeds on the pith. The resultant hollow reed stem provides a residence for the creature when it pupates.

According to the well-known angler/entomologist John Henderson, one of the most common species of Moths that are likely to be blown on to the water surface in sufficient quantities to interest the trout are a small light-coloured species commonly called Grass Moths. However, I have not personally encountered these and I am therefore unable to give any further information on them.

Apart from the artificials mentioned above, there are many patterns and dressings available, including several tried and tested imitations listed in Courtney Williams' book, a *Dictionary of Trout Flies*. In most cases, however, a pattern of each of the most predominant colours, brown, pale brown or white permutated on large, medium or small hooks will suffice.

Moth patterns should be fished on a floating line with a greased leader, and they should be cast to land on the water with a distinct plop, as this disturbance will help to attract any trout in the vicinity, and will simulate the natural falling on the surface accidentally. The artificial should be retrieved in short, sharp jerks in an effort to copy the struggle of the natural in the surface film. The most productive areas in stillwater to fish these patterns at dusk is the sheltered bays lined with sedges, reeds or other fairly heavy marginal vegetation.

Spiders, Aquatic, the Arachnids (Order Araneae)

This Order, unlike the insects, have four pairs of legs instead of the three pairs of the latter. Although an extremely large group, there is, in fact, only one true aquatic species and this is *Argyroneta aquatica* (Plate 11, No. 123). They are quite common and are to be found in all types of stillwater, usually in the vicinity of weed, where they construct what is best described as a diving bell. This is formed from silk (see Plate 8, No. 105) and in due course is filled with air by the spider, and in this it can live for a considerable period, thus obviating the necessity of repeatedly returning to the surface to replenish its air supply. On its underwater travels air is retained on the fine body hairs, and this air or bubble of air around the body gives the spider a distinct silvery appearance. In shape they are very similar to ordinary land spiders, and are commonly found in the weedy margins of lakes and ponds. It is interesting to note that the males of this particular species, the members of which average a little under half an inch in length, are usually a little larger than the females. This is unusual in spiders, as the reverse is most often the norm, and may well account for the fact that the female aquatic spider does not devour her spouse after mating, which so frequently happens in the spider world.

There are several other families of spiders, apart from the above mentioned truly aquatic species that are to be found in the vicinity of water, and they are as follows. The Wolf Spiders, Family Lycosidae, are not very large, growing to about 8 mm. They are hunting spiders and are quite common along the shores of lakes, and usually spin a vertical silken tube among weed or Sphagnum moss in which they live. The bottom of this tube is usually open below the water surface and through it the spider descends into the water encased in a silvery bubble of air when alarmed. When in search of prey it emerges from the top of its retreat and, like the pond skaters, is able to travel along the water surface without difficulty.

Another common species found in swamps and dykes, and occasionally in the shallow margins of lakes, is a species commonly referred to as the Raft Spider. These belong to the Genus *Dolomedes*, which consists of some of the largest of the British spiders. The males are about 14 mm. and the females 20 mm. and they are usually to be found residing on the floating leaves of water plants. Like the previous species, they are hunting spiders, and can also run along the surface of the water. When alarmed they often descend under water via any handy weed stem. The last species worthy of mention belongs to the Genus *Tetragnatha* and is of medium size, averaging 10 mm. Very common in bogs and along the shoreline of lakes, it spins a web low over the water surface in marginal plants, and will ocasionally be blown on to the water surface.

From the above it should be apparent that artificial patterns to represent some of these spiders should, on the appropriate occasion, be effective. It therefore seems strange that up to the present time spiders as a whole are largely ignored by the stillwater fisherman.

This seems even stranger when one considers that the naturals are more likely to be encountered on stillwater than on rivers; and on running water, particularly in the northern part of the country, spider patterns are extremely popular with the river fly-fisherman, although most of these were probably developed to represent nymphs. Furthermore, Courtney Williams mentions in his book that it is beyond dispute that when a spider gets on to the water in the vicinity of a trout, it never progresses very far before it is taken. With this I am inclined to agree, and therefore if any spiders are in evidence at all I think it well worth trying an artificial in an appropriate size or colour, fished either on or under the surface in the shallower water. I am sure there is also considerable scope here for the amateur fly dresser to evolve patterns to represent these spiders under water enveloped in their silvery sheath of air.

The Snail

Apart from terrestrial forms of life, there are also many aquatic insects or other fauna that at some stage in their life cycle provide food for the trout in or on the surface. It is probably not generally realized at certain times of the year some of the common aquatic snails may be included in this category. Most anglers are aware that snails, where they exist in quantities, form a major part of the diet of the stillwater trout. They are normally browsed off the weed or bed of the lake by the fish in their search for food, but it is unfortunately rather difficult to represent successfully the snail with an artificial in its natural aquatic abode. However, on occasions, usually during the hot weather of mid or late summer, there takes place on many stillwaters a mass migration of snails to the surface. This phenomenon is most interesting, and although I have personally observed it on many occasions, I have so far been unable to ascertain the reason for it. I have also discussed this with one or two people who have made a study of the life history of snails but with nil results. Therefore, one can only hazard a guess, and the most likely explanations seem to be that it is due either to a migratory instinct, coupled with mating, or alternatively to the slight de-oxygenation of the water resulting from high temperature which causes the snails to rise to the surface. This seems to be confirmed, as snails are very much more sensitive to the oxygen content of the water than many other forms of underwater life, including fish. To favour this theory it is interesting to note that snails introduced into a tank of water that has previously been boiled, thereby reducing the oxygen content, immediately rise to the surface.

When they rise to the surface in this manner the snails float with their shell below the surface, but their foot or pad adheres to the underside of the surface film. In this way they can move quite rapidly along the underside of the film or, alternatively, they can be carried along in the film by the current or the wind. When one of these mass rises occurs the snails will often remain in the surface for several days, and on at least one small lake I know the snails were to be found over a period of nearly three weeks, but this is probably unusual. From the fisherman's point of view this is a golden opportunity, even though it is probably not realized by the majority. When the snails are up the trout are most selective, as they are then presented with one of their favourite foods in a very accessible position on the surface, and are unlikely to be caught with anything other than an artificial pattern to simulate these floating snails. However, providing you have an imitation with you at the time this phenomenon occurs, wonderful sport is usually assured. My colleague, Cliff Henry, has perfected an excellent cork-bodied pattern which floats beautifully in the surface and has provided us with many good fish in the past.

Without doubt the most difficult aspect of the rise to the snail is to know when it is taking place, but it is worth remembering that it is a typical head and tail rise usually associated with trout feeding on midge pupae, nymphs or *Caënis* spinners, all of which are common during mid-summer. Apart from the difficulty of recognizing the rise, one would assume that it would be an easy matter to spot the snails in the surface, but in fact this is extremely difficult, and it can only be done by looking directly down into the water.

Finally, I should like to recount a little story in connection with the snail that happened to a friend of mine on a day in August at Grafham. Having fished all morning from the south bank with the wind in his face, with little success, he decided to join the majority of anglers on the north bank, fishing with the wind behind them. Upon arrival there was little space left to fish, so he engaged one or two anglers in conversation. He was promptly informed that the fishing was terrible and, despite the fact that numerous trout were rising, none had been caught. His curiosity aroused, he walked down to the water's edge to try and discover what the fish were taking. There at his feet was the answer; snails in profusion floating along the margin. The wind was gradually blowing them out into the lake a few at a time and odd trout, being aware of this, were patrolling near the shore awaiting their arrival. Mounting the appropriate snail artificial my friend was able to attain his limit of trout in a very short time, much to the amazement of the many anglers in the vicinity. Questioned as to the successful fly, he was happy to furnish the information but, unfortunately, none of the fishermen had such a pattern.

It is also worth mentioning that this cork-bodied snail pattern may be fished successfully near the bottom, which is the more common abode of the natural. The method is as follows. Mount the artificial snail on the point, and tie on a weighted nymph pattern on a dropper about twelve inches above it. In the water that you are fishing choose a location that has an area of silkweed or similar type of weed covering the bottom. Cast out and allow your flies to sink to the bottom. In practice it will be found that the weighted pattern on the dropper will sink into the weed, but the buoyant artificial snail will ride just above it. In this manner it will appear quite natural to any patrolling trout, and it is only necessary to give the line a slight twitch occasionally to attract any fish in the vicinity. This method is explained in detail in Dick Walker's new book on modern reservoir trout fishing, shortly to be published.

Sticklebacks

Undoubtedly these and the small fry of other fish form an important part of the diet of trout on most stillwaters, and although they are not adverse to feeding on them at any time of the season, the main period is usually late July/August and early September, when these little fish congregate in vast shoals in the margins of most lakes. It is at this time that some trout become preoccupied in feeding on them.

If one can find a fairly secluded stretch of bank on a lake or reservoir at this time of the year it is no uncommon sight to see large trout making sorties into the very shallow edges and harrying the fry unceasingly. Under these conditions it is often possible to find a trout that is making regular forays into one particular area, and providing you fish a suitable imitation in the correct manner, while keeping out of sight, success is usually assured.

However, a situation such as this seldom occurs on our more crowded reservoirs, and consequently the most popular method is to fish the water with a lure, deep, and in an attractive manner. This is most successfully accomplished from the bank. If possible, areas adjacent to weed beds, old hedgerows or shallow banks where fry are likely to congregate, should be searched, but if the water is featureless the angler has little alternative other than to fish the water at random. This can often be productive, for if the imitation is fished correctly there is a chance that any trout in the vicinity will assume that it is a small fish separated from its brethren and is making a dash for the sanctuary of the shallower water near the shore.

Although a lure or imitation fished deep and fast will yield trout at most times, during this period the fishermen who make the heaviest bags of trout will be those who fish the imitation in a lifelike manner. This can be best achieved by spending a little time in closely studying the actions of sticklebacks and then endeavouring to emulate them with the artificial. It is also most important to mount an artificial that corresponds closely in size and colour to the natural fry on which the trout appear to be feeding. For this style of fishing it is usual to fish only one artificial on the point, and a long leader is usually advantageous. Depending on the depth of water being fished, either a high-density, fast-sinking line or a slow sinker should be used, but for fishing the very shallow or weedy water along the shore a floater is advisable.

So far as a choice of artificials to represent sticklebacks or fry is concerned, we have a very wide selection. For over half a century various eminent anglers have formulated and recommended patterns, and many of them are readily obtainable from the shops. More recently, that well-known angler, Dick Walker, has perfected and popularized a series of imitations which he calls "Polystickles" to represent many of these small fish. They are dressed with a wonderfully translucent body and simulate a small fish to perfection. I would mention that very full information on these most effective artificials is given in his new book shortly to be published, on modern reservoir ₄trout fishing. Apart from dressings specifically copying fry in appearance, there are also many artificials available to approximate them, and these come under the headings of streamer or bucktail flies. The former are basically long-feathered patterns, while the latter, though similar, are made predominantly of hair. Many of these patterns are given in the appropriate chapter at the end of the book.

Water Bugs (*Hemiptera*)

Although the Corixa should officially be included in this category, it was decided to treat them separately in view of their importance. Most of the creatures that come under this heading are of little interest to the fisherman, and it is therefore considered unnecessary to give detailed descriptions and information on all of them. A few that may possibly be of some interest are dealt with briefly.

The Pond Skater (*Gerris* spp.). These are quite a common sight on most ponds or in the margins of larger lakes. They have slender bodies about 14 to 17 mm. in length, very long legs, and skate on the surface in short bursts, hence their colloquial name. In my experience they are seldom taken by the trout and as far as I am aware, there are no dressings available to represent them. **The Water Measurer** (*Hydrometra stagnorum*) is very similar in appearance, although a little smaller, about 9 to 10 mm., and its body is very much more slender. They are also to be found on the water surface often in the company of the previous species. **The Water Cricket** (*Velia caprai*). Also a surface dweller with a slightly stouter body and shorter legs than the two preceding species. They are quite small, about 6 mm. long, and fairly common, usually in the quieter water close to the banks. **The Water Mites**—*Arachnids* (see Plate 5, No. 57). Although of doubtful value to the fisherman, they are worthy of mention as there are quite a few different species and some of them are very common in all types of stillwater, and at least a brief description will enable the angler to recognize them. Of the same order as the spiders, but somewhat dissimilar in appearance, they also have four pairs of legs, and most of them have round or spherical bodies. In size they vary from the smallest species which is less than 2 mm. to the largest of over 6 mm. The predominant colour is bright red, but some species are yellow, blue or green. Purely aquatic, they live in the weed or silt on the bottom and are often to be found in large colonies. One of the most common bright red types is of the *Eylaeis* Genus, and it is often to be found adhering to the underside of corixa which it apparently uses as a host. It is quite often found in trout at autopsies and it may therefore be worth while to fish a pattern to represent it. John Henderson, in a recent article, stated that he has had some success fishing a pattern that he has devised, and I feel that this is a first-class accomplishment in view of their relatively small size.

Tadpoles
Strange to relate, these very common creatures are completely ignored by most authorities on stillwater trout fishing, yet trout will often feed on them avidly during the early part of the summer when they are present in large numbers in many small fisheries. I first became aware of their importance several years ago when fishing some small dams stocked with trout in South Africa.

At the time I developed a simple pattern to represent them which I consequently called the Tadpolly. Dressed on a long shank hook it has a bulbous body formed from Ethafoam blackened with a magic marker or several strands of peacock herl, and a long tail utilizing several strands of black marabou or three black cock hackles. This accounted for many trout at the time, and I have since used it with considerable effect on many waters in the U.K. It is most effective retrieved at a medium pace in long pulls on a slow sink line. I have also used it on occasions later in the summer, with some success even when the naturals are long gone. I think the trout accept the artificial at this time from past memories of the succulent meals they provided.

Daphnia

These tiny crustaceans are found in vast numbers in most stillwaters and while they form an important diet of the trout they are much too small to imitate with an artificial. However, they are most important to the angler from June onwards as they can be an indicator as to what depth of water the trout may be feeding in. Broadly speaking, find your Daphnia and the trout will not be far away, as when they are present the trout feed on them gluttonously. Enormous clouds of them can often be observed in the water, but as they are sensitive to bright light, the sunnier the day the deeper they will be found. Fortunately, when trout are feeding on Daphnia they are not adverse to accepting other forms of food.

CHAPTER XI

COLLECTING AND PHOTOGRAPHY

This chapter on collecting and photography, although not strictly necessary in a book on fly identification, is included because some fishermen may well decide to take advantage of the additional knowledge which can be gained from the pursuit of these two subjects.

Collecting. This can be divided into three categories:
1. The collection of specimens for study at home when it is not convenient to do so at the waterside.
2. The collection of specimens for permanent mounted collections or preservation in formalin.
3. The collection of specimens for photographic purposes.

These various aspects of collecting will be dealt with in detail later in this chapter, as it is necessary first to discuss ways and means of collecting, transporting, etc.

The Net

The most important part of the collector's equipment is the net or nets, as to do the job properly two nets are necessary. Both can be made quite easily using fine mesh curtain netting or muslin. One should be completely flat for lifting floating specimens off the surface of the water, and the other can be of the traditional bag shape for either scouring the bottom or weeds for nymphs or for catching specimens flying in the air. This latter type of net is also useful for collecting specimens by sweeping through long grass, herbage or vegetation, where many insects find refuge.

The ideal net for lifting flies off the surface is one that can be fixed to the top of a rod, so as to enable the collector to capture those elusive specimens that are so often beyond the reach of a normal net. This constitutes a serious problem, as such a device can easily damage a delicate rod top. However, I believe I have solved the problem and I give the details below.

A 19 inch length of brass wire, 20-gauge thickness. This is a very light fine wire but amply strong for the job. Form this into a circle $2\frac{1}{2}$ to 3 inches in diameter at one end and solder, or better still, braze. Cover this circle with flat net. Next braze or solder a small piece of the same wire about an inch long at a very slight angle to the stem about $1\frac{1}{2}$ inches down from the net. Push the stem through the top rings, with the small 1 inch piece acting as a clamp on the top or second ring. This is all that is required, except for a piece of rubber or cork to push on to the end of the stem to prevent it dropping off the end of the rod should it become loose.

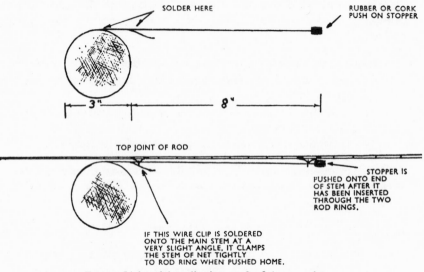

FIG. 22. Lightweight collecting net for fixing to rod top.

As will be seen from the above illustrations, this makes an extremely light and compact net which is very convenient for carrying in your bag or haversack; it can be quickly fixed or detached, and most important of all, cannot possibly damage the rod top in any way, as the only point of fixing is the clamping action on the rod ring.

Collecting Containers

Having caught your specimens, the next problem is their safe transportation. In the case of winged specimens a small glass screw-top jar with a perforated lid for ventilation is probably as good as anything, but the inside should be lined with blotting paper to absorb condensation. This is most important, as if this is not done it is most likely that your insects will reach home in a wet and bedraggled state, completely useless as specimens, through contact with the damp sides. This is particularly liable to happen on hot days.

Most Upwinged flies can easily be transferred from the net to the container by holding the wings of the specimen between forefinger and thumb, but care should be taken to hold very lightly as the wings of these flies are very delicate and easily damaged. Wet fingers incidentally are lethal. (The above method is not recommended if specimens are required for transposing to spinners, as in this case, and in the case of Sedges, the wings must not be touched and the following method should be adopted.)

Captured insects can also be transferred by tapping the net over the open bottle. A mistake made by many people when collecting is to try and introduce the freshly-caught fly into the container through a partly opened lid; this is usually done to prevent specimens already in the container from escaping, but usually it results in the new arrival being injured or escaping as you try to push it through the gap between jar top and lid.

A much more efficient way is to tap the lid of the jar smartly with the palm of the hand (this knocks most of the specimens to the bottom of the container), remove the lid completely, and tap the new specimen in. Providing you are reasonably quick in this operation it is surprising how few flies will escape during the course of a day's collecting.

If you are prepared to take the trouble, the most efficient method of all is to construct a special collecting container. This is fairly simple to make and the construction is as follows:

Any suitable jar will suffice providing it has a good screw-on lid. Line the inside and base with blotting paper. Buy a small plastic funnel, cut off the stem, then trim off the lip until it is very slightly larger than the top of the chosen jar, so that it is a push-fit inside, with the apex and the hole down inside the jar. The resulting container will then be somewhat similar in appearance to a lobster pot and will of course work on the same principle (see photo: opp.).

Some species of flies will travel very well, while others will die quickly unless the container is kept in a cool place. When you reach home, a kitchen refrigerator is a useful place to keep specimens until they are required, but flies kept too long in this way tend either to lose their colour, or to darken considerably; this is particularly so with duns. It is as well to note that if too many specimens are collected in one container, they may damage one another. Therefore, for important specimens it is advisable to carry several small bottles, and limit one specimen to one container.

For those who wish to make an even closer study of entomology, it can be interesting to collect and hatch out nymphs, or larvae. This can be a very hit-or-miss business, but providing the following procedure is carried out, a fair amount of success should be attained.

Collecting and Transporting Nymphs or Larvae

Nymphs and larvae of the various species are fairly easily collected from weeds, under stones, in silt or in mud on the lake bed. They can be kept in a watertight screw-top jar while being collected but the best way to transport nymphs home after collection is in a large canvas water bucket, or in a quantity of wet water weed.

One can with a little luck rear and hatch nymphs and larvae into winged flies under the following conditions. A small aquarium, which is the ideal container, should be treated on the exterior of three of its sides with a dark paint to keep out excess light—this is of course assuming the aquarium is to be positioned in front of a window. It should be covered on top with a hood of muslin-net curtain material, which can quite simply be attached to a wire frame. The purpose of this is two-fold; it allows plenty of necessary air to circulate in the container and it provides a safe resting place for the flies when they hatch out.

The container should be set up with about an inch of gravel for nymphs or silt for larvae at the bottom and filled with water from the same source as that from which the nymphs or larvae were taken. Should this not be readily available, rainwater or tap water that has stood for at least two weeks may be used as a substitute. Also a little weed may be introduced from the same locality. At this stage a word of warning: the water should be strained through a cloth before transferring it to the container, and the weed should be thoroughly washed, to prevent the introduction of aquatic predators which might make short work of your nymphs.

If it is decided to hatch out any larvae (particularly Caddis larvae) or the larger Stonefly nymphs, they should be confined to a separate container, as many of them are carnivorous and include Ephemeropteran nymphs in their diet. With them should be included a piece of jutting rock or stone, to enable them to crawl out of the water in order to transpose; this is essential.

The specimens themselves feed mainly on detritus and decaying vegetable matter, so do not worry about keeping your tank too clean. A fair proportion of the mature specimens collected will usually hatch out within a matter of a week or two, but in practice it has proved very difficult to keep them alive for more than three or four weeks, so some casualties must be expected.

Let us now specifically deal with the Ephemeroptera. Nymphs which have successfully hatched into duns will, if they are allowed to remain on the net cover, within a day or two change into spinners (imagines), superb creatures of shimmering translucency. This is accomplished by the fully adult fly crawling out of its own skin which splits along the top of the thorax. With a little patience it is possible to watch this fascinating transformation take place. When handling spinners for examination, they may be picked up by the wings, and a particularly useful little tool for this delicate job is a pair of ordinary flat-bladed tweezers with a small pad of plastic foam stuck on the inside of each blade.

All these different flies, nymphs and larvae can of course be preserved indefinitely, either pinned through the body and mounted in a case, or kept in formalin for microscopic examination and reference at a later date, but the specimen should first be immersed in a 60 per cent alcohol solution for a short period before placing in the formalin. If this is not done, the specimen will not sink in the formalin properly and will quickly deteriorate.

It is not intended here to elaborate further on either of these two methods, as much has been written on them before. Also they are far more essential to the entomologist, to whom microscopic examination is of prime importance. To the angler/entomologist they are not so important, as with each method the colours of the specimens quickly fade and are of little value for colour reference purposes.

It is possible to preserve an insect indefinitely by casting a block of water-clean resin around it, and do-it-yourself kits can be purchased for this purpose. The insect, after the operation is finished, is permanently embedded within the block and cannot deteriorate, irrespective of the amount of handling it receives, except perhaps for a little loss of colour.

Photographing Nymphs and Flies

If one is interested in photography and can afford the necessary equipment, this is a fascinating subject of itself, offering limitless opportunities for the enthusiast. Reference collections of all the more common species can be built up in true-to-life colour and size, and if you have mastered the art of fly-tying, the advantages of having actual colour photographic models to work to in the winter months are obvious.

The problems that had to be overcome to produce the photographs that illustrate this book were many. Any reader who is thinking of trying his hand at it will find the following information of some use.

Equipment

The equipment and methods suggested here are similar to those used for the production of the photographs in this book, and for which much experimenting was necessary before success was attained.

The first essential is a good camera. The most convenient for this type of work is a 35-mm. direct-lens Reflex, which allows you to look directly through the lens and which gives very accurate focusing and positioning of your subject, most necessary in this type of work.

Film. Kodachrome II 35-mm. film is probably the best for this purpose as this will give colour transparencies which can be studied direct or enlarged through a projector. If the photographs are taken at 1 × magnification, this will give an actual life-size reproduction on the transparency. Kodacolour film can also be used and gives excellent colour prints, but the snag here is that in the printing the subject is considerably enlarged.

Tripod. An adjustable tripod, allowing you to tilt the camera up or down, can be used if you intend to photograph flies from various positions outdoors. This is essential for close-up work.

Electronic Flash. This is necessary for indoor photography, as it gives an exposure of one-thousandth of a second, which is desirable for these fast-moving flies.

Bellows or Extension Tubes are also useful, being far better than close-up lenses.

Various small perspex cells can be made and mounted in or on a sliding extension unit which is clipped or screwed on to the front of the camera. Some white cards will have to be mounted around and under each cell to throw the correct reflection of light on to the subject.

The flash unit should be set at an angle of roughly 45° overhead so that it is trained directly on to the subject. The controls of the camera should be set as follows:

Distance—infinity ∞ Aperture—f 16. Speed—1/25th or 1/30th of a second. The correct exposure is governed by the distance from the face of flash unit to the subject, and for a life-size reproduction the bellows should be set at magnification 1 × and for this setting the face of the flash should be approx. 6 in. from the subject to give correct exposure.

The perspex cells can be made from a 2 in. section of perspex tube with a diameter of between 2 and 3 inches, or a square tube can be made from sheet perspex. This should be sealed at each end with a disc of optically clear glass. These can be stuck on with a watertight glue, and should have a piece of perspex or glass mounted inside to form a platform on which to arrange your flies for photography. The cell should have a ⅝ in. hole in the top centre for inserting and removing your specimens, and may be used in the horizontal position for photographing duns, caddis and other flies in the "at rest" position. It can also be filled with water and used for photographing nymphs in their natural environment.

The second cell is simpler as it need only be sealed with a glass disc at one end. It may be filled with water and photographed either from below, showing us what the trout sees, or from above, so that spinners, for example, can be photographed as the angler sees them.

However, let us first examine the reason for suggesting the set-up as outlined above. Many of these flies could of course be photographed in the field under natural conditions with natural daylight, but it is assumed that the average fly-fisherman will be reluctant to waste good fishing time in the field photographing specimens. Furthermore, this would also necessitate transporting a great deal of equipment to the waterside.

Using electronic flash, daylight conditions can be exactly simulated, and providing specimens can be successfully transported to or bred at home, this work can then be undertaken in comfort with all the equipment at hand under ideal conditions. Also with electronic flash the exposure is constant, whereas in the field the exposure will vary greatly and one is at the mercy of the vagaries of weather.

Photographing a live insect is far from easy, as the subject more often than not refuses to keep still, and when it does finally settle at rest it is seldom in the right position. The correct answer to this problem is to have unlimited patience, but you must be prepared to spend sometimes as much as half an hour jockeying a specimen into the right position for photographing.

We will first of all consider photographing duns, caddis, stoneflies, etc. in the horizontal cell. It has been found necessary to use a cell, as otherwise most of the time will be spent retrieving your specimen from odd corners of the room, and it is quite incredible how even in a small room a specimen can quickly vanish, perhaps never to be found again. This can be disastrous if you have only the one!

The fly should be dropped through the porthole in the top of the cell and constantly kept on the move with a steel probe. The insect eventually tires, and can then be induced to assume the right position where it is only too pleased to take a rest long enough for you to take its photograph.

We will next deal with the problem of photographing a fly from under water in the vertical cell. The only problem here is to keep the fly on the water surface while you are photographing it. Unfortunately, the first reaction of a fly placed on water is to fly off, and some method had to be devised to prevent it doing so. This can be achieved as follows. Fill the chamber with water two or three days before it is required for use. During this time it will form a nearly invisible skin or film on top. The specimen should then be dropped on to this surface from a height of one to two inches; nine times out of ten the fly will land on its feet and the tension caused by the surface skin will firmly hold it in position. Sometimes, particularly with duns, they will violently flap their wings in an effort to free themselves and if you are unlucky a wing will stick in this film. When this happens the fly will have to be picked out and allowed to dry before one tries again.

Finally, with the cell in the other vertical position being photographed from above, you are now ready to take pictures of the various spinners lying spent in the surface film. It is fairly simple to prepare your subject here. Drop the spinner from an inch or two above the surface as in the previous case, and using two small steel wires, spread its wings apart and down on to the surface. Once the wings have touched the water, the fly is trapped in the right position in the surface film.

Care should be taken to ensure that the wings are pressed down evenly, as otherwise the specimen will turn on its side and is virtually impossible to right. This can only be achieved with practice, and it must be emphasized that the two expressions "patience is a virtue" or "practice makes perfect" are particularly applicable to this whole subject.

Finally, I should like to point out that many of the above problems would be simplified if the fly could be killed or doped just before photographing, but in the early stages of experimenting I was unable to find any method or drug which would do this without the specimen contracting or relaxing. It will be realized, of course, that when a fly relaxes its legs will not support the weight of its body and the wings and tails droop down, or when a fly contracts it is impossible to straighten its limbs; in either case it is then an unsuitable subject for photographing. However, I have now discovered two alternative methods which seem reasonably successful. By using a cyanide killing bottle judiciously, some flies can be doped (not killed) and their limbs and wings positioned. This is particularly useful for photographing spinners on the water, or for quietening the very active sedges. By trial and error I have arrived at the correct time to keep various species in the cyanide bottle to reach the desired state. They are as follows:

Trichoptera ..	..	25 seconds
Plecoptera ..	..	35 seconds
Diptera ..	..	50 seconds
Ephemeroptera	..	90 seconds

The other alternative is to contain your specimen in a plain glass tube and then to hold it in front of an illuminated photoflood bulb for a short interval. The heat given off by the bulb will quickly send the insect into a state of exhaustion, but great care must be taken not to over-expose the insect to the heat, as this is fatal. The correct length of time to expose the insect to the heat can only be judged by experience. After correct exposure the specimen will be comatose for a sufficient period for the photograph to be taken.

On occasions it may be desirable to photograph various aquatic species in their natural environment. This is fairly simple to achieve if a small tank is used, in conjunction with extension tubes on the camera to give a magnification of 1 ×. The electronic flash is set up either at the side or immediately over the tank and should be approximately two to four inches away from the subject in the tank being photographed. With this method some very artistic results can be obtained, particularly if the insect is photographed on bright green weed, although personally I seldom adopt this technique as with photographs required for identification purposes a neutral background without incidental distractions is essential.

Note: It is now possible to take excellent close up photographs of insects in the field under natural conditions, by using one of the new electronic ring flashes in conjunction with special close up lenses or extension tubes, using Ektachrome 200 A.S.A. film or 400 A.S.A.

CHAPTER XII

POT-POURRI

Since I completed the original manuscript of this volume several interesting facts have come to light relating to the behaviour of some species of insects. In addition I have realised a few hints and wrinkles in respect of fishing techniques and tackle have been omitted from the original text and these are now included to bring the book up to-date. Many of these items have been based on articles I have submitted and had published in the *Trout and Salmon* magazine during the past four years, and I am indebted to the Editor of this journal for his permission to reproduce these herewith in full or part.

HABITAT OF CERTAIN SPECIES

Over the centuries most species of insect have become acclimatized to live and breed in a certain environment, this depends on a number of factors, among the most important are temperature, humidity, availability of suitable food and breeding conditions as well as the type and flow, or otherwise, of water where aquatic species are concerned. For this reason may species of fauna of interest to the fly fisherman may only be found in predetermined areas or localities. Very occasionally some species may be observed in parts of the country where they have not been previously recorded. This is due either to lack of observation prior to the first sightings, or a change in environmental or climatic conditions which have enabled the species in question to spread to an otherwise hostile area. The discovery or arrival of a species on a water can often be of considerable importance to the fisherman and if possible this should be recorded for the benefit of other anglers.

During research over many years I have discovered several species previously unrecorded in areas I have fished, and most of these have now been recorded in my previous book *Trout Fly Recognition*. However, I recently made two new discoveries and as these could be of interest to the still water fly fisher I am pleased to now provide details. The Gravel Bed *Hexatoma Fuscipennis*. A medium to small

PLATE 15.   Even on a very hot day the odd trout will sometimes oblige.
The author with a nice rainbow trout.

Fishing along the bank for sticklebackers.

A rainbow trout of 5lb. in superb condition, from Chew Valley Lake.

PLATE 16.

PLATE 17.

Cliff Henry with collecting net and special insect container.

This fine brown trout was taken on a black gnat—the right answer as the stomach contents in the dish prove.

Fly with roof-shaped wings—Trichoptera.

A hard-winged fly—Plecoptera.

A flat-winged fly—Diptera.

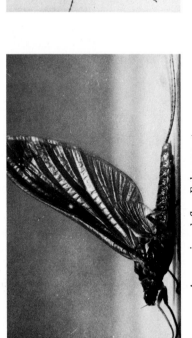

An upwinged fly—Ephemeroptera.

PLATE 18. The Four Major Groups.

THE POLYSTICKLE.
By Dick Walker.
excellent imitation of a
stickleback.

THE HATCHING OLIVE.
By the Author.
represent the Pond or
Olive hatching in the
surface film.

THE ADULT MIDGE.
By the Author.
be dressed in various
colours and sizes.

E 19. Special Patterns.

RED OR GREEN LARVAE
By the Author.
A killing pattern fish
the prescribed manner.

THE SHRIMPER.
By the Author.
A very lifelike patter
simulate the fresh
shrimp.

THE FLEXIFLY.
By the Author.
A new approach to a g
pattern.

THE LAST HOPE.
By the Author.
A tiny artificial—but
fish killer.

PLATE 20. Special Pa

THE FLOATING SNAIL.
By Cliff Henry.
A wonderful pattern when
the snail are "up".

HATCHING MIDGE PUPA.
By the Author.
A very lifelike and successful
pattern.

SEDGE PUPA.
By the Author.
This represents the Sedgefly
in its pupal stage of life and
has proved very killing when
these flies are hatching.

P.V.C. NYMPH.
By the Author.
A weighted nymph pattern
that has accounted for large
numbers of trout where
olives abound.

PLATE 21. Special Patterns.

THE G. AND H. SEDGE.
(*side view*).
Developed by the Author and Cliff Henry this has proved itself time and again when any green bodied sedges are on the water. It is an exceptionally fine floater.

THE G. AND H. SEDGE.
(*top view*)

OLIVE DUN.
By Cliff Henry.
A superb dry fly when Pond or Lake Olives are on the water.

PLATE 22. Special Patterns.

THE POND OLIVE SPINNER.
By the Author.
Should be dressed to float in
the surface film not on top.

THE HATCHING MAYFLY.
By the Author.
A pattern to represent the
adult mayfly emerging from
its nymphal case in the
surface film.

THE SMALL HATCHING
MIDGE.
By the Author.
A pin shows the small size
of this pattern tied to
represent a small midge
hatching in the surface film.

PLATE 23. Special Patterns.

THE BLACK BEARS HAIR
LURE.
By Cliff Henry.
An excellent general lure
should be fished slow to fast
just under the surface.

THE DEMOISELLE NYMPH.
By Cliff Henry.
A very killing pattern most
effective fished a little below
the surface in the mornings
during July and August.

THE MUDDLER MINNOW.
Considered to be a very
good general pattern on
many still waters.

PLATE 24. Special Patterns.

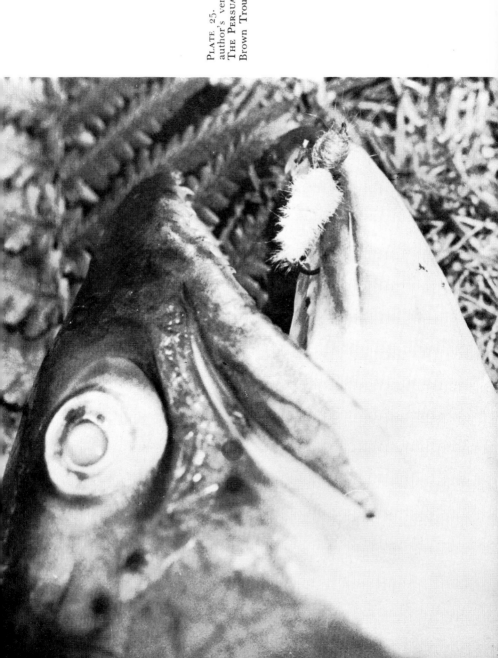

PLATE 25. This close-up shows the author's very successful new pattern THE PERSUADER in the jaw of a large Brown Trout.

member of the *Tipulidae* or crane fly family. A dark brownish grey insect with black legs and two brownish heavily veined mottled wings, it is a terrestrial insect but often found on or over water as the pupa are usually found in the damp gravel or sand bordering rapid streams or rivers of Westmorland and northwards. I am reasonably certain that this species has never been recorded either south of Westmorland or on stillwater. During May and June of 1974 I observed large numbers of these hatching out from the sandy margins on the west bank of Bough Beach reservoir in Kent. Many of these were flying out and low over the water and on several occasions I observed trout feeding on them. The Heather Fly *Bibio pomoni*. This is also a terrestrial species and full details of this fly are given on page 120. Similar in size and appearance to the well known Hawthorn fly as far as I am aware the Heather fly, or Bloody doctor as it is sometimes called, has never been recorded from the South of England, yet in July of 1974 I observed and identified huge swarms of these flies among the herbage along the banks of the river Test at Leckford in Hampshire. Later in the day I also saw numbers of them around a small lake and pond in the same area.

SOME NEW FACTS ON ADULT BUZZERS

A few years ago I remember reading a report in one of our fishing journals which I viewed with some scepticism about trout feeding regularly on adult winged Chironomids or buzzers as they are popularly referred to by many fishermen.

For a long time now I have made a special study of this fascinating family of insects and until recently it has only been on rare occasions that I have personally observed trout feeding upon these adults on the surface. However, I now feel I owe the writer of the article an apology for my doubts as during the early part of this season for a period of two or three weeks on our local resevoir the trout started feeding on these in the evenings and were not interested in any other form of food. This phenomenon was also observed at this time on other reservoirs in the area according to reliable reports I received.

First of all I should like to make it quite clear that the reason for this appeared to be an unusual behaviour pattern on the part of the buzzers not of the trout, after all it is a natural reaction of the fish to feed on the form of food that is most easily accessible and that is what was happening at this time. Let me explain! To start with the trout usually commence feeding on the ascending pupae as they slowly swim to the surface to transpose into the adult. On windy mornings or evenings when the surface is rough and broken, the

pupae hatch at the surface very quickly indeed and almost immediately fly off. The trout being wise in the ways of nature find it
easier to feed upon this ascending pupae at this time and only
occasionally chase one and take it at the surface. However on calm
still days when there is a relatively thick film present on the surface
of the water, the ascending pupae often have difficulty in breaking
through this to hatch, and the trout quickly realize it requires much
less effort to feed upon the pupae hanging in the surface which is
more often than not the cause for those splendid evening rises we
sometimes encounter on calm warm evenings. It is also under these
conditions that I have sometimes seen the odd trout also taking the
newly hatched winged adult, but in my experience until recently
this has been very much the exception rather than the rule.*

The season of 1974 started quite normally with some good
evening rises to the buzzers and plenty of trout were taken on midge
pupae artificials, but by about the third week of May the position
altered dramatically. The evening rises were still as good if not
better, but very few were being caught, and the normally highly
successful midge pupa patterns were steadfastly refused. After a
couple of evenings with very poor results my fishing companion
Cliff Henry and I decided to make a closer study of the feeding
pattern of the trout. First of all we noticed that the trout were
feeding higher out of the water and furthermore instead of the
normal rather slow head and tail rise associated with fish feeding on
the pupae, the movement was more hurried and closer allied to
trout feeding on sedges or similar surface flies. We were extremely
puzzled by this as despite careful observation the only insects
hatching in sufficient quantities were buzzers. The next calm
evening we therefore concentrated on studying the surface of the
water and it was only then that we noticed that there appeared to
be considerable numbers of adult winged buzzers or midges actually
flying low over the water surface.

They flew relatively slowly with their legs actually trailing in the
water, and once we became used to spotting them their flight could
easily be observed as they left a very faint V shaped trail on the
surface, in most cases the wake would suddenly cease as the insect
disappeared in the swirl of a rising trout.

We studied this phenomenon closely over the ensuing three weeks
and after catching many of these adults we ascertained the following
facts. To start with we had never previously seen adult midges
flying for long periods over the surface in this manner since normally,
as soon as they hatch, they fly to the nearest land and mating takes

* So far the first two months of the 1975 season appear to be following the same
pattern, and rises to the adult now appear to be widespread on many still
waters.

place at a later period. The egg bearing females then return to the water usually at dusk to drop their egg clusters over or onto the water. Most anglers will be familiar with the swarms of these females that gather round a boat just as it is getting dark emitting an audible buzzing sound from which of course they obtain their common name. We caught many dozens of these adults on the surface, and for the first week or ten days they were the familiar orange/silver midge, but during the last few days of June and early July, the majority were a medium sized green midge. These were very similar to the common green midge normally to be seen a little later in the season, except that they had a distinctly yellow thorax as opposed to the normal greenish colour. Finally and of particular interest in each and every case they proved to be females, but their gyrations over the surface seemingly had nothing to do with oviposition as in no case were there any traces of eggs.

Now what can we deduce from these facts, and the answer I am afraid is very little. Our first reactions were that this peculiarity could be accredited to a species with which we were unfamiliar, but this theory was quickly dispelled when we found that many we caught were the common orange/silver variety. Secondly we thought it may have something to do with distribution of the eggs onto the surface, but this idea was also quickly discarded as there was no trace of any eggs at all. Could it be due to weather conditions as in this particular year we had had one of the driest springs on record.

Apart from our very interesting study of the natural insects involved, we also tackled the problem of evolving a suitable pattern and technique to catch the trout that at this period were preoccupied in feeding exclusively on these adults. So far, sad to relate, we have only met with mediocre success. After some experimenting we perfected a dressing that floated well and in appearance closely approximated the natural in flight. The method of fishing this pattern however proved to be the most difficult problem. Fished without movement it brought negative results. Fished along the surface with either a slow or fast retrieve resulted in far too much wake which apparently scared the trout. A compromise of giving an occassional slow pull on the line did result in the capture of a few fish, but apart from this the only real success we attained was in the latter part of the evening when the light was fading and the odd trout rose extremely close. When this happened by dapping the artificial lightly on the water immediately in front of the trout, it was immediately accepted without hesitation.*

* The use of a specially made 14 ft rod now appears to be at least a partial answer to this problem as with a light line you can virtually dap your artificial very lightly along the surface.

TO GREASE OR NOT TO GREASE

I am surprised at the comparatively large number of still water trout fisherman I have encountered over the last two or three seasons that seem unaware of the importance of oil or line grease, or lack of it, on their leader or flies. This can often mean the difference between success or failure and is vitally important under most conditions.

Let us first of all take a quick look at some of the preparations available to fly fishermen today. There are several different brands of line grease on the market and most of these have a mucilin base. Personally I use the plain mucilin in the little green tin, as this is freely on sale and I have always found it perfectly satisfactory. This is supplied with a felt pad for application to the leader, but it should be applied sparingly. Oil or floatant for flies is offered either in bottles or aerosol type sprays and there are many different brands on the market each one claiming to be superior to any other. I prefer the preparation first recommended by Dick Walker in *Trout and Salmon** a year or so ago, as I find this far superior. It is in liquid form and is best kept in a wide mouth screw top bottle, so that the whole fly no matter how large can be dipped in the liquid, but this should if possible be carried out some little time before use to allow it to dry out thoroughly. Flies treated with this oil float beautifully for several hours. There are several preparations one can obtain for degreasing leaders or flies from ordinary liquid glycerine to thick mud from the edge of the water which will suffice if nothing else is available. Liquid detergent is very good, but I prefer glycerine mixed with fullers earth.

A basic error made by many anglers is to apply grease too liberally to the leader in an effort to ensure that their dry fly does not become waterlogged. This is a mistake, always apply lightly, and always leave the last six inches completely free of grease. Some fishermen do not realise the amount of disturbance a greased line creates as it is retrieved on the surface; under calm conditions this will be immediately apparent, but in rough water this is not noticeable to the angler, but will be to the trout. A similar situation can apply when using wet flies or nymphs on a floating line, if you require to fish these at any depth it is essential to thoroughly degrease both flies and leader before fishing commences. It should also be appreciated that the application of grease to different sections of the leader can predetermine at what depth various flies on it will fish.

For example, from midsummer onwards when there are a lot of sedge flies about, an extremely effective method is to use, in con-

---

* Now available from many tackle retailers it is marketed under the name "Permafloat".

junction with a floating line, a dry sedge pattern on the dropper with a sedge pupa artificial on the point. In this case the leader above the dry fly is greased whilst the remainder down to the point fly which must be retrieved just below the surface is thoroughly degreased. In another instance you may wish to retrieve a dry sedge, invicta or similar patterns in the surface film. This can be a very killing method when trout are feeding on the adult sedge, as they will often completely ignore a dry sedge fished on the surface, but readily accept the same pattern fished in the film, as they seem to take this for a sedge fly hatching. To ensure that your chosen pattern fishes in the correct position it is necessary to degrease the leader and very sparsely oil the artificial. Too much oil and it will float too high, too little and it will sink too far below the surface.

To illustrate the importance of this aspect of fly fishing I should like to recount an actual incident I was personally involved in last season. The time was early July and I had arranged to take a friend out for a day's boat fishing on one of our larger reservoirs. Fairly new to this style of fishing he asked me if I would be kind enough to guide him on which patterns to use and how to fish them. Upon arrival at the water I was informed that few, if any, fish were rising and anglers were having most successes fishing deeply retrieved lures. Observing several sedge-flies fluttering in the margins I felt it should be possible to take a few fish on the surface despite the complete absence of rises. Under these conditions I knew it would be necessary to attract the trout to our flies, so it was therefore essential to use a large dry, well oiled, sedge on the dropper with an invicta fished just below the surface on the point. I explained this to my colleague and also advised him to grease the leader heavily in this case above the dry sedge. We then commenced a nice drift, over water not too deep where the trout should be able to see the disturbance created by the sedge on the dropper even if they were lying deep. Sure enough this proved succesful and during the next two hours I boated four nice trout and also rose several others which came short. The disturbance created by the sedge attracted them to the surface where most accepted the invicta. Despite the fact that my companion was fishing the same method with similar flies he only rose one fish in this period. I checked his flies, leader and even the distance between flies, but could not account for this, we also changed places in the boat but all to no avail, eventually I suggested we exchange rods and the reason for his lack of success was immediately apparent. The flies were fishing incorrectly as he had greased the leader between the two flies instead of the section only above the sedge on the dropper. I immediately corrected this for him and within five minutes he was delightedly playing a fine plump trout.

This clearly demonstrates the extreme importance of this aspect of fly fishing.

WHY DO TROUT TAKE LURES

At the time I wrote this article I had been reading a piece by Brian Clarke in *Trout and Salmon* magazine with considerable interest, particularly his excellent analysis as to why trout accept lures. Initially he quite rightly pointed out that over the years it has been generally accepted that most lures were intended to represent small fish, fry or sticklebacks on which trout are reputed to feed avidly at all times but in his experience he had not found this to be true. Up to a point I confirm his findings in this respect, as over the years during my own research, particularly apertaining to autopsies, I have seldom found small fish in the stomach contents except on certain waters at specific times of the year. Consequently while I agree that trout do not accept lures as food in the form of fry throughout most of the summer, I must also point out that on those waters where fry in one form or another abound, many trout particularly the larger browns do settle down to feed upon them exclusively, usually during the late summer when the fry start to shoal in the margins or when they emerge from the sanctuary of the weed beds in very shallow water. I can quote many instances at such times when I have caught trout that have been so full of fry that they have been literally spewing them out of their mouths as they have been netted. In fact for two or three weeks during late July or early August on some waters it is all but impossible to catch trout at all unless one is prepared to mount an imitation of stickleback or a perch fry. According to Brian, autopsies carried out over a period of two years by him and several friends does not confirm this, but in fairness the reason for this is probably due to the absence of this phenomenon on the waters they fish.

The other theories advanced are as follows. That trout are motivated to take lures out of (a) fear, (b) aggression, (c) curiosity and (d) as some other form of food. In his final analysis Brian seemed to favour curiosity and while he put forward several excellent theories to substantiate his conclusions I am afraid I do not altogether agree. In my humble opinion I think we have to look at this situation from a far broader spectrum. I feel up to a point we can discount the fear aspect, and also aggression except possibly prior to pairing and mating, or on those few still waters where trout, even rainbows, stake out territorial rights to a certain area of water. Let us now look at the curiosity aspect; here I agree Brian has a good case in some respects as from my own observations I am sure he is right that some trout do follow a lure to investigate it, and then often take it into their mouths to feel or taste this strange invader of their kingdom. On the other hand I am sure many anglers will have had similar experiences to myself, when using a lure, where trout and in some cases the same trout, will follow a lure almost to the rod tip time and time again, but consistently refuse it. Conversely I have on occasions mounted a different lure, and every trout that I have covered has immediately accepted it without hesitation. In the latter case I am sure it is accepted as a form of food.

From the above I am inclined to think that trout accept lures for a number of reasons, depending on a variety of factors appertaining at the time. The weather, water temperature, the depth of the water, the time of day as well as the other reasons put forward. In addition I should like to suggest one other factor which I think Brian has overlooked, which I'm sure is equally valid. This is, the automatic reflex action which all trout seem to possess. How many times have we all experienced the surprised take of a trout almost before your fly has landed in the water, or on other occasions where one casts a lure behind and to one side of a trout you can clearly see, and find it is immediately snapped up by the trout as soon as it appears in his window.

Finally I should like to look a little closer at Brian's reasons for dismissing the motivation of trout to take lures as some other form of food. I definitely disagree with him over this point as I am sure at times certain patterns of lures are taken as a form of food, if (a) the trout is hungry and (b) if the lure loosely represents a form of food on which it has recently been feeding. Brian states: "Where is there anything in either of these natural larders – whether in what we know they do eat, or in what they have available to them if they wish – that looks and behaves like most (or indeed any) of the lures that habitially catch trout". Again I beg to differ and would put forward the following specific examples.

The Worm Fly

This is one of the earlier and most popular lures, and is quite a good representation of either an alder fly larva, or certain of the darker species of sedge pupa.

The Black Lure

A very popular and often effective lure, it is I am sure taken at times for some of the large dark coloured leeches that are common on many stillwaters.

The Baby Doll or My Own 'Persuader Pattern'
This, or in fact, many basically white coloured lures are undoubtedly taken for many of the larger pale coloured species of sedge pupa.
The Woodcock and Green
Typical of many green bodied lures that are probably taken for some of the larger green damsel nymphs.

There are many other examples I could quote, but up to comparatively recently I have always been puzzled as to why many large lures with predominant green dressings should often prove effective as I could think of no true form of aquatic life that even loosely approached such a colour and size. As a result of some research I carried out last season, I discovered by pure chance the probable answer even to this mystery. As this is most interesting I will recount the series of events that led up to it.

On a calm warm summer day in July last season my colleague Cliff Henry and myself decided to spend a complete day on our local reservoir catching and photographing damsel nymphs, in order to establish the reason for the wide range of colours in which they are found. Taking a boat and resisting the strong temptation to take our rods as well as our cameras, we proceeded to a quiet bay where we had previously spotted a lot of these particular nymphs. We anchored the boat close to the branches of a submerged tree that were sticking up out of the water, as we reasoned that any nymphs in the area would be sure to make for these branches as they always transform into the adult winged form via emergent vegetation etc. Sure enough upon our arrival we found several nymphs drying out on the branches in preparation for the final moult, and these we duly removed and photographed. We then settled down to observe the arrival of further specimens, while at the same time idly watched masses of the large adult blue bodied winged males and green bodied females gyrating around the branches. My reverie was suddenly interupted by Cliff saying, "you won't believe this but I am sure I just saw a winged adult emerge from beneath the surface". I was just about to make a sarcastic reply, when to our absolute amazement we both clearly observed a repeat performance literally under our noses. Determined to find the reason for this odd phenomen, we both settled down patiently to a searching appraisal of the situation. It was shortly after this that we both noticed a lot of winged adults were mating in the air and copulating tail to tail. The blue bodied male seemed to be the predominant partner supporting the female who had her wings partially closed. After a short interval a pair alighted on one of the branches and the male still supporting the female proceeded to crawl backwards down the branch until the female at his tail was pushed underwater. As soon as she was fully submerged, they parted and she continued on her own to crawl underwater down the branch to a depth of three or four feet, until she found some weed where she commenced to oviposit her eggs. Fortunately the water was very clear and we were able to note her actions closely. Even now in retrospect it seems quite incredible but she remained underwater moving from weed patch to weed patch quite repidly for over 25 minutes. At the end of this period she was many feet away from where she oringinally descended and having completed her task she then swam or rather struggled to the surface. All this time the male had been slowly circling over the area where they parted company but as soon as she emerged above the surface he darted down and joined her again when they flew off. During the ensuing few hours we observed many other pairs do a repeat performance some females remaing underwater for over 40 minutes.

Over the years many authorities have reported finding adult winged damsel flies in the stomach contents of trout they have caught, and it has always to the best of my knowledge been generally accepted that trout have obtained these by leaping out of the water and intercepting low flying specimens. Due to this chance observation it now seems beyond reasonable doubt that during the mating period of these flies in July and August, trout will feed upon these underwater where this occurs. As many of these adults are upwards of two inches in length this could of course account in some instances for trout readily accepting what are normally considered extremely large lures. Whilst the most common damsel flies are blue or green bodied there are also other species with red and other body colours, so this could well provide room for much experiment on water where they are found. We have now dressed some artificials to specially represent these adults underwater, and we are now eagerly awaiting the next mating period in order to try our luck.

A SUGGESTION

Let us forthwith ban wading in any form on all our bodies of stillwater! To be perfectly fair let us first of all consider the possible advantages of wading as opposed to the disadvantages. These are, I am sure most readers will be forced to agree, relatively few and despite much thought on the matter I can only think of three instances where it would be desirable. These are as follows:-
(a) in areas where your backcast is so restricted it would not be

possible to fish, (b) in extensive areas of very shallow or weedy water, and (c) to reach islands or known hot spots such as old hedgerows, submerged obstacles or old stream beds.

At the moment on most of our waters it is unfortunately necessary to wade, as if one angler in a restricted area wades, all must. Let us now consider the implications behind this a little further. Over the years it has become an accepted fact that it is essential for the bank angler to wade out as far as possible before he commences to fish, under the mistaken impression that the further away from the bank he can cast his flies the better his chances of success. Therefore, the first angler arriving to fish a deserted area of bank usually wades out as far as he can, and in the process of so doing scares any trout in the vicinity that may have been feeding in the shallow water. Other anglers arriving after him have no alternative but to follow suit. Even if the first few anglers arriving are aware that it is far more likely to catch trout in the shallow often weedy margins and accordingly fish from the shore it is inevitable that sooner of later along will come the fisherman who will wade out into the water sometimes almost in front of you. In addition, a further serious disadvantage of wading is the resulting discolouration of the water from disturbed mud or sediment off the bottom, and along an area of shore where many are wading this can often be quite considerable thereby reducing the chance of hooking a fish.

From the above it should be apparent to most thinking anglers that apart from the few advantages previously mentioned which are, after all, not absolutely necessary the full enjoyment of our sport, wading is only essential when other anglers do so, and this in fact decreases, not increases, our chances of sport. It is a very odd facet of human nature but put the same angler that has previously been wading, in a boat and if there be an area of shore that is out of bounds to the bank fisher, he will often fish along this with the utmost zeal – CASTING AS CLOSE TO THE MARGINS AS POSSIBLE.

Apart from the above there are also several other extremely serious consequences that arise from wading that are probably overlooked or not realized by many anglers or water authorities. Most fishermen wade out to a depth of about 30″ and it is this very area on most Lakes or reservoirs that many of the more common water weeds are most prolific. These in turn offer sanctuary and shelter to a large proportion of the aquatic insects or other fauna that provide the bulk of the food for the trout inhabiting the water. Anglers wading not only uproot, destroy or crush the weed in which eggs or larvae of future generations of insects may be residing, but in many cases crush the adult forms of life as well, particularly snails, sedge larvae and other relatively slow moving creatures such as freshwater shrimps and louse.

It is of course possible that I may have overlooked other factors that are advantageous to wading but if not, in the light of the above facts, I can only hope that at least some of our authorities will seriously consider either a complete ban on wading or at least restrict wading to certain specified sections of bank.

A TIP

During the past two seasons I have been using shooting heads made from silk lines, and in practice I am certain their use has resulted in higher catches. I find I can cast a silk head with more precision, and place it on the surface with much less disturbance. Futhermore, for added delicacy I now find I can use a lighter head in silk than I used to use in plastic. Previously my heads were normally formed from No 7 plastic lines, I now use a No. 6 silk. My favourite stillwater rod is a 9 ft 3 in Richard Walker Superlight rod made by Hardy's and with a silk shooting head between 30 and 33 feet long formed from a No. 6 double taper line silk line, I can still comfortably cast well in excess of 30 yards.

THE 'PERSUADER'

As no doubt many fly fishers are aware I always advocated the close imitation approach to stillwater trout fishing, not that I am opposed to lure fishing, but I find it less interesting. During the past few years I have perfected and popularised many new patterns, but all without exception have been imitative dressings. It is therefore with some trepidation for the first time ever I have departed from my usual practice and produced a new pattern which is basically a general attractor and does not simulate any particular aquatic insect. Before I proceed to explain my thinking behind this new fly I should like to briefly discuss new patterns in general.

I am quite horrified at the number of new artificials that have been published in the fishing press during the past four or five years, and I and many of my colleagues are of the opinion that editors in many cases are doing a disservice to their readers, by adding unnecessarily to the multitude of patterns already on the market. This can only make life more difficult for the proffesional fly dresser as well as the newcomer to the sport. Most experienced fly fishers will agree that at times it is possible to catch a trout on anything from a

cigarette butt to a bare hook, for this reason it is all too easy for a
new pattern to be borne overnight. An angler invents a new dressing,
catches a few fish on it, informs the press, anglers may try it and
find it reasonably successful at the time, and from then on it escalates
as the more people use a pattern the more trout are caught. This
does not of course mean it is necessarily a genuine killing pattern
In my opinion any responsible fisherman that perfects a new
artificial should test this very thoroughly over a whole season under
varying conditions before rushing into print. Likewise editors can
assist by ensuring as far as possible that this has been carried out
before recommending to their readers.

I would hope that my new pattern comes into this latter category
as it has been thoroughly tested over two seasons. During this period
it accounted for many of the larger trout I have caught, this despite
the fact that it was not used to the exclusion of many of my normal
dressings. I am now convinced this is a genuine killer. For many
years I have held a season ticket on Hanningfield water which is
typical of many of our larger resevoirs. In the past the trout have
always been free rising, but for the two seasons during the evolvement
of this new pattern they were rather dour and reluctant to rise, consequently most fish were taken on or near the bottom on sunken
lines. This reservoir is one of the windiest I know and is often difficult
to fish with conventional nymphs and pupae, I therefore decided
these conditions called for a new pattern.

The new artificial, which I have christened I trust appropriately
the 'Persuader' (see Plate 25), was needed to fulfil the following
requirements. (a) A fairly large size in order to attract the attentions
of a trout from a reasonable distance, (b) an attractive colour or
colour combination and (c) a juicy succulent looking body. Finally
I wanted, if possible, a pattern that would at last loosely resemble
some of the more common forms of food on which trout feed. The
result after much experimentation turned out as follows. White and
orange for the two basic colours as over the years dressings in either
of these have proved exceptionally effective. I decided on white
ostrich herl for the main body, as this material is particularly
translucent, and I used seal's fur of an orange colour for a similar
reason for the thorax. Hook was a long shank size 8 or 10 and for
silhouette I settled on a shape which vaguely simulated a sedge
pupae. I found that there were two particularly effective methods of
fishing the new fly. Either on a sinking line fished slowly as near to
the bed of the reservoir as possible – this proved very good
for the larger browns. Alternatively, retrieved fast just below the

surface on a floating or sink tip line in fairly shallow water, or over deep water if there are odd fish rising here and there. As many fly fishers have probably discovered this latter method is in itself a very killing way to fish a large number of patterns, in spite of this few writers to my knowledge have emphasised this.

The 'Persuader' accounted for 12 fine trout between three and four pounds apiece spread over seven days fishing between May and June as well as many smaller trout. Since this pattern was first introduced in the third edition it has proved very popular and has now accounted for great numbers of trout. It has subsequently proved to be exceptionally killing when fished on the drop—utilizing a long leader on a floating line.

DRESSING FOR THE PERSUADER

HOOK. No. 8 or 10 D/E. Long shank.

TYING SILK. Orange.

BODY. Five strands of white ostrich herl (trim after tying).

RIB. Round silver tinsel No. 20.

THORAX. Orange seal's fur.

WING PADS. Three strands of dark brown dyed turkey herl from tail feather.

CHAPTER XIII

MONTH BY MONTH AT THE WATERSIDE

As previously mentioned, on occasions popular general artificial patterns prove to be as killing as those tied as specific representations of the natural. If this situation always applied, there would be no point in writing this book, but this is not always the case as often the trout become preoccupied when feeding upon a particular form of aquatic fauna, and will be caught only on an artificial that is a close imitation. This is no drawback as it provides a constant challenge to the angler, and keeps his interest alive, in what otherwise could become a rather dull and uninteresting branch of our sport.

One of the most difficult problems to overcome in this respect, assuming the angler is provided with close artificial representations of the natural insects, is when and at what time to fish them. To the novice this may appear to be an insurmountable problem, and on occasions even the expert may be perplexed, due to the fact that we are seldom able actually to see what the trout are feeding on under water. Naturally, the problem is never quite so acute when trout are feeding on or in the surface, but even then it can be tricky, as at such times the fish often have a large variety of food to choose from.

There are, of course, plenty of clues which may assist the reader to come to a decision, and I hope I have covered most of them within the various chapters of this book, but as it will take time and much experience for the novice to absorb all these various factors, I feel it is necessary to limit the field to a certain extent. It seems to me that the easiest way to do this is to give brief details of the more common insects and other fauna which may be expected throughout each month of the fishing season, and furthermore, for quick reference, also to present this information in concise table form at the end of the chapter.

Before giving this information, however, there are several other factors that must be taken into consideration, and I feel it would be wise to present them before proceeding. In the first place, it should be pointed out that weather conditions from day to day affect the emergence of insects quite considerably. In really adverse conditions the emergence of a complete species may be delayed by as much as a week or even two. Under these circumstances it will be appreciated that at times it is quite possible that certain species which would normally be anticipated one particular month, may not turn up till early the next month.

Another important factor is the distribution of different species of insects, for I am sure it will be readily understood that only the very common varieties are likely to be found on all stillwaters. Therefore, readers should tailor the monthly lists to include only those species known in their localities. Should the angler be fishing a water with which he is unfamiliar, information regarding the insect population may be gleaned from other fishermen, but it is sometimes best for him to rely upon his own judgment from observations at the waterside.

In some cases the field may be narrowed still further, due to the fact that certain fauna in stillwater, with which we are concerned are broadly speaking normally confined to known areas or localities. To quote a few examples, such creatures as Water Lice, Shrimps or Corixa are unlikely to be found in deep water. Pond Olives are usually found in shallow water, while the similar Lake Olive often prefers the deeper water. Adult Sedge-flies are more likely to be found in the vicinity of bank-side vegetation or adjacent to trees or copses than in open water. Certain species or Orders of insects often show a preference for thick weedbeds, or for muddy or perhaps hard or stony bottoms. The list is endless, but as this aspect may be difficult for the beginner to observe, I only mention it as it can be of considerable value as his knowledge increases.

I intend to commence the season from the month of April, as the majority of stillwaters open either during this month or in May. Localized or uncommon species are not included.

April. During the early part of the season the fishing is usually patchy, as there is little insect life to tempt the trout, and therefore throughout this month general attractor or flasher patterns, such as a Butcher or a Dunkeld, will often prove effective when there is nothing apparent for the fisherman to imitate. Two species of fauna that are present in most waters at this period are the Shrimp and the Water Louse, and where concentrations of these are found it is always worth trying the appropriate artificial. The first of the Upwinged flies, the Sepia Dun, appears on some waters usually in mid or late April and although it is sometimes possible to take trout on a floating artificial to imitate the Dun or Spinner, the sunk nymph is usually most effective. In areas where they occur a few species of Stoneflies may be in evidence and also at least two species of the more common Midges. They are the Black and the Orange Silver Midges. Hatches of the latter are seldom seen in large numbers so early in the year, but sometimes a reasonable emergence may occur late in the afternoon, and may produce a fair rise of trout to the pupae. The other common species, the Black Midge, is a very useful early season insect. In Wales and Scotland it is very common during March and April and in these areas it is often referred to as the Duck fly; it emerges during the middle part of the day, and the appropriate artificial should be fished on or just under the surface. The Blagdon Green Midge may be encountered at this time also, but it is of little consequence so early in the year.

May. By this time of the year the better weather should be with us, and it may be possible to take fish regularly, early in the morning and late in the evening, as well as during the day. Many of the species that first appeared in the previous month are still with us, while many new ones are about to emerge. The Sepia Dun is often very prolific early on in certain localities, but by the middle of the month, except for stragglers, will be seen no more till next season. Hatches of the Blagdon Green Midge are now on a larger scale, particularly during the day, and some trout may commence to feed on the pupae as they do at spasmodic intervals throughout the rest of the season. During the late evenings, and occasionally in the very early mornings, good buzzer rises to the Orange-Silver or Ribbed Midge may be expected, particularly in the latter part of the month. At the very end of April or early May the Alder larva should be much in evidence, and an artificial to represent it is often killing; also about this period we are likely to encounter the first hatches of Lake Olives and, later in the month, Pond Olives. A less common Upwinged fly, namely the Claret Dun, should be encountered in some areas towards the end of the month, while at the same period on certain waters, particularly on the Irish loughs, the Mayfly, the largest Upwinged fly of all, will be making its début. During this month two new Orders of insects, Beetles and Sedge-flies, join the assembly. Among the former Order the Cockchafer, a large terrestrial insect, may be encountered on windy evenings, and so may some of the aquatic members of this Order in both larval and adult stages. By the middle of the month certain species of the Sedge-flies may be observed in fair numbers, particularly the Small Silver and the Small Red Sedge, but this early in the year the trout are usually a little reluctant to come to the surface for them.

June. Without a doubt this is the most pleasant month of all by the waterside, as the warmer weather is now with us, and early morning and late evening rises are of fairly regular occurrence. Hatches of most of the Upwinged flies are now at their maximum and it is often possible to find odd trout cruising about during the early evening sipping down the spinners of the various species, or taking the ascending nymph in the mornings. Many types of Sedge-flies are now on the wing, and close attention by the fisherman should be well rewarded, particularly by fishing appropriate artificials of the pupae of those insects which can be successfully imitated. Various species of Beetles are also commonly encountered in certain areas, including the Coch-y-bonddu and the Soldier and Sailor Beetles, as well as many aquatic species and their larvae. Other fauna that are with us throughout the season, such as the Shrimp, the Water Louse and, on a few localized waters, various species of Stoneflies, should not be forgotten. Heavy hatches of many of the Midges (Buzzers) are now to be expected in the early morning as the sun rises, and again in the very late evenings, the predominant species being the Ribbed or Golden Dun or Orange Silver Midges, although the latter usually disappears by the middle of the month. One of the smaller species also appears for the first time during June; this is the Small Brown Midge, and the angler will be well advised to keep in mind the rather unusual rise form of the trout to these small insects which usually takes place during the day. Towards the end of the month Corixa and Damsel nymphs are likely to be in evidence in sufficient quantities to interest the fish, and often in the late afternoons emergence of fair numbers of the Large Red Midge are likely, and will often bring about a spasmodic rise of trout to the pupae in the surface film. In late June the first hatches of the Angler's Curse (Caenis) are fairly certain, usually in the early evenings.

July. The early part of this month is often very pleasant and productive of trout, but by the end of the second week, particularly during a spell of hot weather, conditions deteriorate, and the trout usually become dour and disinclined to feed; at least during the hours of bright sunshine. However, there are certain compensations as by this time of the year many species of Sedge-flies are prolific, and it is timely to commence fishing the artificial Sedge on the surface as a dry fly. Around this period, Crane-flies are beginning to appear in ever increasing numbers and in some areas an artificial representation fished dry is killing. The Upwinged flies are now seldom encountered, except for odd hatches of Claret Duns or Pond Olives, but emergence of the Angler's Curse is now likely in ever-increasing numbers. Many of the species previously mentioned are still likely to be seen and of these the following are of particular interest during July; Damsel nymphs, Corixa and some species of Beetles. Two types of fauna that often appear for the first time in July, particularly should the weather be very hot, are floating Snails and Ants, and as the appropriate artificials can be extremely effective when these are about, a careful watch should be maintained. In the early mornings and late evenings occasional buzzer rises are still encountered, but towards the end of July heavy rises are again likely to the pupae of the Large Green Midge. During the day, if the sun is not too fierce, trout may sometimes rise to the Small Brown or Small Red Midge, and later on in the afternoon to the pupa of the Large Red Midge. About this time of the year, in the evenings, emergence of the very tiny Black Midge, often in incredible numbers, is to be expected, and in localities where they occur they are likely to be encountered at spasmodic intervals throughout the remainder of the season. Although a rather difficult month, July provides one further item on the menu of the trout, this is the Stickleback, and by the middle of the month the fry of these or other fish are usually in sufficient concentrations to provide both interest to the fish and the angler.

August. Often referred to as the "dog days", the month of August is usually very difficult, although not hopeless, as if the fisherman is fortunate enough to pick a cool or even better a wet day, sport can be most rewarding. By this time many species of insects are on the wane, and consequently less volume of food is available to the trout, and the effect of this, combined with high water temperature and bright sun, seems to make the fish dour and disinclined to feed. However, should a few days of cooler wet weather come along, the trout may recommence feeding, and at this time a dry sedge or a stickleback imitation will often provide the angler with an unexpected heavy bag. On the other hand, should the weather prove unkind, the best chances of killing a few fish are undoubtedly during the very early mornings or late evenings, as there is often

MONTHLY EMERGENCE TABLE (Common Species)

	April		May		June		July		August		Sept		Oct	
THE MAYFLY				X	X									
,, POND OLIVE AND NYMPH			X	X	X	X	X	X	X	X				
,, LAKE OLIVE ,, ,,			X	X	X	X			X	X				
,, CLARET DUN ,, ,,				X	X	X	X							
,, SEPIA DUN ,, ,,	X	X	X											
,, CAENIS ,, ,,						X	X	X	X	X				
,, STONEFLIES			VARIOUS SPECIES ALL SEASON											
,, ALDER LARVA		X	X	X	X	X								
,, ANT							X	X	X	X	X			
,, BEETLES			X	X	X	X	X	X	X	X				
,, DAMSELFLIES (NYMPHS)						X	X	X	X					
,, LOUSE							ALL SEASON							
,, SHRIMP							ALL SEASON							
,, CORIXA						X	X	X	X	X	X			
,, STICKLEBACKS							X	X	X	X	X	X		
,, LARGE GREEN MIDGE							X	X	X					
,, LARGE RED MIDGE						X	X	X	X	X	X			
,, ORANGE SILVER MIDGE	X	X	X	X	X									
,, GOLDEN DUN MIDGE				X	X	X	X	X	X	X				
,, RIBBED MIDGE			X	X	X	X			X	X	X			
,, BLACK MIDGE	X	X					X	X	X	X				
,, BLAGDON GREEN MIDGE							ALL SEASON							
,, SMALL BROWN MIDGE					X	X	X	X	X					
,, SMALL RED MIDGE							X	X	X	X	X	X		
,, SMALL BLACK MIDGE	X					X	X	X	X	X	X	X	X	
,, SEDGE-FLIES			VARIOUS SPECIES ALL SEASON EXCEPT APRIL											
,, SNAILS (FLOATING)							X	X	X	X	X			

some activity at this time, with artificials to represent Sticklebacks, Corixa or Midges offering the best chances of success. Finally, under favourable conditions, a rise to floating Snails or Ants may be anticipated, and should provide an unexpected bonus to the observant angler.

September and early October. By this time of the year the trout are often very wary and difficult to catch, and in addition natural food is becoming increasingly scarce. Fortunately for the angler the fish apparently anticipate the lean months of winter, and consequently a comparatively small amount of insect activity will often bring the trout on the feed, and provide the more experienced fishers with fair bags. For a brief period in late August and September, spasmodic hatches of Pond and Lake Olives are likely, and during this same period the Ribbed Midge is the predominant species among Buzzer rises. Early in the month it is still possible that rises to the Ant or floating Snail may be observed, and also at this period it is still worth while fishing an artificial Corixa. On some waters Sticklebacks and other fry are still about, and may even extend into early October. During the whole of September the Small Red, Small Brown and Small Black Midges are again quite common, the latter extending well into October. It is to the Sedge-flies that the angler should look for his best chances during the closing stages of the season, as September is undoubtedly one of the peak months of the year for the emergence of a great variety of these insects. On some occasions during the warmer periods the dry artificial will still prove effective, but artificials to represent the various pupae of these Sedge-flies are usually most productive under average weather conditions. On those waters that remain open until the middle of October, general attractor patterns again give good results, for a similar reason to those of the early season fishing in April.

SUMMARY OF SEASONAL METHODS

This is only a general guide and does not take into account specific techniques required when fishing certain patterns.

Spring In the early part of the year, before the temperature of the water rises significantly, the trout will feed in deeper water and it will therefore be necessary to fish your artificials on or near the bottom. Choose your fly line according to the depth to be fished: floaters with long leaders for shallow water, sink tips or slow sinkers for water of minimum depth or fast sinkers for very deep water. During this period slow retrieves give the best results.

Early summer   As the temperature of the water rises, surface activity will increase, particularly during the early evenings, when good hatches of chironomids (buzzers) may be anticipated. During the day however, most trout are still to be found on or near the bottom, but a faster retrieve is to be favoured when using lure type artificials.

Mid-Summer (Calm Conditions)   With a high water temperature and little wind, lure or attractor patterns are best fished slow and deep, while nymph and imitative patterns seem to be most effective retrieved very slowly in midwater during the day, or near the surface early mornings or late evenings.

Mid-Summer (Windy Conditions)   Trout, particularly rainbows, at this time are likely on or just under the surface, so it is seldom necessary to fish your artificial deep.

Late Summer   As the temperature begins to drop it will once again be necessary to seek your trout in deeper water. However, surface activity may still occur on odd days, particularly when weather conditions favour late hatches of fly.

USEFUL TIPS
Coloured Water   In windy conditions a good place to fish is in areas where clear water meets coloured.

Wind   Where possible, fish the bank or shore onto which the wind is blowing, but if it is too strong, move to the bank which the wind is blowing along.

Fishing at Anchor   Unless there are special circumstances, move the boat at frequent intervals until you find the fish.

Algea and Wind Lanes   Always be on the lookout for these particularly when boat fishing, as food tends to congregate along these lanes and the trout will not be far away.

Early Season   Black or white lures are often most productive at this time of year, but you will have to find out which is the taking colour of the day as they seldom produce trout at the same time.

Drift Fishing   If the trout are continually coming short, try altering the size of your artificial, speeding up your retrieve, or both.

Colour   Orange seems particularly attractive to trout during July and August.

Inlets–Outlets   Any such places where there is an unusual movement of water are likely to attract trout and are well worth trying.

CHAPTER XIV

MODERN BOATFISHING TECHNIQUES

Since this volume was first completed in the late 1960s, tremendous advances have been made in boatfishing techniques on stillwater. While some of these methods are to say the least somewhat controversial, and in fact are now banned on many stillwaters, I have decided to give full details as on waters where there are no restrictions fly fishers may wish to experiment and decide for themselves which techniques are acceptable to their own personal standards.

Trolling

While it is debatable whether or not this method can be construed as fly fishing, there is no doubt it accounts for a lot of trout where it is permissible. Although trolling or trailing a fly from the back of a slowly moving boat is in itself not new and requires little expertise, the same cannot be said about the latest techniques now being employed. Some fly fishermen have developed trolling into a highly skilled operation, making full use of the wide variety of modern fly lines now available. The first requirement is to find out at what level or depth in the water the trout are feeding, and this can be established by trial and error or from personal experience of conditions at the time. It will then be necessary to mount the correct fly line—a floating, slow sink or sink tip line if they are feeding on or near the surface, a fast sink line for midwater or for trolling along or near the bottom, in waters of medium depth a high D or one of the new super fast sinking fly lines. For trolling in very deep water many anglers now use shooting heads formed from lead cored line, used in conjunction with large lures often in excess of six inches in length. Within the last two years this latter method alone has accounted for many exceptionally large brown trout, which up to a point justifies its use, as these are probably fish that seldom leave the sanctuary of very deep water and are unlikely to be caught by traditional fly fishing methods. Apart from the importance of choosing the correct fly line for trolling, the area or depth of water to be fished must also be taken into account. The movement of the boat in relation to the lines you are trolling must also be seriously considered. For instance, an exaggerated zig-zag course will cover a greater area of water, while a sharp zig-zag will cause the lure to sink and rise again in an enticing way at each alteration of course. It is also worth noting that, under windy conditions, it is often more effective to troll across the wind. The experienced troller will also take into account the type of fly or lure to be used, and his choice will be dictated by the type of food upon which he thinks the trout may be feeding at the time. This may vary from sedge pupa to leeches or fry and small fish up to as much as six or eight inches in length.

Lead Cored and HI.D Super Fast Sinking Lines

In the latter half of the summer small fish leave the shallows and tend to congregate in deeper water along the edges of dam walls and valve towers. These areas are usually inaccessible to bank anglers, and even from a boat it is not possible to present your fly by traditional methods to the large trout that are often to be found feeding in their immediate locality. The answer to this problem lies in the use of the above new lines. Make up a shooting head from either of these lines, very short—seven to eight yards if you are using the lead cored—as it is difficult to cast with a longer length. Mount a very large white marabou type lure (one six inches in length is not too big) on a short leader, and anchor the boat just within maximum casting distance of the wall or tower. Try to cast your lure so that it just hits the structure, and immediately strip off four or five yards of backing under tension. If you have executed the movement correctly your lure will be pulled directly underwater down the front of the wall, and will be taken on the drop. Usually the first indication you will have that a fish has accepted your offering will be the sight of a trout leaping high out of the water. While it is still necessary to watch the backing entering the water from your rod tip it is seldom necessary to strike as most of these fish will hook themselves. For this style of fishing always use a strong point on your leader, at least seven pounds test, as it will often account for some of the biggest trout in the water. These super fast sinking lines may also be used in a similar way from a drifting boat. Utilizing a drift control rudder or drogue streaming from the stern of the boat, cast your line out at ninety degrees to the drift of the boat, and feed out several yards or backing until you feel your line hit the bottom. If you then immediately commence the retrieve the lure will start to come back to you in the opposite direction to the path of the boat for at least a few seconds. It will then suddenly change direction, and this will often prove to be the undoing of many trout, who have been used for much of the season to following the same old lures moving in the same direction.

The Drift Controller

This in reality is a large rudder which is clamped to the transom of the boat, and was originally developed by those two maestros of the stillwater scene, Bob Church and Dick Shrive. Few boats available for stillwater trout fishing are fitted with rudders, and even where they may be found the conventional type is hardly large enough to give the degree of control essential for this relatively new technique. It will therefore be necessary to construct your own. The actual blade of the rudder should be about 18in. x 14in. and this is slotted and riveted into a steel shaft about ⅝in. in diameter. Brackets are then formed to take the shaft and these should be welded or riveted onto a plate which is used to clamp the contraption to the stern of the boat. These brackets should be drilled and tapped to take two large wing bolts which may be tightened by the operator to lock the rudder in any desired position, providing the required direction of drift. Finally, a short bar to form the tiller handle is made to clamp on top of the shaft.

A drift controller can only be used in winds of light to medium strength; in a strong wind it is useless, as the rate of drift will be far too fast. The main use of the rudder or controller under the right conditions is to enable the fisherman to gain some semblance of control over the direction of the drift. In more expansive days this was the job of the gillie using his oars. With the rudder this can be accomplished equally well and of course much more silently, and in addition leaves both fishermen in the boat free to concentrate on their casting without the encumbrance of a third person aboard. The amount of control given by the rudder is surprisingly good, and although the basic drift will still be found to be downwind, quite a reasonable angle down or across wind can be accomplished with a little practice. This will enable you to keep the boat roughly parallel to any shore or dam wall a given distance out, and will also allow you to follow the contours of the bank or underwater shoals. In addition to this, the rudder can be set to give you a long downward drift bow first across a reservoir, which will allow each angler to face in opposite directions and fish across the wind. Admittedly, the same effect can be created with a drogue trailed over the stern, but in light winds the drogue will slow the boat down too much.

The Leeboard

This is another idea that came from the inventive mind of that most accomplished stillwater trout angler, Dick Shrive. Like many good ideas it is basically simple, and the only materials required are a plank five feet six inches in length, about 12 inches in width, and approximately one inch in thickness, plus a large G clamp. The leeboard is clamped to the curved section of the bow on the lee side of the boat (the downwind side), hence its name. When in position, it projects well below the keel of the boat and acts like a centreboard on a sailing boat. The wind blowing into the side of the boat tries to push the boat directly downwind while water pressure on the other side of the board endeavours to prevent it. The net result of these two forces operating against one another forces a compromise, so the boat drifts across and only slowly downwind. With the leeboard in position the wind, often your enemy, can be turned into an ally, as the boat can be held over chosen areas for much longer periods. For example, you may wish to fish a productive section of shallow water immediately offshore. If the wind is blowing directly onto or offshore you will drift over this very quickly, but with your leeboard in position you will be pushed across it, and if you turn the boat smartly and refix the board in the same position on the other side of the bow, you will probably succeed in tacking back again before running ashore or into deeper water.

When using the leeboard, both anglers should fish downwind, but extra care must be taken by the fisherman in the stern, as it is only too easy to hook the other angler in the bow when casting. For this style of fishing, lures or flasher patterns should be used, as the retrieve should be fairly fast. If you wait too long after casting or retrieve too slowly, your fly line and flies will be swept astern of the boat, and tangle with the keel or other projections. If your retrieve and timing is correct the fly will be presented to the trout diagonally across the path of the wind and will be clear of the disturbed water over which your boat has just drifted. On occasions this can be a most effective method of fishing, as trout, especially rainbows, seem to take a fly which is moving across their path more confidently than one being retrieved directly upwind, which is more often than not the case from a boat drifting directly downwind in the conventional manner.

A word of warning; a leeboard can be a dangerous tool in the hands of an inexperienced person, so it should never be used unless the following points are strictly adhered to. Never attempt to use one in very strong winds or if there are a lot of other boats, particularly yachts, in the vicinity. Do not stand up in a boat with a board fitted

as they tend to be less stable. Never try fitting your board on the
upwind side, and above all do not attempt to turn the boat around
to go on the other tack with the board in position; remove it well
before you turn and do not reclamp until the boat has been completely reversed. Apart from the above points, care should be taken
not to cross the paths of other boats drifting downwind in the
traditional style as it is, to put it mildly, most discourteous to disturb
the water over which they will shortly be fishing. Leeboards are now
banned on many waters, as many authorities now consider they are
too dangerous or encourage the illegal practice of trailing which
unfortunately is all too easy from a boat on the move in this manner.
On those waters where they are allowed, the leeboard itself when not
in use makes a most comfortable seat when placed across the
thwarts.

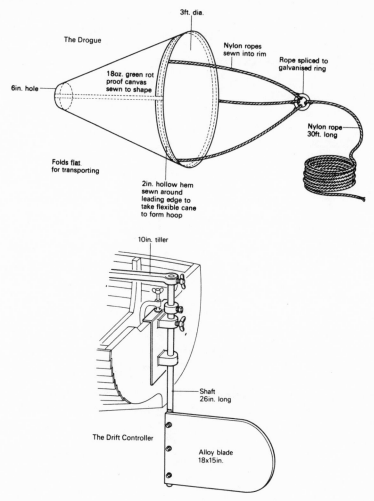

ARTIFICIAL FLIES

The following lists have been compiled to provide the Stillwater fisherman with a quick and easy means of reference as to the most suitable choice of artificial to match the natural fly, together with the appropriate dressings. I have also included lists and dressings for many of the more popular general patterns, incorporating Lures, Bucktails and Streamer flies. Unfortunately, lack of space has rather restricted the number of patterns listed, and although it is reasonably comprehensive I must beg the indulgence of the reader if any particular favourites have been left out.

I am deeply indebted to Mr. John Veniard of Messrs. E. Veniard & Sons, the well-known purveyors of fly-tying materials, for his invaluable assistance in compiling this list of dressings. Many of these have been taken from his new book, *Reservoir and Lake Flies*, published by Messrs. A. & C. Black Ltd. This excellent volume is the first of its kind to deal extensively with artificial patterns for the stillwater fisher. It is a veritable mine of information and is the ideal companion to this volume.

ARTIFICIALS SUGGESTED TO MATCH THE NATURAL

UPWINGED FLIES

The Mayfly	Grey Wulf—Nevamis—Hatching Mayfly—Green Drake Upright
Spent Mayfly	Various Spent Gnat patterns
B.W.O.	Orange Quill—B.W.O.
Sherry Spinner	Pheasant Tail Spinner—Sherry Spinner
Small Spurwing	Little Marryatt—Last Hope
Little Amber Spinner	Yellow Boy—Lunn's Particular
Pond Olive Nymph	P.V.C. Nymph

Pond Olive Dun (*Wet Patterns*)	Greenwells Glory—Gold Ribbed Hare's Ear—Hatching Olive
Pond Olive Dun (*Dry*)	Rough Olive—Olive Quill—Grey Duster
Apricot Spinner	Pond Olive Spinner—Apricot Spinner
Lake Olive Nymph	P.V.C.—Lake Olive Nymph
Lake Olive Dun (*Wet*)	Hatching Olive—Lake Olive Hatching—Olive Upright
Lake Olive Dun (*Dry*)	Olive Dun—Lake Olive
Lake Olive Spinner	Pheasant Tail Spinner—Port Spinner—Lake Olive Spinner
Large Summer Dun	Large Summer Dun
Large Summer Spinner	Large Summer Spinner
Yellow May Dun	Yellow Dun
Yellow May Spinner	Yellow Boy (Large)—Yellow Evening Spinner
Dusky Yellowstreak (*Wet*)	Dark Watchet—Snipe and Purple
Dusky Yellowstreak (*Dry*)	Iron Blue (Large)
Dusky Yellowstreak Spinner	Pheasant Tail Spinner
Claret Nymph	Claret Nymph
Claret Dun	Various Claret Dun Patterns
Claret Spinner	Various Claret Spinner Patterns
Sepia Nymph	Sepia Nymph
Sepia Dun	Various Sepia Dun Patterns
Sepia Spinner	Pheasant Tail—Sepia Spinner
Autumn Dun	August Dun
Autumn Spinner	Great Red Spinner
Caenis Nymph	Caenis Nymph—Last Hope (Fished Wet)
Caenis Dun	Last Hope
Caenis Spinner	Lunn's Yellow Boy (Small)—Caenis Spinner—Cream Spinner (Small)

STONEFLIES

Large Stonefly	Stonefly (Wooley)
Medium Stonefly	Stonefly (Veniard)
Yellow Sally	Yellow Sally
Willow-fly	Winter Brown—Willow Fly
Small Brown	Grey Duster
Needle-fly	Dark Spanish Needle

SEDGE-FLIES

Sedge Pupa	Various Sedge Pupa Patterns—Amber Nymph
Great Red Sedge	Large Sedge
The Caperer	The Caperer—Large Red Sedge
Large Cinnamon Sedge	Large Red Sedge

Mottled Sedge	H. and G. Sedge
Cinnamon Sedge	Cinnamon Sedge—Medium Sedge
Welshman's Button	Welshman's Button
Medium Sedge	Light Sedge
Brown Sedge	Brown Standard Sedge
Black Sedge	Dark Sedge
Black Silverhorns	Black Silverhorns
Brown Silverhorns	Brown Silverhorns
Grouse Wing	Grouse Wing
Silver Sedge	Silver Sedge
Longhorns	Longhorns or G. and H. Sedge (Small)
Small Red Sedge	Small Buff Sedge—Little Red Sedge—Little Brown Sedge
Dry (General) Sedge Patterns	Various by Richard Walker, G. and H. Pale Sedge, or Red Palmer, etc.
Sedge Larva	Sedge Larva
Emerging Sedge	Hatching Sedge

OTHER FLIES

Chironomid Larva	Red or Green Larvae
Chironomid Pupa (Buzzers)	Various Hatching Midge Patterns—Buzzer Nymph—Footballer
Chironomid Pupa (Small)	Small Hatching Midge
Adult Chironomids	Blagdon Green Midge—Blagdon Olive Midge—Black Duck-fly—Adult Midge
Hawthorn-fly	Various Wet or Dry Patterns
Heather-fly	Heather-fly
Black Gnats	Knotted Midge—various Black Gnat patterns
Crane-flies	Various Crane-fly or Daddy patterns
Phantom Pupa	Phantom Pupa
Phantom-fly	Phantom-fly
Reed Smuts	Jassid—Reed Smut
Mosquito	Mosquito Pupa
Alder-fly	Alder Fly
Alder Larva	Alder Larva
Ant (Black)	Black Ant
Ant (Brown)	Brown Ant
Coch-y-bonddu	Coch-y-Bonddu
Soldier Beetle	Soldier Beetle
Cockchafer	Cockchafer
Beetles	Bracken Clock—Eric's Beetle—Doctor— Governor—Little Chap
Dragon-fly Nymph	Large Dragonfly Nymph—Big Dragonfly Nymph
Damsel Nymph	Demoiselle—Blue Damsel Nymph—Damosel Nymph
Louse	Louse

Shrimp	Various Patterns
Caterpillar	Green Caterpillar
Grasshopper	Dapped Live
Corixa	Various Patterns
Moths	Hoolet—White Moth—Ermine Moth—Brown Moth.
Spiders	Wolf Spider
Snail	Floating Snail
Stickleback	Polystickle and various patterns
Water Mite	Water Mite
Black Leech	Black Lure or Black Bear's Hair Lure

RECOMMENDED GENERAL PATTERNS

(Wet unless otherwise stated)

Alexandra
Blae and Black
Black and Orange Marabou
Black and Peacock Spider
Black Pennell
Butcher
The Chief
Chompers
Coachman (Dry)
Dogsbody (Dry)
Dunkeld
Grenadier
Grey and Red Matuka

Invicta
Pale Sedge (Dry)
Mallard and Claret
Mole-fly (Dry)
Peter Ross
Silver Doctor
Silver March Brown
Teal Blue and Silver
Teal and Green
Water Hen Bloa
Wickham's Fancy
Woodcock and Yellow
Worm-fly
The Persuader

LURES—STREAMERS—BUCKTAILS, ETC.

Appetiser
Baby Doll
Black Lure
Broffin Trout Streamer
Church Fry
Cree Streamer
Hairy Minnow
Jersey Herd
Minnow Streamer

Muddler Minnow
Orange Muddler
Orange Streamer
Orange Bucktail
Sweeney Todd
Sweeney Todd Tandem
Texas Rose Muddler Minnow
Black Bear Hair Lure

DRESSINGS

The Adult Midge (John Goddard) (See Plate 19)

A dressing to represent the newly hatched adult winged midge as it rests on the surface after hatching. This pattern should be fished as a dry fly with little or no movement when the adults are on the water, and the trout appear to be taking them as they occasionally do. It should be tied in several colours and sizes to match the adult that happens to be hatching at the time.

HOOK.   Up-eyed No. 10 to 14.

TYING SILK.   Brown.

BODY.   Marabou silk in red, brown or green wound thickly to give body a cylindrical appearance. This is ribbed with silver lurex and covered with opaque P.V.C.

HACKLE.   Dark honey or rusty dun cock.

WINGS.   Pale blue cock hackle tips tied in spent fashion but at an angle towards tail.

The Alder (John Henderson)

This fly is to be seen along the shores of most reservoirs from the middle of May to the middle of June. The female fly is considerably larger and more bulky than the male, being about ¾-inch long whereas the male is only about ½-inch long. As the natural fly when on the surface of the water is usually fluttering, the hackle pattern is the most practical to use.

Dressing of Hackle Pattern

HOOK.   For male No. 1 or 2, for female No. 3 or 4 (14 to 11).

TYING SILK.   Brown nylusta (No. 17 Gossamer).

BODY.   Five fibres of a cock pheasant's tail feather, tied in by the butts at the bend of hook, the tag ends being bound firmly along the top of the shank. The five fibres are now twisted together and wound up to shoulder to form body.

RIBBING.   Brown nylusta.

BODY HACKLE.   Rusty dun cock's, trimmed from ½-inch to ¼-inch, tied in by the stem at shoulder and wound down body to bend so that only the tip of the hackle remains, this is fixed on the top of the shank by two turns of the ribbing which is then wound up body to shoulder and fixed with two half hitches.

WING HACKLE.   A dark brown, slightly speckled feather from the back of a mallard, or a dark brown mottled feather from the breast of an old cock grouse, this is tied in by the stem in front of the body hackle and given the necessary turns and finish off with whip finish.

Note: With regard to the fibres from a cock pheasant's tail feather, if the reverse side of a tail feather is examined, it will be noted that a considerable portion of the fibres from the mid-rib outwards are black or heavily mottled with black, the remaining portions of the fibres to their tips being a reddish brown, hence the reason for tying in the fibres by the butts for the blackish brown body of the Alder and by the points for the reddish brown of the P.T.

The Alder

Dressing of the Winged Pattern

BODY AND BODY HACKLE similar to hackle pattern.

WINGS. The marginal covert feathers from the wings of a blue game cock or hen. These feathers are to be found on the edge of the wing close to the wrist joint. They have very strong mid-ribs and one margin is more convex than the other. Select a feather from the right wing and another from the left wing to match it. Tie one on each side of the shoulder so that the convex edges are uppermost and come flush together over the body, pent house fashion. In order to do this satisfactorily, it will be found necessary to trim the tops of the body hackle fibres.

HEAD HACKLE. A dark rusty dun cock's hackle, about four turns in front of the wings, finishing off with whip finish.

A fly so dressed makes a very realistic imitation of the natural fly, giving it the characteristic hump-backed shape. However it requires much practice to set the wings properly and it does not stand up to wear so well as the hackle pattern.

Alder Larva (C. F. Walker) (Wet)

HOOK. Long shank No. 10 or 12 D/E.

ABDOMEN. A mixture of brown and ginger seal's fur the former predominating, tapered steeply from head to tail.

RIB. Gold tinsel.

GILLS. A pale sandy hen's hackle.

HACKLE. Brown partridge.

THORAX AND HEAD. Hare's ear dubbing.

TAIL. The point of a ginger hackle, or none.

Amber Nymph (Dr. Bell)

Another of Dr. Bell's patterns for lake fishing, of which there are two versions. They have been very successful in both Blagdon and Chew Valley lakes.

Large Amber Nymph for use in May and June and usually the first dropper, and the Small Amber Nymph for use in July.

HOOK. No. 11 10. For the large pattern. No. 12 for the small.

BODY. Amber yellow floss silk or seal's fur tied rather thick.

THORAX. Brown floss silk or seal's fur, approximately one third the length of the body.

WING CASE. A strip of any grey-brown feather, tied in at the tail and finished behind the thorax.

LEGS. A few fibres of pale honey hens hackle, tied in under the head and extending backwards.

The only difference in the smaller pattern is that the thorax should be of hot orange floss silk or seal's fur.

Ant—Black or Brown (John Goddard)

Although this pattern may not be used very often, it is extremely effective on those somewhat rare occasions when a fall of ants occur. It is fished as a dry fly but with occasional animation.

HOOK.   Up-eyed No. 14.

TYING SILK.   Black, brown or orange according to colour of natural ant on water.

BODY.   Two small cylindrical pieces of cork split and bound round shank of hook, one near bend the other near eye. Cover with above choice of tying silk from bend to eye and varnish.

WINGS.   Two white hackle tips tied spent but at an angle towards rear.

HACKLE.   Black or Rhode Island red cock hackle to match tying silk used.

Apricot Spinner (Oliver Kite)

HOOK.   No. 14.

TYING SILK.   Golden olive.

BODY.   Swan primary herls dyed apricot.

THORAX.   Same herls doubled and redoubled.

HACKLE.   Palest honey dun.

TAILS.   Pale yellow.

August Dun (Dry) (Roger Woolley)

HOOK.   No. 12 to 14.

TAIL.   Fibres of dark ginger cock hackle.

BODY.   Brown floss silk or brown quill.

RIB.   Yellow silk.

Big Dragon Fly Nymph (Col. Jocelyn Lane)

HOOK.   No. 10 to 12.

TYING SILK.   Green.

TAIL.   Three lengths of thick knitting wool ¼-inch long; one medium green and two nigger brown.

BODY.   Two long pieces of similar wool, one medium green and one nigger brown, twisted together and wound on tightly. Make the body nearly ¼-inch thick in the middle and slightly tapered at both ends, leaving room for one turn of hackle at head. Bind it down with open turns of tying silk.

HACKLE.   One turn of brown speckled partridge hackle dyed very dark green.

Black Duck Fly (Dry)

(Alternate names: Black Midge or Black Buzzer.)

HOOK.   No. 13 or 14.

BODY.   Black floss, thicker at shoulder.

WINGS. Two dun or cream cock hackle points tied sloping backwards.
HACKLE. Rusty black cock, short in fibre, tied in front of wings.

Black Duck Fly (Wet)

HOOK. No. 12 to 14.
BODY. Black silk or wool, wound thicker at shoulder.
HACKLE. Black cock.
WING. Starling wing quill fibres, tied short, divided, and inclined
towards tail.

Black Gnat (Dry) (Halford)

Male
HOOK. No. 16.
BODY. Undyed peacock quill with four close turns of black horsehair
at shoulder.
WINGS. Points of two pale blue dun cock hackles.
HACKLE. Glossy black starling body feather.
HEAD. Two close turns of pale maroon horsehair.
Female
HOOK. No. 16.
BODY. Stripped peacock quill dyed jet black.
WINGS. From pale starling wing quill, tied sloping back over body.
HACKLE. Glossy black starling body feather.

Black Gnat (Dry) (Cliff Henry)

HOOK. No. 16.
TYING SILK. Black.
BODY. Black cock hackle, flue trimmed to $\frac{1}{32}$-inch of stalk.
WINGS. Pale starlings, tied sloping back.
HACKLE. Black cock short in flue.

Black Gnat (Dry) (J. W. Dunne)

HOOK. No. 16 to 17.
TYING SILK. Olive.
BODY. Black floss silk.
RIB. Black tying silk.
WINGS. A mixed bunch, consisting of about twenty fibres cut from a
hackle dyed bottle-green, and about ten fibres cut from a hackle
dyed fiery red-wine.
HACKLE. Several turns of darkest honey. Wind long and then clip till
fibres stand out from shank a length equal to about two-thirds of the
fly. Cut a narrow V out below.

The Black Hackled Dry-fly (Black Palmer)

This I consider to be the most useful all-round dry-fly on reservoirs as it not only represents The Black Midge but many other insects such as beetles and Black Silver Horn sedges.

HOOK. No. 15.
TYING SILK. Dark Claret or black.
BODY. Black ostrich or three fibres from a Magpie's tail.
RIBBING. Thin gold wire or nylusta (Dark grey).
BODY HACKLE. Black cock's trimmed to taper from ¼ inch to ⅛ inch.
SHOULDER HACKLE. Black cock's untrimmed.

Black Sedge (Dry) (Terry Thomas)

HOOK. No.14 to 10.
BODY. Black wool or chenille with black hackle tied in reverse so it slopes forward.
WING. Black moose tied on flat with the cut end to the rear.
HACKLE. Black cock.

The Black Silverhorns (John Henderson)

HOOK. No. 15.
TYING SILK. Nylusta (Gunmetal), (No. 10 Gossamer).
BODY. Black Polymer dubbing or three fibres from a magpie's tail.
RIB. Pale green gossamer thread.
BODY HACKLE. Black cock's trimmed to taper from ¼ inch to $\frac{1}{16}$ inch.
SHOULDER HACKLE. Black hen's or a small feather from a black hen's breast.

Blagdon Green Midge

A stillwater fly, hatching in June and lasting throughout the rest of the season. A good dry-fly for all pools, lakes and reservoirs.

HOOK. No. 14 to 16.
BODY. Emerald green wool.
WINGS. Stiff white cock hackle wound at shoulder only.
Or
BODY. A strand from a swan's feather dyed emerald green.
HACKLE. A plymouth rock (grizzle) cock's hackle wound from tail to shoulder, cut to shorten the fibres.
WINGS. Two light grey cock hackle points.

Blagdon Olive Midge

Another fine dry-fly for lake fishing.

HOOK. No. 14 to 16.
BODY. Natural heron's herl.
HACKLE. Stiff olive cock's hackle at shoulder only.
WINGS. Two bue dun cock hackle points.

Blue Damsel Nymph (Dragon Fly)

BODY. Blue Lurex ribbed with black wool on weighted tubes up to 1 inch long.
HACKLE. Dyed blue guinea fowl, or blue bucktail fibres.
HEAD. Peacock herl.

Bracken Clock (Wet)

HOOK. No. 10 to 12
BODY. Bronze peacock herl and red silk.
HACKLE. From cock pheasant neck, brown with black edge.

Brown Moth (Dry) (Courtney Williams)

HOOK. No. 10 to 14.
TYING SILK. Orange.
BODY. Brown floss silk, rather thick.
WINGS. From a dark owl's wing feather.
HACKLE. Dark red cock hackle from shoulder to tail.

Brown Standard Sedge (Dry) (Terry Thomas)

HOOK. No. 10 to 12.
BODY. Dark pheasant tail fibres wound on thick with a body hackle of ginger cock, tied in reverse so it slopes forward.
WING. Grey deer hair tied on flat with the cut end to the rear.
HACKLE. Ginger cock.

The Brown Silverhorn (John Henderson)

HOOK. No. 14.
TYING SILK. Nylusta (Medium brown).
BODY. Dark green Polymer or seal's dubbing mixed with hare's ear.
RIBBING. Nylusta (Gunmetal shade). (No. 10 Gossamer.)
BODY HACKLE. Rusty dun cock's trimmed from $\frac{1}{4}$ inch to $\frac{1}{16}$ inch.
SHOULDER HACKLE. Wood cock's neck or Landrail's feather from wing.
The method of dressing for both the above is the same as for the Black Hackle Dry-fly. The dressing of the light brown sedge (*Tinodes waeneri*) is the same as for the Brown Silverhorn, but with a light brown body.

Brown Silver Horns Sedge

HOOK. No. 10 to 14
BODY. Olive tying silk.
RIB. Fine gold wire.
BODY HACKLE. Darkish brown or furnace, tied "paler" and clipped.
WING. Strip from grouse tail or wing feather (well marked) and tied low over body.
HORNS. Two striped hackle stalks from a large grizzle hackle. These are realistically marked, and very durable. Note the curved effect.

HACKLE.   Darkish brown, wound over wing roots, and clipped. The clipping makes this fly an excellent floater.

Buzzer Nymph (Dr. Bell)

From the same stable as the Amber Nymph, this should be fished in June and from mid-August to the end of September.

HOOK.   No. 12 10.

BODY.   Black floss silk taken partly round the bend of the hook.

RIBBING.   Flat gold tinsel.

WINGS.   A short tuft of white floss silk tied in just behind the head, about ⅛ inch long.

LEGS.   A few fibres of brown mallard shoulder feather tied in under the head and sloping backwards.

B.W.O. (Dry) (David Jacques)

HOOK.   No. 14.

TYING SILK.   Orange.

BODY.   Plastic (P.V.C.) sheet dyed olive (or immersed in picric acid for half hour) wound over ostrich herl dyed dirty yellow. The best results are obtained by dyeing a "grey" ostrich feather. The air in the fibres of the herl is trapped when covered by the plastic, and gives the fly buoyancy. The final colour should be that of a ripening greengage.

WINGS.   Rather full, two pair from the wings of a coot.

HACKLE AND WHISKS.   Light olive, particularly the stem.

Caenis Nymph (John Henderson)

HOOK.   No. 16.

SILK.   Light flesh coloured Nylusta, (3 or 9A Gossamer).

WHISKS.   Four or five short fibres from a white cocks hackle.

BODY.   Natural ostrich herl (pale stone colour).

RIBBING.   Thin gold wire.

THORAX.   Several turns of bronze peacock herl or dark brown polymer dubbing.

Caenis Spinner (John Henderson)

HOOK.   No. 16.

SILK.   Light flesh coloured Nylusta, (3 or 9A Gossamer).

WHISKS.   Four or five long fibres from a white cock's hackle.

BODY.   Fibre from a white swan's feather, dyed cream.

RIBBING.   Light flesh coloured Nylusta.

WINGS.   White cock's hackle spread out horizontally and trimmed to shape and size.

LEGS.   Light stone coloured ostrich herl, two turns behind the wings, one turn between the wings and two turns in front of wings. The details of dressing split hackle horizontal wings will be found under Spent Drake.

Caperer (Large Sedge Dry) (William Lunn)

Winged

HOOK. No. 12 to 14.

TYING SILK. Crimson.

BODY. Four or five strands from a dark turkey tail feather, and two strands from a swan feather dyed yellow. The swan to make a ring of yellow in the centre of the body.

WINGS. From a coot's wing quill feather which has been bleached and dyed chocolate brown.

HACKLES. One medium red cock hackle and one black cock hackle, wound together in front of wings.

Cinnamon Sedge (John Henderson)

HOOK. No. 11 or 12.

TYING SILK. Nylusta, light brown, (No. 6B Gossamer).

BODY. Light yellowish brown seal's fur mixture for males, Green seal's fur dubbing for females of L. lunatus.

RIBBING. Fine gold tinsel.

BODY HACKLE. Light red or ginger cock's.

SHOULDER HACKLES. Light red cock's followed by a light brown feather from a brown hen's breast.

Cinnamon Sedge (Cliff Henry)

HOOK. No. 10 D/E.

TYING SILK. Light Brown.

BODY. Pale olive seals fur.

BODY HACKLE. Ginger cock.

RIB. Gold wire.

WINGS. Light brown cock tail, natural.

HEAD HACKLE. Ginger cock, slightly darker than body hackle, hackle fibres to be trimmed away on top of hook to shape of a Sedge's head.

Claret Dun (J. R. Harris)

HOOK. No. 14.

SHOULDER HACKLE. Dark blue dun cock, six or seven turns with a V clipped underneath.

BODY. Dark heron herl dyed dark claret, or mole's fur and dark claret mohair mixed on claret tying silk.

RIB. Fine gold wire.

TAIL. Dark blue dun cock.

Claret Spinner (J. R. Harris)

HOOK. No. 14.
HACKLE. Blue dun or rusty dun cock.
BODY. Very dark claret seal's fur, on claret tying silk.
RIB. Fine gold wire.
TAIL. Dark blue dun cock.

Claret Dun (John Henderson)

HOOK. No. 13.
TYING SILK. Dark claret.
WHISKS. Five dark fibres from a rusty dun cock's spade feather.
BODY. Very dark claret seal's fur.
RIBBING. Fine gold wire.
HACKLE. Very dark rusty dun cock's.

Claret Nymph (John Henderson)

HOOK. No. 13.
TYING SILK. Dark claret.
WHISKS AND BODY. Three fibres from a cock pheasant's tail, dyed dark claret the points forming the whisks (short), the remainder are wound up shank to shoulder to form body.
RIBBING. Fine gold wire.
THORAX. Very dark claret seal's fur.
HACKLE. Two turns of dark dun hen's.

Claret Spinner (John Henderson)

HOOK. No. 13.
TYING SILK. Dark claret or dark brown Nylusta.
WHISKS. Five fibres from a very dark dun cock's spade feather.
BODY. Dark claret seal's fur.
RIBBING. Fine gold wire.
HACKLE (WINGS). Light dun cock's, long in fibre.
HACKLE (LEGS). Very dark dun cock's.
The method of dressing the spinner with wings spent, is similar to that of the Spent Drake.

Claret Dun (C. F. Walker)

HOOK. No. 14 or 15.
WINGS. A bunch of fibres from a back or breast feather of the waterhen of the darkest shade procurable.
BODY. Grey brown condor herl, without ribbing.
HACKLE. Cock's hackle dyed sepia.
TAILS. Very dark grey or black fibres from a cock's spade or saddle feather, splayed apart.

Claret Spinner (C. F. Walker)

HOOK. No. 14 or 15.
WINGS. Palest blue or brassy dun cock's hackle.
BODY. Dark brown and yellow seal's fur.
RIB. Gold tinsel.
HACKLE. Dark furnace or Coch-y-bonddu cock or none.
TAILS. Brown mallard fibres.

Claret Nymph (C. F. Walker)

HOOK. No. 15 D/E.
BODY. Dark brown seal's fur mixed with a little ginger.
GILLS. The body material well picked out with a dubbing needle.
RIBBING OR TAG. Silver tinsel or lurex.
THORAX AND WING PADS. Black seal's fur.
LEG HACKLE. Dark brown hen.
TAILS. Fibres from a black hen's hackle as long as the body and well splayed apart with a turn of tying silk.

Coch-y-Bonddu (Dry)

HOOK. No. 12 to 14.
BODY. Two strands of bronze peacock herl.
TIP. Flat gold tinsel.
HACKLE. Coch-y-Bonddu. (A red hackle with black centre.)

The Cochybonddu Beetle (John Henderson)

This beetle has been given various names; Ronalds calls it the Marlow Buzz and it is also known as the Hazel-fly, Shorn-fly and the June Bug. It is about ¼-inch long, the thorax, head, underparts and legs being a dark shiny green and the wing cases a bright reddish brown. It begins to appear about the end of May and continues to the end of June. On a sunny afternoon in June, on a reservoir in the Welsh mountains, I have seen the surface of the water, which a few moments before, was void of all insects and no fish rising, suddenly become agitated with rising fish and the surface speckled with quantities of the beetles. This queer urge to shift their quarters does not usually take place before noon and the usual time to expect it is from then to about 2 p.m. They seem to require a certain amount of sun and warmth for them to take wing. On a dull wet day they remain roosting in the foliage.

HOOK. No. 13 or 14.
TYING SILK. Nylusta (brown), (No. 17 Gossamer).
RIBBING. Fine gold tinsel.
BODY. Five or six peacock herls twisted together and wound up body to shoulder.

BODY HACKLE.   A black cock's trimmed from $\frac{1}{4}$ inch to $\frac{1}{8}$ inch, tied in
by the stem at the shoulder and wound down body to bend where
it is fixed on top of shank by the ribbing, leaving the point of the
hackle (which should be at least $\frac{1}{4}$ inch long) as a tail, the ribbing
is then wound up body to shoulder and fixed by tying silk.

SHOULDER HACKLE.   A bright reddish brown Cochybonddu hackle, tied
in at shoulder, immediately above the body hackle, take two or three
turns into the body hackle and then back towards the eye, at least
six turns in all. Finish off with whip finish.

The Cockchafer (John Henderson)

This, is one of our largest beetles, being from 1 inch to $1\frac{1}{8}$ inch in length
and $\frac{1}{2}$ inch in width. Its wing cases and legs are a reddish brown and the
under-parts of its body banded black and grey. It makes its appearance
from the middle of May to the middle of June. In some years they may
occur in great numbers but this can be followed by an interval of many
years when few are seen. As in the case of most beetles, the Cockchafer,
when it pitches on the surface of the water, is unable to fold its wings
under the wing cases and they remain unfolded and projecting beyond
the end of the body. This tendency of floating beetles to have their
wings trailing beyond the end of the body is of some practical use to the
dry fly fisherman as it enables him to dress his imitation with a feathered
projection at the tail which helps to hold the fly up on the surface and
improve its flotation. I have experimented with three different dressings:

(1) With cork body.
(2) With Condor fibre body.
(3) With Caribou fur body.

HOOK.   Long May No. 7 to 8.
SILK.   Nylusta, brown, (No. 17 Gossamer).
TAIL.   Two light dun cock hackle points $\frac{3}{4}$-inch long.
BODY.   Cork, oval shape with flat underside, about 1-inch and $\frac{1}{2}$-inch
wide.

A groove is cut with a fine saw down the centre of the body about
$\frac{1}{16}$-inch deep this is filled with Durofix or Bostick. The shank of
the hook is now pressed down into the grooves so that the tail end of
the cork body is at the bend of the hook and leaving sufficient room
at the head for tying on the hackle and wing cases. It is then left to
dry for some hours and then painted a dark grey all over and if one
wishes to be very exact in the imitation, thin white bands can be
painted on the underside.

Corixa Weighted (Cliff Henry)

HOOK. No. 12 D/E. Tying silk wound from eye to bend of hook, then one layer of fine copper wire wound over the silk.

TYING SILK. Black.

WING CASES. Black Squirrel hair tied in at bend of hook and then after the body has been wound on, brought over the top and tied down at the head.

BODY. White chenille, Dressed Fat.

HACKLE. Light badger hen hackle one turn.

Corixa

HOOK. No. 12 or 13.

BODY. White or cream floss silk dressed very fat.

RIBBING. Beige or brown silk.

WING CASE. A strip of woodcock wing fibres tied in at the tail, brought over to lay on top of the body and tied in at the head.

LEGS. A few fibres of white or cream hen's hackle tied in under the head.

Note: If the hook is first painted white, it will prevent the white floss body becoming dull when wet.

Crane-fly (Geoffrey Bucknall)

HOOK. No. 12.

BODY. Detached plastic Mayfly body.

LEGS. Cock pheasant tail, knotted in the middle.

WINGS. Brown cock hackle points tied "spent".

HACKLE. Red cock.

Cream Spinner (John Goddard)—small for Caenis

HOOK. No. 15 or 16.

TYING SILK. Cream.

BODY. Baby seal fur, cream.

RIB. Thin gold wire.

WINGS. Tips of two small pale blue dun cock, hackles tied "spent".

HACKLE. Cream cock hackle tied sparsely two turns only.

TAILS. Pale blue cock fibres.

Daddy-Long-Legs (Dry) (T. J. Hanna)

HOOK. No. 10 to 12 long shank.

LEGS. Six fibres from a cock pheasant's tail—knotted in the middle to form joints. Four fibres tied in to point back and two to point forwards.

BODY. A thin piece of bicycle tube rubber wound up shank between the legs, to form a segmented body.

WINGS. Two brownish cock hackle tips tied "spent".

HACKLE. Natural red-brown cock hackle tied and wound behind wings.

The Daddy-long-legs (John Henderson)

HOOK. Long May Fly 10.
BODY AND LEGS. Four fibres from a peacock's wing feather, about two inches long.
RIBBING. Fine gold tinsel.
WINGS. Mottled cock's hackle points.
HACKLE (FOR FLOTATION ONLY). A light dun or ginger cock's hackle.

Method of Dressing

The four fibres from the peacock's wing feather, which is of a light fawn colour, are knotted about ¾ inch from the tips to represent the leg joints, and are then tied in by their butts together with the ribbing at the bend of the hook, the tying silk is wound up the shank to the shoulder and fixed with a half hitch. The hook is then taken from the vice and replaced up-side down, so that the point of the hook is above the shank. The four fibres are now turned up the shank to the shoulder, not twisted together before doing so, but spread out as much as possible while making the turns. About four turns will bring them to the shoulder, where they are held vertically and fixed in this position by the tying silk. They should be about 1½-inch long, which is about the right length for the legs. The fibres are now separated, two on each side and the tying silk brought figure-of-eight wise between them, this is followed by at least two turns between the pair of legs on each side. The ribbing is now wound up body, through the legs and finished off beyond them. The hook is now taken from the vice and replaced in normal position. The two mottled hackle points for the wings are now tied in at the shoulder, are separated by the tying silk, figure-of-eight wise between them, they should slope somewhat towards the tail end. The hackle is tied in by the stem in front of the wings, then brought down, under and behind the wings where at least four turns are made, then one turn between the wings and three or more in front of them, depending on the length of the hackle. Finish off with whip finish.

Dark Sedge (Terry Thomas)

HOOK. No. 14 to 4 as required.
BODY. Black wool or chenille.
BODY HACKLE. Black cock.
WING. Black deer hair tied on flat with cut end to rear.
FRONT HACKLE. Black cock.

Dark Spanish Needle (Dry) (Pritt)

HOOK. No. 14.
BODY. Orange silk.
WING. A hackle from the darkest part of a brown owl's wing.
HEAD. Bronze peacock herl.

Dark Spanish Needle (Roger Woolley)

HOOK. No. 15.
BODY. Waxed orange or waxed claret tying silk.
HACKLE. Small dark dun feather from shoulder of a starling's wing.
HEAD. Magpie herl, from tail.

Dark Watchet (Wet) (Edmonds and Lee)

HOOK. No. 14 to 16.
BODY. Mole fur spun on orange and purple tying silks, these silks to
show as alternate ribs when wound on.
HACKLE. Small feather from a jackdaw's throat. This is a very dark
silvery grey feather.

Damsel Nymph (Cliff Henry) (Plates 14 and 24)

HOOK. No. 8 long shank.
TYING SILK. Green.
TAIL. The tips of three olive cock hackles, to extend $\frac{1}{4}$ inch beyond
bend of hook.
BODY. Medium olive seal's fur, tapering to tail for two-thirds of hook
length.
RIB. Eight turns heavy gold wire to finish at wing cases.
WING CASES. Brown mallard shoulder feathers tied in before thorax,
then after the thorax has been wound on, tied down at head.
THORAX. Dark olive seal's fur slightly thicker than body.
HACKLE. One turn light olive hen hackle trimmed short on top of
the hook.

Demoiselle

HOOK. No. 10.
TYING SILK. Golden olive.
TAIL. A big bunch of dyed olive cock's hackle fibres, cut off square
to a length of 1 inch.
BODY AND THORAX. Carrot shaped. Of olive floss silk or 3X Nylon,
tapering from tail up to a full $\frac{1}{4}$ inch at thorax.
RIBBING. Finest gold wire ending short of thorax.
LEG. A bunch of dyed olive cock hackles fibres, tied in under the
throat to lie close beneath body.

Doctor

A fly designed to imitate beetles, which can be used throughout the season on rivers or lakes.

HOOK.   No. 12 to 14.

BODY.   Rear quarter, white rabbit fur dyed yellow, remainder black rabbit fur. It should be dressed full to represent a beetle-like body.

TAIL WHISKS.   Fibres form a large stiff coch-y-bonddu cock's hackle.

HACKLE.   One large coch-y-bonddu cock's hackle wound full—ten or eleven turns.

The Devonshire Doctor from which the above pattern was derived, is usually ribbed with flat gold tinsel and does not have the yellow rear quarter. This is also a very good wet fly.

Dry Sedges (Richard Walker)

Despite the opposite views expressed by some reservoir anglers, there are times when dry Sedge imitations can be deadly, and can catch fish when no other fly would do nearly as well.

All can be dressed on the same principle, as follows, and the dressings are given after the tying instructions:

On a long-shanked hook, wind the tying silk from behind the eye to the beginning of the bend. Tie in a wisp of daylight fluorescent floss or wool and form a tag. Tie in two to five strands of dyed ostrich herl (more for big flies, less for small ones), and carry the silk in close turns back about two thirds of the distance between the tag and eye. Varnish the turns of silk, twist ostrich herl ropewise, and wind to form the body. Tie in, cut off waste ends and clip the flue of the body close with sharp scissors. A velvety appearance is achieved by this means.

Tie in a bunch of hackle or feather fibres to lie close to the body and to form the wing. Varnish the roots and cut off the butts of the fibres, and then clip the ends of the fibres flush with the bend of the hook.

Tie in, wind on and tie down, two good long stiff cock hackles ahead of wing. Form head with tying silk, whip-finish and varnish.

Do *not* use a spiral body hackle, as is so often advised for Sedges.

After tying, the Sedges should be doped with silicone dressing, and then again immediately before use. A little paraffin-wax disolved in the dope is a great help with regards to floatability.

Fish these Sedges on a fully greased leader, greased right up to the fly. Try letting the fly sit immobile and just giving it an occasional tweak. If that fails skate the fly across the surface very fast so that it sits up on its head hackle like a speed-boat on its step. This is done by pulling the line with the left hand and simultaneously raising the rod, but don't raise the rod farther than about 60–70 degrees to the horizontal, or there will be no room to strike. After each pull lower the rod about 10 degrees and recover the slack line. Takes may come when the fly is moving, or after it has stopped. This skimming technique can be used at very long range.

Choose whichever Sedge matches those you see on the water, but the cinnamon will often catch trout when no naturals are to be seen, especially in August.

Eric's Beetle (Eric Horsfall-Turner)

HOOK.   No. 8.
BODY.   Bronze peacock over a double thickness of yellow wool, the wool left showing for two turns at rump.
HECKLE.   Black hen, two turns.

Ermine Moth (Dry) (Revd. Edward Powell)

HOOK.   No. 10 to 14.
TAG.   A loop of two-ply orange wool tied in flat, protruding a quarter of an inch beyond the bend of the hook and then cut off so as to make a short fork.
BODY.   White rabbit fur.
RIB.   One strand of black knitting wool or coarse black thread.
HACKLES.   Two large grey speckled partridge back feathers.

Footballer (Geoffrey Bucknall)

HOOK.   No. 12 to 14.
TYING SILK.   Grey or dun.
BODY.   Black and white horsehair wound from well round bend of hook, to form a slim body of alternate bands of black and white.
THORAX.   Mole fur.
HEAD.   Peacock herl.

Fresh-water Louse (C. F. Walker)

HOOK.   No. 12 to 14 wire-loaded.
BODY.   Mixed grey and brown hare's ear flattened horizontally.
RIB.   Silver tinsel.
LEGS.   A grey-brown partridge hackle half-way up body.

The Goddard Caddis (formerly G. and H. Sedge) (See Plate 22)

This pattern has been developed by Cliff Henry and myself in an endeavour to attain a more natural silhouette than is possible with most standard dressings. It is an excellent floater, and to date appears to be a very killing pattern. Although this has been tied to represent the Mottled Sedge it is also a good general pattern for any of the lighter Sedges tied on the appropriate size of hook.

HOOK.   Long shank No. 8 to 10.
TYING SILK.   Green.

UNDER BODY.   Dark green seal's fur dubbed on to silk and tied in at
   bend. After the body of deer hair has been tied in and shaped, the
   seal's fur is stretched along under body and tied in at the eye.
BODY.   This is formed from several bunches of deer hair, it is then
   trimmed to the shape and silhouette of the wings of the natural
   Sedge-fly. (This is tied in as instructions for a Muddler Minnow.)
HACKLE.   Two rusty dun cock's tied in together at eye, and wound
   slightly down body. The top of the hackle is then trimmed off to
   approximate head of natural. The stripped butts of these two hackles
   may be left in to form antennae of Sedge if so desired.

Gold Ribbed Hare's Ear

Another "champion" fly with a fine reputation all over the U.K.,
fished wet or dry. It is thought to represent the nymph in the process of
shedding its shuck, and should therefore be fished only slightly submerged
for the best results.

HOOK.   No. 14 to 16.
BODY.   Dark fur from the root of the hare's ear spun on yellow silk.
RIBBING.   Fine flat gold tinsel.
HACKLE.   Long strands of the body material picked out with the dubbing
   needle.
WHISKS.   Three strands as hackle.

If a winged pattern is preferred, these should be formed of fibres from a
starling's primary wing feather, low over the body for the wet fly, upright
and double for the dry fly.

Governor (Dry)

HOOK.   No. 10 to 12.
BODY.   Bronze peacock's herl, with golden yellow floss silk tip,
   followed by one turn of flat gold tinsel at tail-end of body.
WINGS.   Feather from a hen pheasant's wing.
HACKLE.   Natural reddy-brown cock's.

Great Red Sedge

TYING SILK.   Orange.
HOOK.   No. 8 long-shank.
TAG.   Yellow fluorescent floss.
BODY.   Mahogany ostrich herl.
WING.   Dark natural red cock hackle fibres, preferably barred, or cock
   pheasant tail fibres.
HACKLES.   Natural red cock.

Great Red Spinner (Roger Woolley)

TAIL WHISKS. Fibres from a red game cock hackle.
BODY. Red seal's fur.
RIB. Gold wire.
WINGS. Tips of two medium blue dun cock hackles tied spent, or medium blue dun cock hackle fibres tied spent.
HACKLE. Red cock hackle.

Green Caterpillar (Dry) (Courtney Williams)

HOOK. No. 12 to 14.
BODY. Emerald green wool.
HACKLE. Stiff emerald green cock hackle wound length of body and clipped short.

Green Drake Upright (Dry) (David Jacques)

HOOK. A "Mayfly" hook, iron as light as possible.
TYING SILK. Olive or straw colour.
BODY. Build up shape with floss silk, then cover with natural raffia.
HEAD HACKLE. Two short stiff cock hackles dyed green drake.
TAIL HACKLE. Two or more long cock hackles, as stiff as possible, same shade as head hackles.

Grey Drake Upright (David Jacques)

As above, but the hackles to be dyed medium grey.

Greenwell (Greenwell's Glory)

Invented by Canon William Greenwell of Durham, this is probably the best known of this whole list. In fact it is more likely the most well-known fly of all! It is effective no matter which of the duns the fish may be taking, and is a pattern which can be fished with confidence during the entire season. The dressing can be varied to suit particular conditions, but the original was as follows:

HOOK. No. 14.
BODY. Yellow silk (sometimes ribbed with fine gold wire).
HACKLE. Light coch-y-bondhu, cock or hen.
WINGS. Hen blackbird wing feather.

The yellow silk of the body is more often than not waxed with cobblers wax to impart an olive hue, and what is called a "Furnace" hackle is usually in place of the coch-y-bondhu. The furnace hackle does not have the black tips of the coch-y-bondhu.

For a dry hackled pattern, a blue dun cock's hackle should be wound with a furnace cock, and tail consisting of a few fibres of furnace cock hackle also added.

Grey Duster (Dry)

One of the best all-round dry-flies, which will take fish throughout the season, being particularly good during the Mayfly hatch.

HOOK.   No. 12 to 14, larger for Mayflies and lake fishing.

TYING SILK.   Brown.

BODY.   Dubbing of light rabbit's fur mixed with a small amount of the blue under-fur.

HACKLE.   Stiff badger cock's hackle with a good dark centre.

TAIL WHISKS.   Can be added on smaller patterns if the "Duster" is used during a hatch of olives.

Grey Wulf Mayfly (Hair-winged)

HOOK.   No. 10 to 11, long shanked.

TAIL.   Fibres from a brown bucktail.

BODY.   Blue-grey seal's fur.

WINGS.   Brown fibres from a bucktail, divided and sloping forward.

HACKLE.   Blue dun cock's hackle.

Tied on a size 15 hook, and using fibres from a brown barred squirrel tail for the wings, this makes an excellent representation of smaller hatching nymphs.

Grouse Wing

TYING SILK.   Black.

HOOK.   No. 12 long-shanked.

TAG.   White fluorescent floss, very small.

BODY.   Dark chocolate ostrich herl or dyed swan herl.

WING.   Grouse wing or tail fibres, or dark sepia and brown speckled turkey.

HACKLES.   Dark Furnace or dark Coch-y-Bonddu.

Hatching Olive (John Goddard) (See Plate 19)

HOOK.   No. 13 to 16.

TYING SILK.   Brown.

BODY.   Olive green condor—three fibres, leave ⅛ inch of the tips projecting to form tails of nymph, tie in a silver lurex rib and cover body up to thorax with strip of olive dyed P.V.C.

THORAX.   Form from Peacock Hurl with three dark pheasant tail fibres doubled and redoubled. To represent wing cases.

HACKLE.   Two turns of pale honey or dark red.

Hatching Olive Nymph

HOOK.   No. 12 to 14.

TAIL.   A slim strip of light olive goose feather.

BODY.   As tail, in fact the body can be wound from the buts of the tail strip.

RIB. Fine gold tinsel, oval, or flat, up to thorax only.

THORAX. A "knob" of dark olive seal fur.

WING CASES. A strip of waterhen or any dark wing feather, over thorax only.

HACKLE. A clipped medium or light olive cock hackle.

The Hatching Mayfly (John Goddard) (Plate 23)

This pattern has proved very effective and is also an excellent hooker. It is tied to represent the adult insect emerging from its nymphal case in the surface film, and is fished with the tail section of the artificial submerged.

HOOK. Long-shank fine wire No. 8.

TYING SILK. Yellow.

BODY. Tail half—cock pheasant tail fibres. Head half—cream seal's fur.

RIB. Gold wire or narrow gold lurex.

WINGS. V-shaped hackle fibre wings using a large pale blue dun cock.

HACKLE. Small furnace cock tied thickly.

TAIL. Tips of three pheasant tail fibres used for body.

The Hatching Midge Pupa (John Goddard) (See Plate 21)

As this pattern has to be fished either without movement or exceedingly slowly, it is important that the artificial pupa resembles the natural as closely as possible. The method of fishing is equally important and is as follows. A floating line is used with the cast lightly greased. A large well-greased dry Sedge pattern is fished on the point, with two or three pupae tied directly on to the cast at twelve-inch intervals; the nearest should be at least a yard away from the dry sedge on the point. They should be tied on straight eyed hooks and either tied directly into the cast or held in position on the cast by blood knots. This pattern and method have proved most effective during calm conditions, during a widespread rise to the pupa (buzzer) when trout are often most difficult to catch. The artificial pupae may be cast in the path of a rising fish without movement or may be cast at random and retrieved with occasional very slow pulls. The colour and size of pupae used should be dictated by the colour and size of the natural pupae hatching at the time. An effective alternative method of fishing this artificial when the trout are not feeding on the surface is to use a weighted nymph on the point and one or two artificial pupae on droppers. Fish sink and draw with a floating or sinktip line in water of medium depth but retrieve as slowly as possible.

HOOK. Straight-eye round bend No. 10 to 14.

SILK. As body colour.

BODY. Black, brown, red or green marabou silk or firebrand fluorescent wool rib with silver lurex and then cover with opaque P.V.C. The red pattern tied to represent the orange-silver Midge pupa should be ribbed with wide silver lurex, leaving only a narrow band of red showing between each turn of lurex.

TAG. White hen hackle fibres projecting about ⅛ inch from tail tied in well round bend of hook.

THORAX. Green peacock or brown dyed turkey.

HEAD FILAMENTS. Loop or Bunch of white hen hackle fibre tips or white firebrand fluorescent wool tied through thorax but facing upward and forward over eye of hook.

N.B. For tag strands of white glass fibre cloth may be used as an alternative, and these certainly give the fly a longer life.

Hatching Sedge (John Hamp)

HOOK. No. 12.

TYING SILK. Green.

BODY. Dubbed with a mixture of fox fur and mole fur both dyed in picric acid, with a black rib, usually of two strands from the black part of a turkey tail feather.

WING CASES. Black wing feather, tied on the underside of the shank, facing backwards, to reach almost to the hook point.

LEGS. Two speckled black and white fibres from a guinea-fowl (or Mallard) feather tied along each side, sloping backwards. Two cock pheasant tail fibres are tied in fairly short at either side of the thorax, the fine end pointing backwards then two of the same fibres are tied in on either side in the same way, but with the root end pointing backwards also quite short. Finally, two more are tied in on either side in the same way, with the root end pointing backwards but this time extending the whole length of the hook.

Hawthorn (Dry) (Courtney Williams)

HOOK. No. 12.

BODY. Black ostrich herl, thin.

WINGS. From a starling's wing feather.

HACKLE. Black cock's hackle, fairly long in fibre.

Hawthorn (Dry) (Roger Woolley)

BODY. Two strands from a black turkey tail feather, tied and wound so that the shiny black quill shows up well. The two ends of the strands are tied back to represent the legs of the fly.

WINGS. From a jay's primary wing feather, as pale as possible.

HACKLE. Black cock's hackle.

Heather-fly

HOOK. No. 12.

BODY. Black ostrich herl.

WINGS. Palest starling feather.

HACKLE. Rich red coch-y-bonddu.

Hoolet (Moth)

HOOK.   No. 8 to 10.
BODY.   Bronze peacock herl wound over a strip of cork.
WINGS.   Owl or woodcock wing feather tied low over body, either rolled or flat.
HACKLE.   Two light red cock hackles wound over wing roots. An excellent dapping or "wake" fly.

HOOK.   No. 10 or 12.
TAIL.   Iron blue hackle fibres.
BODY.   Mole fure dubbing.
HACKLE.   Iron blue.

Jassid

HOOK.   No. 20.
TYING SILK.   Black.
BODY.   Black hackle tied palmer fashion and then clipped away on top and underneath.
WING.   One jungle cock eye feather tied in at the eye and flat along the body over the hackle.

Knotted Midge (Wet)

HOOK.   No. 12 to 14.
BODY.   Black tying silk.
HACKLE.   Black cock, one at tail end of hook, and one at shoulder.

Lake Olive (John Henderson)

HOOK.   No. 13.
TYING SILK.   Olive.
WHISKS.   Five fibres from a dun cock's spade feather.
BODY.   Three grey fibres from a blue game cock's tail feather dyed light olive or three light heron herls dyed light yellow.
RIBBING.   Fine gold wire or yellow silk.
HACKLES.   Light dun cock's dyed light yellow followed by a medium dun cock's (undyed).

Lake Olive Nymph (John Henderson)

HOOK.   No. 13.
TYING SILK.   Olive.
WHISKS AND BODY.   Three fibres from a blue game cock's tail, dyed light olive, the points forming the short whisks, the remainder being wound up shank to form body.
RIBBING.   Fine gold wire or yellow silk.
THORAX.   Dark olive seal's fur mixture.
HACKLE.   Two turns of small dun hen's.

Lake Olive

This is the dressing of this fly invented by Mr. J. R. Harris the well-known Irish entomologist, and recommended by Colonel Joscelyn Lane in *Lake and Loch fishing*.

HOOK. No. 12 to 13.
WINGS. Dark starling tied forward.
BODY. Pale blue heron herl dyed brown olive.
RIBBING. Gold wire.
HACKLE. Green olive cock's hackle.
TAIL. Fibres from a brown olive cock's hackle.

During the autumn the hackle should be brown olive, and the body swan herl dyed brown olive.

Lake Olive Spinner (J. R. Harris)

HOOK. No. 14 or 15.
BODY. Deep amber or mahogany seal's fur on orange tying silk.
RIB. Gold Wire.
HACKLE. Good quality rusty or pale grizzled dun cock tied spent or half spent.
TAIL. Rusty dun or reddish cock hackle fibres.

Lake Olive Spinner (C. F. Walker)

HOOK. No. 14 or 13.
WINGS. Pale brassy dun cock's hackle.
BODY. Dark red seal's fur.
RIB. Gold tinsel.
HACKLE. Pale brown or honey dun cock, or none.
TAILS. Fibres from a medium blue dun cock's spade or saddle hackle.

Large Dragonfly Nymph

HOOK. No. 8 or 10.
TYING SILK. Green.
TAIL. Three lengths of thick knitting wool ¼ inch long. One medium green and two nigger brown.
BODY. Two pieces of the same wool, one medium green and the other nigger brown, twisted together and wound on tightly. The body should be ¼-inch thick in the middle and taper at both ends, and be tied down with open turns of the tying silk.
HACKLE. One turn of a brown partridge back feather dyed very dark green.

Large Red Sedge (John Henderson)

HOOK. No. 6 new No. 9, Old Redditch scale.
TYING SILK. Nylusta, brown, (No. 17 Gossamer).
BODY. Yellowish brown seal's fur mixture.

RIBBING. Gold tinsel.

BODY HACKLE. Red cock's.

SHOULDER HACKLES. Red cock's followed by a Rhode Island hen's hackle or a feather from the breast of a Rhode Island cock or hen.

Also the dressing I have given for the Cockchafer, No. 2, with thick Condor fibre body, ginger hackle, with two feathers from the breast of a cock pheasant, tied one on top of the other, so as to rest along the top of the body.

Large Red Water Mite (John Henderson)

HOOK. No. 15 to 14.

TYING SILK. Nylusta, brown, (No. 17 Gossamer).

BODY. Loaded by winding round the shank several layers of thin copper wire, so as to make the body as bulky as possible. On top of the layers of copper wire, red Polymer or seal's fur dubbing is wound over them to represent the globular body.

HACKLE. Two turns of black hen's or starling's to represent the legs.

Large Summer Dun (C. F. Walker)

HOOK. Long shank No. 11 or 12.

WINGS. A bunch of grey fibres from near the tip of a mallard scapular feather.

TAIL. Brown mallard fibres.

BODY. Medium grey-brown condor herl lightly stained in picric acid.

RIBBING. Gold tinsel.

HACKLE. Brown-olive dyed cock.

Large Summer Spinner (C. F. Walker)

HOOK. Long shank No. 11 or 12.

WINGS. Medium brassy dun cock's hackle.

BODY. A mixture of grey-green, dark brown and yellow seal's fur, the last showing towards tail.

RIB. Gold tinsel.

HACKLE. Medium brown cock, or none.

The Last Hope (John Goddard) (See Plate 20)

An exceptionally killing pattern originally developed to represent the Pale Watery dun or any small pale coloured river insects. It has now proved to be equally effective to represent the Angler's Curse (Caenis) of stillwater. A very simple pattern to tie but it is essential to use a very short-fibred hackle. Although this is essentially a dry fly, it is also extremely effective fished very slowly as a wet fly in the surface film to represent the Hatching Caenis Nymph.

HOOK. No. 17 or 18 up-eyed fine wire.

TYING SILK. Pale yellow.

BODY.   Two or three Norwegian goose or condor herls grey buff.
HACKLE.   Dark honey very short in flue.
TAIL.   Honey dun cock, six to eight fibres.

Light Sedge (Terry Thomas)

HOOK.   No. 14 to 4 as required.
BODY.   Fibres from a light cock pheasant tail wound on as thickly as possible.
BODY HACKLE.   Ginger cock.
WING.   Brown deer body hair tied flat with cut end to rear.
FRONT HACKLE.   Ginger cock.

Little Brown Sedge (Dry) (Courtney Williams)

HOOK.   No. 14.
BODY.   Orange tying silk dubbed with light brown wool.
RIB.   Fine gold wire.
BODY HACKLE.   Short fibred natural red cock hackle from shoulder to tail.
WINGS.   From wing feathers of Rhode Island Red hen.
FRONT HACKLE.   Natural red Cock's hackle, tied in front of wings over wing roots.

Little Marryat (Dry) (Skues)

HOOK.   No. 15 to 16.
TYING SILK.   White or pale straw.
TAIL WHISKS.   Creamy dun.
BODY.   Cream fur from a baby seal.
WINGS.   Pale starling wing feather.
HACKLE.   Creamy dun.

Little Red Sedge (Dry) (Skues)

HOOK.   No. 14.
TYING SILK.   Hot orange, well waxed with brown wax.
BODY.   Dark fur from hare's ear.
RIB.   Fine gold wire.
BODY HACKLE.   Short fibred, deep red cock's hackle from shoulder to tail.
WINGS.   Brown hen's wing quill rolled and tied, sloping well back over body.
FRONT HACKLE.   Deep red cock tied in front over wing roots five or six times.

The Longhorns (John Goddard)

This is a new pattern developed in conjunction with Cliff Henry, dressed to represent this particular natural, it is a very good floater. It also has the distinct advantage of being a relatively simple pattern to tie.

HOOK. Long shank No. 12 or 14.

TYING SILK. Green.

BODY. This is formed from two or three strands of dull green dyed ostrich herl. This is tied thickly along body and then trimmed cylindrically leaving the herl as long as possible at the bend and tapering down to zero at the eye, to simulate the wings of a Sedge.

HACKLE. Pale cream dun cock, tied along body palmer fashion, but the butt of the hackle should be tied in at bend and not point as normal palmer tying. Tied in this way the hackle does not break down tapered outline of body herl.

Lunn's Particular (Spinner) (William Lunn)

HOOK. No. 14 to 16.

TYING SILK. Crimson.

TAIL WHISKS. Fibres from a large Rhode Island Red cock hackle.

BODY. Undyed hackle stalk of a Rhode Island Red.

WINGS. Two medium blue dun cock hackle tips put on flat.

HACKLE. Medium Rhode Island Red cock hackle.

Medium Sedge (Dry) (Halford)

HOOK. No. 11 to 13.

BODY. Unstripped condor herl dyed medium cinnamon. (Or cinnamon turkey tail fibres as an alternative.—Veniard.)

BODY HACKLE. Short fibred ginger cock hackle.

WINGS. Well-coloured red hen wing quill.

FRONT HACKLE. Ginger cock wound in front of wings over wing roots.

Mosquito pupae (David J. Collyer)

This fly is a pattern which will prove worth a trial on a bright summers day, preferably in a shady part of the lake. It is simple to dress and should be used just under the surface film on a greased leader. A very gentle twitch of the line every ten seconds or so is all the movement that this fly needs, a twenty yard cast should take at least half-an-hour to recover.

BODY. Stripped peacock herl, taken from the eye feather.

THORAX. Mole or muskrat for dubbing.

METHOD OF DRESSING. Tie in black tying silk at the head and wind down the body in *close* turns, take it well round the bend in the hook. Tie in the stripped peacock herl and wind this almost to the head. Dubb on the fur and wind this just behind the hook eye and tie off. The thorax should be a pronounced round ball.

HOOK SIZE. No. 12.

The Nevamis Mayfly (John Goddard)

Is a pattern developed specifically to overcome the bad hooking properties of many Mayfly patterns. Although originally tied as a river pattern it has proved very effective on some of the large Irish Loughs.

HOOK. Long-shank fine wire No. 8 up-eyed.

TYING SILK. Yellow.

BODY. Cream seal's fur wound thickly—body hackle large honey cock tied in at tail and wound to shoulder and then clipped to $\frac{1}{4}$ inch of body at shoulder sloping to $\frac{1}{8}$ inch at tail.

RIB. Oval gold tinsel.

WINGS. V-shaped hackle fibre wings using a large pale blue dun cock.

HACKLE. Small furnace cock ($\frac{1}{2}$ inch fibres).

TAIL. Three long pheasant tail fibres.

Nymph Imitations (Richard Walker)

The Sepia Nymph, tied on a No. 12 or 14 hook, has light sepia ostrich herl, dark sepia feather fibre (swan, goose, turkey etc.), and black floss. The tails should be long and the ostrich herl long in the flue. Tying silk should be black.

The Green Nymph can be tied in all sizes from 12 down to 18. For sizes 16 18, dyed swan herl, can replace ostrich, and for sizes 12 to 14 the ostrich herl should be short in flue. Floss and feather fibre can be any shade from brown-olive to greenish-olive, as the naturals vary tremendously. Tails should be shorter than in the Sepia Nymph.

Both types can be weighted by means of fine copper wire, two layers of touching turns, then built up thicker under the thorax.

Fish these nymphs very slowly at all times. Near surface on a greased leader when trout are showing, otherwise deep on an ungreased leader. In either case *always slow*.

Instructions for making

At the bend of the hook tie in three or four strands of suitable dyed feather fibre as tails, and at the same point two strands of dyed ostrich herl and one strand of floss, all of suitable colour. Now wind the tying silk back to where the junction of the abdomen and thorax will be, in touching turns, and then varnish these turns with clear celluloid varnish. While this is wet, wind on the ostrich herl with strands twisted rope-wise. Tie down and cut off the waste ends. Wind the floss over the ostrich in open spirals to achieve the desired effect; tie in but leave waste ends— *do not cut off*.

Tie in a bunch of feather fibres, same as tails, with points projecting over the eye of the hook. Carry silk to behind the eye, wind on the remainder of the floss to form the thorax, tie down and now cut off the waste ends.

Manipulate some of the points of the feather fibres with fingers and silk so that they slope slightly backwards to imitate legs. Bring the rest of the fibres forwards and tie in behind eye to imitate wing cases. Cut off waste and whip-finish and then varnish the head.

Olive Dun (Cliff Henry) (See Plate 22)

HOOK. No. 14 or 16.
TYING SILK. Green.
TAIL. Grey-blue whisks.
BODY. Hen hackle stalk from light olive cape.
WINGS. Mallard duck quill feather.
HACKLE. Pale gingery olive.

Olive Quill (Dry)

HOOK. No. 14 to 16.
TAIL WHISKS. Fibres from a medium olive cock hackle.
BODY. Stripped peacock quill from "eye" part of tail, dyed olive.
WINGS. Dark starling wing quill feather.
HACKLE. Medium olive cock hackle.

Olive Upright (Wet)

HOOK. No. 14 to 15.
TAIL WHISKS. Fibres from an olive cock hackle.
BODY. Stripped peacock quill from "eye" of tail, dyed yellow.
HACKLE. Softish olive cock or olive hen hackle.

Orange Quill (Dry) (Skues)

HOOK. No. 13 to 14.
TYING SILK. Orange.
TAIL WHISKS. Fibres from a natural bright red cock hackle.
BODY. Pale condor quill, stripped and dyed hot orange. (Condor is difficult to strip, and I have found stripped ostrich herl equally effective.—Veniard.)
WINGS. Pale starling wing quill, rather full.
HACKLE. Natural bright red cock hackle.

The Phantom Fly (John Goddard)

A dry fly tied to represent the female as it alights on the water to oviposit this is usually in the margins of lakes in the late evening.
HOOK. Up-eyed No. 14.
TYING SILK. Orange.
BODY. Grey condor herl with a wide rib of olive dyed P.V.C.
HACKLE. Honey cock, tied in well back from eye.
WINGS. White hackle points tied spent.

The Phantom Pupa (John Goddard)

This species is very prolific on many waters. The artificial should be fished on its own on the point, and retrieved in small jerks a little off the bottom.
HOOK. Down-eyed No. 16.

TYING SILK. Brown.
BODY. One strand of white marabou silk with a narrow silver lurex rib.
THORAX. Formed from two strands only of orange marabou silk.
Finally the whole body and thorax is covered with clear P.V.C.

Pheasant Tail Spinner (Skues)

HOOK. No. 14 to 16.
TYING SILK. Hot orange.
TAIL WHISKS. Two or three strands of honey dun cock spade feather.
BODY. Two or three strands of rich-coloured ruddy fibres from centre feather of a cock pheasant's tail.
HACKLE. Rusty or sandy dun cock, bright and sharp.

The Polystickle (See Plate 19)

Richard Walker first put forward his theories on the imitation of small fish to be used on our larger lakes such as Chew and Grafham in an article in *Trout & Salmon* magazine in November 1966.

Basically the "flies" consisted of floss silk bodies of various colours, wound to simulate the shape of a small fish, tinsel ribbed, and backed by a strip of feather fibres—turkey or brown mallard—tied in so that a section was allowed to project from the bend of the hook and cut in the shape of a fish-tail. A wisp of red wool was tied underneath as a sort of throat hackle, and a bold head built up with turns of tying silk.

The first one had a white floss body and a silver rib, but variations were soon introduced—one with a yellow silk body and gold rib, another with pale green floss, silver rib, and a ginger throat hackle, and even a pink-bodied one. For muddy water a black variation was devised, all items used being black except the silver rib. Finally, in recognition of success of the better known traditional flies, Stickles using the same materials as the Dunkeld, Peter Ross, and Butcher also made their appearance.

As time passed, however, and the Stickles became increasingly popular, it became apparent that durability was not one of their best features, particularly with regard to the feather backs and even the floss bodies.

An article in *Angling Times* by Ken Sinfoil triggered off the idea of using polythene strip, and the first Stickles using this material began to appear—hence the name "Polystickle".

When Richard Walker first began to use polythene for the bodies, he thought that the transparent effect was too great, but it was discovered that polythene went white when soaked in water, a most convenient coincidence.

The white floss as an under-body was retained, and the silver ribbing, and a few windings of red floss approximately a third back from the eye was added to represent the internal organs of our small fish. The result was a most realistic effect of translucence through which the silver rib and red "gut" gleamed most naturally. Furthermore, the polythene was found to be most durable, and there was no ribbing to slip or break.

The feather back and tail remained at first, but was soon replaced with another plastic—a synthetic version of raffia aptly named Raffine. This also had convenient side effects when immersed in water, where it lost its metallic appearance and became beautifully translucent, and it also bulged and improved the shape of the "fly". Furthermore the new "fly" started to catch fish!

Fundamentally the making of the Polystickle now follows a set pattern, the only variations being in the colours of materials used and the methods of adorning the hook before making up the body.

HOOK.   Originally No. 6 Standard or No. 8 long-shank. The latter is now the most popular.

BODY.   Silver tinsel wound on to the bare hook or a contrasting colour of floss silk so that a ribbed effect is achieved. Front third to be of red floss to simulate the "gut", and fluorescent flosses have been tried with some success.

BODY COVERING.   Polythene strip (clear P.V.C.). This has to be cut in strips from the original sheet, and if it is pulled so as to stretch it during the winding, a firm neat body will result.

BACK AND TAIL.   Raffine. This is already in strip form like raffia so does not have to be cut. This material should be dampened and stretched before tying in, and sufficient left extending from the bend of the hook so that a shaped tail can be cut. The raffine should be tied in before the body is wound, then brought down on top of the completed body and tied down at the head. Most popular colours are brown, brown-olive, buff, yellow, orange, green and green-olive.

THROAT.   The "hackle" can be either a slip of red wool or floss, or hackle fibres tied in underneath as a "false" hackle.

HEAD.   Built up with turns of dark tying silk and well varnished. A small "eye" can be painted either side if so desired.

The Pond Olive Spinner (John Goddard) (See Plate 23)

Often referred to as the Apricot spinner due to its very distinctive colouring, it is one spinner that does really call for a special artificial to specifically represent it. Should be fished in, not on, surface film.

HOOK.   Up-eyed 12 or 14.

TYING SILK.   Orange.

BODY.   Apricot coloured condor herl covered with pale olive dyed P.V.C.

WINGS.   Pale blue hackle tips tied spent.

HACKLE.   Dark honey cock. A bunch of these fibres tied in under each spent wing in place of the traditional type of hackle.

TAILS.   Fibres from a pale badger hackle.

Port Spinner (Cliff Henry)

HOOK.   No. 14 to 16.

TYING SILK.   Crimson.

TAIL.   Pale blue cock fibres.

BODY.   Hen hackle stalk from dark Rhode Island Red. (Port wine colour.)

WINGS.   Pale blue dun hackle points tied "spent".

HACKLE.   Two turns of light olive.

P.V.C. Nymph (John Goddard) (See Plate 21)

Initially developed as a river pattern to represent any of the Olive nymphs it has proved an exceptionally killing pattern, and has since proved to be equally effective on stillwater where Lake and Pond Olive nymphs are found. Fish in the vicinity of weed in shallower water to represent the Pond Olive nymph or deeper water for the Lake Olive. Most effective method sink and draw as slowly as it is possible to retrieve.

HOOK.   Down-eyed No. 12 or 14.

TYING SILK.   Yellow.

BODY.   Cover shank of hook with fine copper wire, forming hump near eye to represent thorax. Tie in silk at bend then body materials; first of all three strands of olive condor herl leaving the fine tips protruding to represent tails. Follow with narrow silver lurex, and then a ⅛ inch wide strip of olive dyed P.V.C. Take herl up to eye and tie in, wind silk back over hump to rear of thorax, bring lurex rib up and tie in followed by P.V.C. to cover body to this point, then continue back to eye with silk and tie in three blackish pheasant tail fibres doubled and redoubled over top of thorax.

N.B. The strips of PVC have to be cut from original sheet, and if it is pulled to stretch during tying a neat firm body will result.

Red or Green Larvae (John Goddard) (See Plate 20)

A simple dressing to simulate the larvae of some of the larger Chironomids. The larvae of these flies are found in large numbers in or on the silt or mud. When they move it is with a figure of eight lashing movement which is quite impossible to imitate, but as they are often observed lying almost still on the bottom the most effective method of fishing this pattern, if one has patience, is as follows. It may be fished from the bank or anchored boat. Cast into medium or deep water using a sinking line preferably. Allow the artificial to lay on the bottom for a period occasionally giving the line a slight twitch (ideal for fishing during the lunch break). It is suggested a weedless hook may be used with this pattern.

HOOK.   Long-shank down-eyed No. 8 to 12.

TYING SILK.   Brown.

TAIL.   A piece from the curly section of an Ibis quill (red). This should be approximately ½ inch long, and must be a piece from a curled feather, otherwise the right action cannot be imparted when the fly is fished. The stop-start motion will cause the curled part of the tail to straighten out and recurl, providing a certain amount of animation. As an alternative, a curved tip of a red or green cock hackle may be used, or two or three fibres from a red or green dyed condor or heron feather.

BODY. Crimson or olive condor herl covered with fluorescent floss of same colour.

RIB. Narrow silver lurex.

THORAX. Several turns of buff condor herl.

Reed Smut (Preben Torp Jacobsen)

HOOK. No. 16 to 18.

HACKLE. Black cock tied parachute.

BODY. Black condor herl behind and in front of hackle.

Rough Olive (Dry) (Roger Woolley)

HOOK. No. 13 to 14.

TAIL WHISKS. Dark olive cock hackle fibres.

BODY. Heron's herl dyed olive.

RIB. Fine gold wire.

WINGS. Dark starling or hen blackbird wing quill.

HACKLE. Dark olive cock's hackle.

Sedge Larvae (Geoffrey Bucknall)

HOOK. No. 10 or 12 long shank, wire-loaded.

TAIL. Honey hen hackle points.

BODY. Cream floss silk, coated with cellular varnish to which is stuck fragments of wood or grains of sand.

HEAD. Peacock herl.

Sedge Pupa (John Goddard) (See Plate 21)

A very killing pattern from July onwards. It is intended to represent the pupae of various Sedge-flies, as they ascend to the surface in the first stages of transformation to the winged fly. It should be fished fairly slowly in medium to shallow water. The artificials are dressed in several colours to represent the most common colours of the naturals.

HOOK. Long-shank wide gape No. 10 or 12.

TYING SILK. Brown.

BODY. Cream, dark brown, orange or olive green seal's fur, the latter two colours may be covered lightly with fluorescent floss of same colour and all are ribbed with narrow silver lurex.

THORAX. Dark brown condor herl.

WING CASES. Pale brown condor herl. Four strands are brought over the top of thorax and tied in at eye, and then doubled and redoubled to form the wing pads.

HACKLE. Honey or rusty hen hackle, tied sparsely 1½ to 2 turns.

N.B. The cream pattern is particularly good during September.

Sepia Dun (Dry) (Oliver Kite)

HOOK. No. 13.
TYING SILK. Brown.
BODY. Dark undyed heron primary herls.
THORAX. Same herls doubled and redoubled.
RIB. Gold wire.
TAILS. Black cock.
HACKLE. Reddish black cock.

Sepia Dun (C. F. Walker)

HOOK. No. 12 or 13.
WINGS. A bunch of fibres from a mallard scapular feather.
BODY. Grey-brown condor herl without ribbing.
HACKLE. Cock's hackle dyed sepia.
TAILS. Very dark grey or black fibres from a cock's spade or saddle feather, splayed apart as in the nymph.

Sepia Nymph (C. F. Walker)

HOOK. No. 12 or 13.
BODY. Dark brown seal's fur mixed with a little ginger.
GILLS. The body material well picked out with a dubbing needle.
TAG. Silver tinsel.
THORAX AND WING PADS. Black seal's fur.
LEG HACKLE. Dark brown hen.
TAILS. Fibres from a black hen's hackle, tied well splayed apart.

Sepia Spinner (C. F. Walker)

HOOK. No. 12 or 13.
WINGS. A ginger and grey cock's hackle, tied in with a slight rake aft.
BODY. Dark brown seal's fur, mixed with a little yellow.
RIB. Gold tinsel.
HACKLE. Dark brown or honey dun cock, or none.
TAILS. Fibres from a dark grey or black cock's spade or saddle hackle.

Sherry Spinner (Skues)

HOOK. No. 14.
TAIL WHISKS. Three fibres from a pale honey dun cock's hackle.
BODY. Amber seal's fur (Skues advocates a mixture of orange, light orange, and green seal's fur, with a small fine amount of fur from a hare's poll added).
RIB. Fine gold wire.
HACKLE. Palest honey dun, with a darkish centre if possible.

Shrimp

One of the most difficult creatures to imitate, and the following dressing is by Col. Joscelyn Lane, given in his book *Lake and Loch Fishing for Trout*.

HOOK. No. 12 or 13.

TYING SILK. Medium olive.

TAIL. A bunch of speckled brown partridge hackle fibres ⅜-inch long, tied on the bend of the hook with fibres pointing downwards.

BODY. Of hare's ear dubbing tied well round bend of hook, padded to suggest the humped back, and as fat as possible without obstructing the gape of the hook.

HACKLE. One or more brown partridge hackles wound over the body, spaced as for ribbing, with fibres upright. Trim off closely all fibres at the sides and top, and then trim the ends of the fibres below the body level with the point of the hook. Touch the coils of quill on top of the body with varnish.

Note: For deep fishing, coils of fine wire can be wound over the hook shank before the fly is dressed.

The Shrimper (John Goddard) (See Plate 20)

This is a tying to imitate the freshwater shrimp. It is tied as a weighted pattern to sink quickly and should be fished on a floating or sinking tip-line in the shallow margins in the vicinity of weed. It should be retrieved slowly along the bottom with frequent pauses.

HOOK. No. 10 to 14 down-eyed Limerick.

TYING SILK. Orange.

BODY. Copper wire wound from eye to bend, thickening in centre to form hump. Tie in strip of natural P.V.C. about ⅛ inch wide at bend (wider in the middle) followed by a honey coloured hackle and olive marabou silk. Wind olive marabou to eye followed by hackle palmer fashion, and then stretch strip of P.V.C. over the top of the body and hackles and tie in at eye. Finally trim excess hackles from along side of body.

N.B. To represent mating colour of shrimp during June, July tie in orange fluorescent silk sparsely on top of marabou.

Silver Sedge (Dry) (Courtney Williams)

HOOK. No. 10 to 14.

BODY. White floss silk.

RIB. Fine silver wire, and a sandy ginger cock's hackle.

WINGS. From a landrail's wing (or substitute) tied low over body.

HACKLE. Sandy ginger cock wound over wing roots.

Silver Sedge (F. M. Halford)

HOOK. No. 10 or 12.

BODY. White floss silk ribbed narrow silver lurex.

BODY HACKLE. Ginger cock.

WINGS. Coot.
HACKLE. Ginger tied in front of wings.

Small Buff Sedge

TYING SILK. Primrose.
HOOK. No. 12 long-shank.
TAG. None.
BODY. Pale buff ostrich or swan.
WING. Buff cock hackle fibres.
HACKLES. Buff.

The Small Hatching Midge (John Goddard) (See Plate 23)

At certain times during the summer on most waters occur quite large hatches of some of the smaller midges, usually of a brown, red or green coloration. When these small pupae are hatching, usually during the hours of daylight, the trout often become preoccupied feeding on them and are very difficult to catch. With this pattern I have achieved a certain amount of success but it must be fished only partly submerged in the surface film, as it is meant to represent the adult midge transposing from the pupal case. When trout are feeding on these emerging midges the rise form is unmistakable as they usually rise repeatably upwind in a ripple or in a circular pattern during a flat calm, barely breaking the surface with their neb as they sip them down. This pattern should be fished with little or no movement, on the point, or on the point and top dropper from a boat.

HOOK. Down-eyed No. 16 or 14.
TYING SILK. Brown.
BODY. Two turns of silver lurex round bend of hook followed by main body of dark red, green or orange-brown condor herl, or firebrand fluorescent wool.
RIB. Narrow silver lurex.
THORAX. Brown dyed turkey herl.
HACKLE. Small honey cock hackle tied in sparcely immediately behind eye.

The Floating Snail (Cliff Henry) (See Plates 14 and 21)

During most seasons there occurs on many stillwaters a mass migration of snails to the surface where they float in the surface film, for hours or sometimes even days. When this takes place the trout will nearly always become preoccupied feeding on them to the exclusion of all other forms of food and only a pattern to represent these snails will succeed. This artificial was originally developed by the well-known amateur fly dresser Cliff Henry, and over the years has accounted for very many trout.

HOOK. No. 10 to 14 Down-eyed wide gape.
TYING SILK. Black.
BODY. A flat-topped pear-shaped section of cork is formed partly split

and bound lightly over shank of hook with flat section facing eye. This is then covered with stripped peacock quill except for last two turns near flattened top representing pad of snail for which bronzed peacock herl should be used.

Snipe and Purple

HOOK. No. 14.
BODY. Purple floss silk.
HACKLE. Small feather from outside of a Jack snipe's wing.

Soldier Beetle (Dry) (Skues)

HOOK. No. 14.
TYING SILK. Hot orange.
BODY. Bright red-orange seal's fur.
WING CASES. Fibres from a cock pheasant's breast tied in at tail, brought down over body and tied in at head.
HACKLE. Natural red cock, rather sparse.

Spent Mayfly (John Veniard)

HOOK. No. 10 to 12 long shank.
TAIL. Three cock pheasant tail fibres.
BODY. White floss silk or natural raffia.
WINGS. Dark blue dun hackle points tied "spent".
HACKLE. Badger cock hackle.

Spent Mayfly (John Veniard)

This is a personal favourite which I have used with much success during the height of the hatch.

HOOK. No. 10 to 11, long shanked and of fine wire.
TAIL. Three fibres from a cock pheasant tail.
BODY. Natural raffia.
RIB. Oval silver tinsel.
WINGS. A very stiff black or dark blue dun cock's hackle wound in the normal way, the fibres then being split into two equal halves and tied "spent".
HACKLE. None. I rely on the stiffness of the wings to float the fly, but if a hackle is preferred I would recommend a short fibred stiff badger hackle.

Standard Sedge (Terry Thomas)

HOOK. No. 14 to 4 as required.
BODY. Fibres from a dark cock pheasant tail, wound as thickly as possible.
BODY HACKLE. Ginger cock.
WING. Grey deer body hair tied on flat with cut ends to the rear, and splayed out.
FRONT HACKLE. Ginger cock, wound over wing roots.

Stonefly (Roger Woolley)

HOOK.   No. 11 long shank.

BODY.   (1) A mixture of two-thirds dark olive seal's fur, and one-third dirty yellow seal's fur.
Rib—Yellow sewing silk.

(2) Dark olive-brown raffia over a foundation of yellow wool, also ribbed with yellow sewing silk.

WINGS.   The tips of four dark grizzle cock hackles tied low and flat over the back of the fly, and projecting well beyond the hook.

HACKLE.   Grizzle cock dyed brown-olive.

Stonefly (Veniard)

BODY.   A mixture of dark hare's fur/dark yellow seal's fur.

RIB.   Yellow silk, close wound at tail end.

WINGS.   Four dark dun cock hackles tied low over back and projecting beyond hook.

HACKLE.   Dark grizzle cock wound in front of wings.

Alternative wings: Fibres from the dark part of a hen pheasant's wing quill, rolled and tied low over body.

Welshman's Button (John Henderson)

HOOK.   No. 3.

TYING SILK.   Nylusta (Chestnut), (No. 17 Gossamer).

BODY.   Four fibres from a cock pheasant's tail, tied in by the butts at the bend, and wound up body to shoulder.

RIBBING.   Fine gold tinsel.

BODY HACKLE.   Dark rusty dun cock's, trimmed to taper from ⅜ inch to ¼ inch. Tied in at the shoulder by stem and wound down body to bend. Fix point of hackle by a turn of the ribbing which is then wound up body to shoulder and tied in.

SHOULDER HACKLE.   Cock Copper Pheasant's breast feather, fibres about ¾-inch long. Rhode Island Red breast feather or that of a cross between a Rhode Island and a Sussex will do as well.

White Moth

HOOK.   No. 10 to 14.

BODY.   White wool rather thick.

RIBBING.   Silver wire.

HACKLE.   White cock from shoulder to tail.

WINGS.   From a light coloured owl's wing.

Willow Fly (*Leuctra geniculata*)

This is essentially an autumn fly and does not appear in any numbers until September, mostly on upland reservoirs, where on a day of sun and cloud, whenever there is a burst of sunshine, they may appear in large numbers,

The length of the body of the fly is about ⅜ inch, the wings when closed extend behind the body by about ⅛ inch. The colour of the thorax and legs, is a dark olive but the body shades off to a golden yellow towards the tail.

HOOK. No. 1 or 2 (14 or 18).

BODY. Seal's fur, shading from golden yellow at tail to dark olive at shoulder.

HACKLE (BODY). Medium dun cock's trimmed a little if necessary, tied in by stem at shoulder and wound down body to bend where the tip of the hackle is bound on top of shank by the ribbing (fine gold wire) which is then wound up body to shoulder.

HACKLE (SHOULDER). Medium dun cock's.

The hackle point left at the tail can be shortened and rounded so as to represent the folded wings of the natural fly which extend beyond the body.

Winter Brown (Dry) (Roger Woolley)

HOOK. No. 13 long shanked.

BODY. Dark brown quill from the stem of a peacock's tail, dyed dark brown.

WINGS. Two dark cree (brown grizzle) cock hackles dyed dun, and tied flat along back.

HACKLE. Dark brown dun cock's hackle.

Hackled Pattern

BODY. As for the winged pattern.

HACKLE. A dark, well-rusted blue dun cock hackle.

Wolf Spider (Wet) (Col. Jocelyn Lane)

HOOK. No. 12.

TYING SILK. Pale olive.

BODY. Cork covered with brown Silko. One-eighth of an inch thick in the middle and tapered at both ends, covering rear half of shank only.

THORAX. Brown ostrich herl, leaving a gap between body and thorax.

HACKLE. Two turns of speckled brown partridge hackle between thorax and body.

Yellow Boy (Spinner) (William Lunn)

HOOK. No. 13 to 16.

TYING SILK. Light orange.

TAIL WHISKS. Pale buff cock hackle fibres.

BODY. White hackle stalk dyed medium yellow.

WINGS. Two light buff cock hackle tips put on flat.

HACKLE. Light buff.

Yellow Dun (Dry) (Harris)

HOOK. No. 14.
TAIL WHISKS. Fibres from a ginger cock's hackle.
BODY. Bright orange floss, or light orange quill.
RIB. Gold wire.
WING. Bunch of fibres from a pale yellow cock's hackle tied so as to incline slightly forward.
HACKLE Ginger cock's hackle.

Yellow Evening Spinner (Harris)

HOOK. No. 14.
TAIL. Fibres from a ginger cock's hackle.
BODY. Light orange seal's fur spun on orange tying silk.
RIB. Gold wire.
WING. Honey dun or pale ginger cock hackle fibres tied "spent" or "half spent".
No hackle.

Yellow Sally

HOOK. No. 12.
BODY. Yellowish buff dyed seal's fur ribbed primrose tying silk.
WINGS. Any fine fibred wing feather dyed a deep primrose.
HACKLE. Natural light ginger cock's.

GENERAL PATTERNS

Alexandra (John Veniard)

A fly that needs little or no introduction, being one of the most well-known lake and sea trout patterns. Lauded by some and condemned by others, I personally have found it a real "killer" in lakes stocked with Rainbow trout, particularly the "Jungle" version.

HOOK. No. 10 to 12.
TAIL. Red Ibis, to which is sometimes added a strand or two of green peacock herl.
BODY. Flat silver tinsel.
RIB. Fine oval silver.
HACKLE. Black hen's.
WINGS. Strands of green herl from the "sword" tail of the peacock usually with a thin strip of ibis on each side.

Blae and Black

HOOK. No. 10 to 14.
BODY. Black seal's fur.
HACKLE. Black hen.
WINGS. Wild duck wing feather.
TAIL. Fibres of golden pheasant tippet.

Black and Orange Marabou (See Plate 14)

Marabou flies are extremely popular in the U.S.A. for most species of game fish. This is due in the main to the excellent mobility of the feather in the water, which the fish find irresistible. Fished deep, early in the season when the water is cold, and the fish hungry, it can be a killer.

TAIL. Orange or red D.F.M. wool.

BODY. Oval or flat silver.

WING. Black Marabou feathers, strip the fibres and tie them in small bunches.

CHEEK. Jungle cock not too long.

HACKLE. Hot orange cock.

HOOK. Three-quarter long-shanked No. 8 to 10.

Black and Peacock Spider

Also one of the patterns recommended for reservoirs by Col. Drury.

HOOK. No. 7 to 11.

BODY. Bronze peacock herl.

HACKLE. A relatively large and soft black hen's hackle.

Black Pennell

The "Pennell" series were the invention of H. Cholmondely Pennell, English poet, sportsman and author, who also had much to do with the evolution of our present day hook styles.

These flies should be dressed with the hackle rather longer than is usual, and the number of turns kept to a minimum. Pennell himself recommended three patterns besides the black; brown, yellow and green.

HOOK. No. 10 to 13.

TAG. Fine silver tinsel.

TAIL. Tippet fibres, to which are sometimes added a small golden pheasant crest feather.

BODY. Very thin, of black floss silk.

RIBBING. Oval silver—fine.

HACKLE. Black cock, long in fibre and dressed sparsely.

For the other patterns it is merely necessary to alter the colour of the body silk and hackle, natural light red game hackles sometimes being preferred for the yellow and green patterns.

The "Pennell's" are primarily lake and sea trout flies, and dressed much heavier in the hackle are very much in demand for "dapping".

Butcher

With the Peter Ross and Alexandra, this is undoubtedly one of the most well-known flies in the world. It is deadly, particularly early in the season, for lake, river and sea trout.

HOOK. No. 10 to 14.

TAIL. Red Ibis or substitute.

BODY.   Flat silver.

HACKLE.   Black cock or hen's hackle.

WINGS.   From the blue-black section of a feather from a mallard drake's wing.

The Chief (Roy Masters)

HOOK.   No. 8 to 10 long-shanked hook.

TAG.   Silver tinsel.

BODY.   Firebrand fluorescent floss silk, scarlet.

RIB.   Oval silver tinsel.

WINGS.   Two yellow hackles back to back inside, with two scarlet hackles outside with a jungle cock eye each side. (See note at bottom.)

HACKLE.   Mixed scarlet and yellow cock.

HEAD.   Black varnish.

The yellow inside hackles of the wing may be hen hackles, but the outside scarlet hackles must be cock hackles.

The cock hackles also must be a bright scarlet and of the slim pointed type; this gives a striking contrast to the Fly.

Chompers (Richard Walker) (see Plate 14)

These are perhaps the easiest of the reservoir flies to tie, and very effective at times.

Instructions for making:

Take a piece of damp raffine, or a bunch of feather fibres and tie in at the bend of the hook. Also at this point tie in three or four strands of ostrich herl. Colours to use are given at the end of these instructions.

Wind the tying silk along the hook-shank in touching turns over the butts of the raffine or feather fibres, leaving plenty stick out at the back to form the "shell-back" of the fly. Finish winding just behind the eye and cut off any forward-projecting ends which may still protrude. Varnish the windings of tying silk and, twisting the ostrich herl strands into a rope, wind them along to just behind the eye of the hook while the varnish is still wet, tie in and cut off waste ends. (The idea of using the varnish before forming the bodies etc., in the dressings, is for increased durability. John V.)

Bring the raffine or feather fibres forward, pull taut and tied down behind eye. Cut off waste, from head and whip-finish. Varnish head.

Useful colour combinations for these patterns are:

Brown raffine and olive ostrich herl, olive silk.

Clear raffine and golden-yellow ostrich, black silk.

Brown speckled turkey and golden-yellow ostrich, black silk.

Pale buff raffine and buff ostrich, brown silk (Shrimp).

Pea-green raffine and white ostrich, olive silk (small Corixa).

Brown speckled turkey and white ostrich, olive silk (large Corixa).

Black raffine of feather fibres, peacock herl instead of ostrich, black silk (Water Beetle).

These Chompers should be fished slowly in small jerks or very slow long pulls (sink and draw). They can be tied in various sizes—choose the size appropriate to the natural insect that the colour combination suggests. They can be very easily weighted by layers of copper wire or lead wound underneath the dressing.

Coachman (Dry)

This very well-known fly is thought to be the invention of a coachman to the British Royal family many years ago, although there are other versions of its origin. It can be used dry or wet, but has been found to be most successful as a dry fly for lake fishing, particularly in the smaller sizes.

HOOK. No. 16 to 10.
BODY. Bronze Peacock herl.
WINGS. White duck wing quill.
HACKLE. Natural red cock's hackle.

When tied with wings of starling wing or grey duck wing quill, it becomes the Lead-winged Coachman.

This fly is as popular, if not more so, in North America as it is in Great Britain, and has several variations in those parts. One of these variations is the Royal Coachman which differs from the original in that it has a centre section of the body composed of red floss silk, the peacock herl forming a "butt" and a "thorax".

The Americans are particularly fond of fan-winged examples of this fly, and any of the variations can be thus formed by using the round breast feathers of the Mandarin Duck as wings.

Dogsbody (Dry) (Harry Powell)

HOOK. No. 14 to 16.
BODY. Brown tying silk dubbed with camel-coloured dog's hair. Seal's fur dyed this colour can be used as an alternative.
HACKLES (2). Grizzle (Plymouth Rock) cock's hackle, with a natural red cock hackle wound in the front.
TAIL WHISKS. Three strands from a cock pheasant's tail.

Dunkeld

This is the trout fly version of the famous salmon fly of the same name, and it has had a very large measure of success during the last few years, particularly in the reservoir type of lake such as Chew, Blagdon, Weir Wood and Grafham.

HOOK. No. 12 to 8 (or larger for sea trout).
TAIL. Golden pheasant crest.
BODY. Flat gold tinsel.
RIBBING. Gold wire or oval gold tinsel.
HACKLE. Dyed orange (wound from shoulder to tail on larger patterns).

WINGS. Brown (bronze) mallard.
"EYES". Two small jungle cock feathers tied close to head.

Grenadier

This pattern is one of several described by Col. Esmond Drury in an article in the *Fishing Gazette* of April 1958. They were designed by Dr. Bell of Wrington particularly for the lakes and reservoirs of Chew Valley and Blagdon. The other patterns are the Large Amber Nymph, Small Amber Nymph, Buzzer Nymph and Corixa, and the dressings of all these are included in this book. See Index.

HOOK. No. 13.
BODY. Hot orange floss or seal's fur.
RIBBING. Oval gold tinsel.
HACKLE. Two turns of ginger or light furnace cock.

Grey and Red Matuka (David J. Collyer)

I have yet to see a British trout angler with a Matuka in his fly box, I find this rather surprising as these patterns can be most effective in conditions when no other fly will be accepted. It can be perhaps put down to the fact that these flies require a rather different approach from the normal trout wet-flies in their dressing. As we are so often reminded the British angler is notoriously conservative, an unwillingness to experiment with foreign flies may be the reason for it. In New Zealand all the Matukas have proved their worth, their trout don't differ very much from ours therefore these flies should prove equally effective here. The Grey and Red Matuka is simply a variation of the New Zealand style of dressing that I have found to be most likely to be accepted by British fish. It should be fished either very deep on a sinking line or just under the surface on a floater, the depth of fishing depends on the prevailing conditions.

RIB. Oval silver tinsel.
BODY. Silver grey chenille.
HACKLE. A large bunch of scarlet hackle fibres.
WING. Hen pheasant body feather.

Method of Dressing. Wind black tying silk down the hook shank almost to the bend and tie in the ribbing tinsel and the chenille. Take close turns of the chenille up the body almost to the head, cut off surplus. Reverse hook in the vice and tie in the beard or false hackle. Turn the hook up the normal way and tie in two hen pheasant body feathers, back to back, after having previously stripped the underside of almost all its fibres, just leave the fibres at the very tips of the feathers. These make the tail. Lay the feathers vertically along the body and separate the fibres toward the tail, then wind the ribbing tinsel through the wing. Work your way up the body to the head winding the tinsel and at the same time separating the fibres. Tie off at the head.

Invicta

Always a very popular fly for lakes, this famous pattern is now having a run of success on the large reservoirs that have come into being since the Second World War. This, I think, is mainly due to the large hatches of sedge to be found on them, of which the Invicta is a fine imitator for wet-fly fishing. When used for this purpose, good results can be expected right through the season.

HOOK. No. 10 to 14.
TAIL. Golden pheasant crest feather.
BODY. Seal's fur dyed yellow.
RIBBING. Oval or round gold tinsel.
BODY HACKLE. Red game from shoulder to tail.
FRONT HACKLE. Blue jay, from the wing.
WINGS. From a hen pheasant's centre tail.

Pale Sedge (David Jacques)

A highly successful Sedge pattern on rivers and stillwaters. It is tied in two sizes, large (Hook 10) and small (Hook 14), the former for use at dusk, and the latter for use during the day. In the appropriate size, it represents closely a number of sedges, including the Caperer, the Grouse Wing and a number of others that have no colloquial names. On still-waters, it is an advantage to move the artificial so that it makes a definite stir on the surface.

HOOK. 14 (small) and 10 (large).
SILK: Hot orange.
BODY: Either cinnamon Turkey Tail or a swan herl dyed emerald green. Sometimes one is preferred to the other.
RIB: Ginger cock overtied with gold twist.
HACKLE: Ginger cock.
WING: From the undyed wing of a hen pheasant, bunched and rolled.

Mallard and Claret

The best known of the Mallard series of lake and sea-trout flies, and probably the most successful pattern ever invented for wet-fly fishing. Its reputation is high in every part of the British Isles, both for lake and sea trout fishing. Tied in the smallest sizes it can be also used for nymph fishing for brown trout. In fact the best all-rounder one is likely to find.

There are several patterns in the Mallard series, but it is the Claret which reigns supreme.

HOOK. No. 10 to 14. (Up to size 8 for sea trout.)
TAIL. Golden pheasant tippet fibres.
BODY. Claret seal's fur.
RIBBING. Oval gold tinsel. (Fine gold wire in very small sizes.)
HACKLE. Natural red cock's, or one dyed the same colour as the body.

WINGS. Bronze speckled feathers from the mallard shoulder, usually referred to as "Bronze Mallard".

Mole-fly (Dry)

Although predominantly popular in Europe, particularly in France, this fly is of English origin, taking its name from the river Mole in Surrey. Very effective on slow flowing rivers, where its forward style of winging enables it to cock up very nicely. It will take fish during a hatch of Olives, Mayflies or Sedges.

HOOK.   No. 14 to 16.
BODY.   Dark olive tying silk.
RIBBING.   Gold wire.
WINGS.   Mottled hen pheasant tied forward.
HACKLE.   Red/black (Furnace) wound from shoulder to tail.

Another pattern, and the one most popular in France is as follows:

HOOK.   No. 14.
TAIL WHISKS.   Coch-y-bondhu.
BODY.   Mustard—yellows floss.
RIBBING.   Gold wire.
WINGS.   Speckled hen wing quill (as light as possible).
HACKLE.   Coch-y-bondhu, ribbed down body.

This dressing makes it a very good imitation of the Oak Fly.

Peter Ross

Undoubtedly the most popular pattern for wet fly fishing ever invented. Its originator was Peter Ross of Killin, Perthshire, and although he only produced it as a variation of the Teal and Red, the slight variation turned a good fly into one of the most killing patterns known to anglers. Its main reputation is as lake fly, but is reckoned by many to be equally good for sea trout.

HOOK.   No. 8 to 14.
TAIL.   Fibres from a golden pheasant tippet feather.
BODY.   In two halves, the tail half of flat silver tinsel, and the front half of dyed red seal's fur.
RIBBING.   Oval silver over both halves.
HACKLE.   Black cock or hen's.
WINGS.   From the breast or flank feather of a teal.

Silver Doctor

This is the trout version of the popular salmon fly of the same name, dressed much simpler of course. Ideal for lake and sea trout when big fish are expected.

HOOK.   No. 10 to 6.
TAIL.   Fibres of golden pheasant tippet.
BODY.   Flat silver tinsel.

RIBBING. Oval silver.

HACKLE. Bright blue.

WINGS. Strips of goose or white duck wing feathers, dyed green, yellow and red, with a strip of mallard's grey breast or flank feather each side.

A small golden pheasant crest feather is sometimes added to the tippet fibres of the tail, and in larger patterns a few fibres of speckled guinea fowl neck feathers are added in front of the blue hackle.

Silver March Brown

TAIL. Two fibres from a brown speckled partridge hackle or speckled partridge tail feather.

BODY. Flat silver tinsel.

RIBBING. Oval silver.

HACKLE. Brown partridge back feather.

WINGS. From the hen pheasant's mottled secondary wing feather.

Teal Blue and Silver

HOOK. No. 8 to 14.

TAIL. Fibres of golden pheasant tippet.

BODY. Flat silver tinsel.

RIBBING. Oval silver tinsel, or silver wire.

HACKLE. Bright blue.

WINGS. Teal breast or flank feathers.

Teal and Green

The Teal series are standard wet fly patterns for both sea trout and lake trout flies. This fly, the Teal Blue and Silver, and the Peter Ross, are the best known of the series.

HOOK. No. 8 to 14.

TAIL. Two or three golden pheasant tippet fibres.

BODY. Green seal's fur.

RIBBING. Oval silver tinsel, or fine flat silver tinsel on the smaller patterns.

WINGS. Teal breast or flank feathers. (Flank feathers are larger.)

HACKLE. Natural light red, or dyed green.

There are many colour combinations for this series of flies, achieved by varying the colour of the body fur and the hackle, i.e. Teal and Black would be the same dressing as above, but with black seal's fur and a black hackle.

Water-Hen Bloa (Wet) (Pritt)

HOOK. No. 14.

BODY. Yellow silk, dubbed with the fur of a water-rat (alternatively mole's fur).

WINGS. Hackled feather from the inside of a moor-hen's wing.

Wickham's Fancy

HOOK. No. 10 to 12.

BODY. Alternate ribbing of flat gold tinsel and natural red cock's hackle.

WINGS. From the wing feather of a starling.

HACKLE. Natural red cock.

TAILS. Three strands of red cock.

Woodcock and Yellow

The Woodcock series resemble the Teal, Mallard and Grouse series in that they are standard patterns for lake and sea trout fishing. The Woodcock and Yellow is particularly successful as a lake or reservoir fly, as a sedge imitation.

HOOK. No. 8 to 14.

TAIL. A few fibres of golden pheasant tippet.

BODY. Yellow seal's fur.

RIBBING. Oval silver.

HACKLE. Natural medium red, or a yellow one the same colour as the body.

WINGS. From the wing feather of a woodcock.

Worm Fly

This is another pattern which has come very much to the fore with the advent of reservoir fishing, and is another of the flies mentioned in Col. Esmond Drury's list of patterns. It is best described as two Red Tag flies in tandem.

HOOKS. Two ties in tandem—No. 12 or 13.

(Tail Fly)

TAG. Red floss silk.

BODY. Bronze peacock herl, with a small tip of flat gold tinsel wound under the tail (optional).

HACKLE. Dark red cock or hen.

(Front Fly)

Same as for tail fly but without the red tag.

LURES—STREAMERS AND BUCKTAILS, ETC.

Ace of Spades (see Plate 14)

Typical of the new breed of lures that has appeared during the last decade, this pattern has enjoyed considerable success since it was first introduced by the celebrated professional fly dresser David Collyer in the early 70's. The wing is tied in the matuka style, which originated in New

Zealand and proved to be so effective on artificials dressed to take the monster trout inhabiting the famous Lake Taupo in that country.

HOOK. D/E 60 to 12 long shank.

SILK. Black.

RIB. Oval silver tinsel.

BODY. Black chenille.

WING. Black hen tied matuka style as a crest.

OVERWING. Dark bronze mallard.

HACKLE. Guinea fowl.

Appetiser (see Plate 14)

This is one of the more recent creations of that fine stillwater angler Bob Church, and follows a series of successful patterns that commenced in the mid-1960's. As Bob tends to specialize in lure fishing most of his better known pattern are lures or attractors and this new pattern is no exception. First introduced in 1973, it was designed specifically to tempt the larger trout when they were feeding on fry during the latter half of the season.

HOOK. D/E Long Shank 6 or 8.

SILK Black.

TAIL. Orange, green and silver mallard fibres mixed.

RIB. Silver tinsel.

BODY. White chenille.

WING. White marabou herl—large spray.

OVERWING. Natural grey squirrel tail.

THROAT HACKLE. Same mixture of fibres as used in tail.

Aylott's Orange

I had great difficulty in deciding in which section to place this pattern as it is more suggestive than lure-like. However, mainly due to its very bright body coloration, I decided it probably favoured this group. Designed in the late 70's by Richard Aylott it is undoubtedly his most successful pattern. It is now a well known and popular artificial on many reservoirs in the southern part of the country and has accounted for many large trout both brown and rainbow.

HOOK. D/E 12 or 14.

SILK: Black.

BODY. Arc Chrome D.F. wool.

HACKLE. Light red cock tied sparsely.

HEAD. Two or three strands of peacock herl.

Baby Doll (see Plate 14)

Here we have a pattern that will no doubt upset the purists, as anything less like a fly is hard to imagine. Let this not fool you, as it has proved to be one of the best lures to appear in recent years. It was originally devised in the early 70's by Brian Kench for use at Ravensthorpe reservoir. Since then it has been popularised largely by Bob Church. Now well established nationwide as a top lure it has accounted for many large trout both browns and rainbows as well as many limit bags.

While this pattern is a quick lure to dress, the method of tying is a little unusual and may cause some problems initially. It is most important to use the right kind of brilliant white nylon wool, and 'Sirdar' brand baby wool was found to be the best, hence the lure's name. When tied with this wool, it stands out like a neon sign in the water. First of all, well varnish the hook shank then cut off about nine inches of wool. This should be laid along the top of the shank as a large loop facing the eye, leaving an inch long single strand and a loop of similar length projecting for the tail. After securing both loops and short single strand with black tying silk, take the silk down to the eye of the hook. Next take the long single strand of baby wool left and loop this over the back of the long loop once. Then build up a long slim body and secure. Pull the long loop tightly along the back and tie in. Cut off any wool projecting over the eye, and then build up a large head with the silk. Finally, cut the short tail loop to about half an inch. Then with a needle shred the three strands and cut into a bushy fish-tail shape.

Black Bear Hair Lure (Cliff Henry) (See Plate 24)

TYING SILK.   Black.
HOOK.   No. 8 or 10 long shank.
BODY.   Black seals fur spun thickly round shank.
RIB.   Oval silver tinsel.
BODY TOP. $\frac{1}{8}''$ wide strip of black bear hair with skin cut slightly longer than hook and bound on top Matuka fashion.

Black Lure (Black Leech)

The Tandem Hook Lure, originally evolved for estuary fishing for sea trout (fry imitation), has become very popular on the reservoirs now, particularly early in the season. Fished deep and fast it has accounted for many "bags" on Chew and elsewhere.

HOOK.   Two hooks in tandem
BODY.   Black floss silk.
RIBBING.   Oval or fine flat silver tinsel.
WINGS.   Two black cock or hen's hackles tied back to back to form a single wing, or the other way round if a "V" effect is required.
HACKLE.   Black cock or hen.
A "tag" of red wool on the rear hook is sometimes added.

Broffin Trout Streamer (Taff Price)

Whilst fishing the outflow of our lake for a large brown trout that lay under some trees, I had a thumping take, a trout I thought until I netted a Jack Pike of just under 3 lb. I believe a lot more work is to be done in the field of streamer flies for Pike in this country as they are fished most successfully in the U.S.A.

TAIL. A tuft of olive green hackle.
BODY. Thin tapered green floss.
RIB. Flat gold tinsel or lurex.
WING. Six cock hackles; two fiery brown hackles back to back, two dark olive hackles either side, followed by two badger hackles.
HACKLE. Dark green olive tied false with a few strands of long white hackle fibres the length of the body tied under the dark olive.
CHEEK. Jungle cock a quarter the length of wing.
HOOK. Long-shank No. 4, 6 and 8.

Church Fry

Bob Church's variation of the Sweeney Todd.
HOOK. Long-shanked No. 10 to 4.
BODY. Orange floss silk.
RIB. Flat silver tinsel or Lurex.
THROAT. Magenta (DFM) wool or silk.
HACKLE. A "false" hackle consisting of some fibres from an orange cock hackle.
WING. Grey squirrel tail fibres.

The Cree Streamer (Roy Masters)

HOOK. No. 8 long-shanked.
TAIL. A thick bunch of light brown hen hackle fibres.
BODY. First wind lead wire along hook shank, then coat with varnish and wind in silver lurex from ready-cut reel or cut from a strip. Allow to dry.
WINGS. Cock hackles from the Cree (coloured grizzle) cape. Take four hackles; two small, about the length of the silver body, and two large. The large hackles when tied in should just extend past the tail.
Put the small hackles back to back inside the large hackles and tie in, then tie in jungle cock eyes.
HACKLE. Mixed yellow and scarlet cock swept back over wing when tied in.
HEAD. Black varnish.

Hairy Minnow (Taff Price)

Not only has this bucktail taken Rainbows and Brown trout, it took a Roach of over 1¼ lb. on what would have been a blank day.
TAIL. Small tuft of DFM Red wool (fluorescent).
BODY. Flat silver.
RIB. Oval silver.
WING. Dark green bucktail, white bucktail underneath.

UNDER WING OR HACKLE.   Reverse hook in the vice, tie in white bucktail
to bend of hook then a small tuft of red bucktail at the throat.
HEAD.   Black, with white painted eye, black pupil.
HOOK.   Long-shanked No. 8 to 10.

Jack Frost (see Plate 14)

Without doubt this is an excellent name for this new lure, which is the
latest creation of that fine stillwater angler Bob Church. It would seem
that this is a natural development, following the success of his Appetiser
lure which incorporated a relatively new material. This was marabou,
which he used in conjunction with hair for the wings. The new pattern
relies entirely on marabou for the wings, which seems to indicate that Bob
now thinks very highly of this material. It is so very fine that the slightest
movement brings the marabou to life; and for this reason it seems to be
more effective fished slowly with frequent pauses, rather than fast.

HOOK.   D/E No. 6 to 10 long shank.
SILK.   Black or white.
TAG.   Crimson wool.
BODY.   White 'Sirdar' baby wool covered by a ⅛" wide strip of poly-
thene.
WING.   Generous spray of white marabou.
HACKLES.   Long fibres crimson cock followed by a white.

Jersey Herd (T. C. Ivens)

HOOK.   No. 9 long-shank.
BODY.   Bold underbody of floss silk thickening at centre. Rib with
copper coloured flat tinsel or alternatively a strip of milk cap foil.
Now tie in twelve strands of bronze peacock herl along top of body,
leaving ⅙ projecting beyond bend of hook to form tail. The
strands projecting over eye are used to form head after the hackle
has been tied in.
HACKLE.   Hot orange short fibred cock hackle tied in doubled for two
turns.

Minnow Streamer (Taff Price)

This fly is fished when the trout are obviously taking the species, it
should be fished with slow pulls, with occasional pauses and faster spurts
now and again. In fact all Streamers and Bucktails should be fished with
movement as near to a natural fish as possible, not as a jet-propelled
aquatic rocket; fished fast, sometimes—yes, but alternate with common
sense.

TAIL.   Blue dun hackle fibres.
RIB.   Silver lurex.
BODY.   White floss tapered fish-like.

HACKLE. Scarlet cock false hackle for the male minnow, Blue dun for female.

WING. Two cock hackles dark olive; either side, strips of black and white barred teal.

CHEEK. Jungle cock very short.

HEAD. Olive green white underneath.

HOOK. Long-shank No. 8.

Missionary

This lure is an old, almost forgotten New Zealand pattern, that has been resurrected and brought up to date by Dick Shrive. Due to his astonishing success in recent years with this pattern it has now become extremely popular particularly on many of the Midland reservoirs. In addition it is highly recommended by Bob Church, so with the backing of two such experts it is obviously worthy of very serious consideration. There are two major variations of this pattern, the first incorporates the use of a whole feather for the wing tied in flat along the top of the body. This whole feather acts rather like a tiny parachute, so that when the fly is cast on the water it sinks slowly with a most attractive action. Under certain conditions this seems irresistible to any trout in its vicinity, which results in a lot of takes coming on the drop. Apart from this it is also very effective when retrieved at a medium pace, and it is now looked upon by many anglers as an excellent all season pattern on most waters. The second variation which Bob Church and his friends have found particularly successful has been modified for a much faster retrieve. This has been achieved by replacing the whole wing feather with a bunch of barred teal feathers taken off the quill.

HOOK. D/E No. 6 to 10 long shank.

SILK. White or black.

TAIL. Bunch of scarlet dyed cock hackle fibres.

THROAT HACKLE. Bunch of scarlet dyed cock hackle fibres.

RIB Silver tinsel.

BODY. White chenille.

WING. A whole silver mallard breast feather.

HOW TO DRESS THE MUDDLER MINNOW (PLATE 22)

The American fly known as the Muddler Minnow achieved a remarkable list of successes in this country during the latter part of the 1967 season. I can vouch for its qualities, not only from actual use but also from the comments I have received from many anglers. The method of dressing this fly is unusual and it is apparently causing some difficulty to many amateur fly dressers. I hope these few notes will help them.

The fly was originated on the Nipigon river in Northern Ontario, by Don Gapen of the Gapen Fly Company, Anoka, Minnesota. It was an attempt to imitate the Cockatush minnow that lives in the waters of the Nipigon watershed. This is a flathead type of minnow that has its habitat under the rocks in streams.

The nickname for these minnows in Wisconsin is "muddlers". They are held in high regard by the Indians of the Nipigon area, who spear them at night with a straightened hook, or even a table fork. They use torch-light for this purpose, since the muddlers come from under the rocks only at night. I am indebted to Joseph D. Bates, Junr., author of *Streamer Fly Tying and Fishing*, for the foregoing information on this fly.

Firstly, here is the dressing as given by the originator:

HEAD.   Black (red for weighted flies).

HOOK.   Sizes No. 12 to No. 1 long-shank.

TAIL.   A small section of turkey wing quill (oak), slightly longer than the gape of the hook.

BODY.   Flat gold tinsel.

WING.   A moderately large bunch of grey squirrel tail hair, on each side of which is a fairly large section of mottled (oak) turkey wing feather tied on nearly as long as the bucktail, extending to the end of the tail and pointing upward at a 30 degree angle. (I assume that the reference to bucktail at this stage is an indication that alternative hairs can be used in the wing besides squirrel-tail hair and, in fact, subsequent dressings I have seen, quoted Impala hair and black and white bucktail fibres. In fact, in the very largest of the patterns, these longer and more robust hair fibres would be essential.—J.V.).

SHOULDERS.   Natural deer body hair, spun on to surround the hook, flattened and clipped short at front and tapering longer backwards, leaving a small part as long as possible. (Use care when applying the wing to leave room at the head for the clipped deer hair part of the shoulders. This can be rather heavily, perhaps using three or four spinnings of the hair.)

It is this last part of the dressing which is causing furrowed brows, the rest of it being quite straightforward streamer-fly procedure.

The use of deer hair on fishing flies is an old-established North American custom, no doubt having its origins in the lures used by the Indians. Its use as a wing material is obvious, but its qualities as a body material are not so well known. The adaptation to of the hair as a body material also calls for a little-known tying technique, and this can be difficult for tyers who have not come across it before.

Most important to remember is that it is only the stiff body hairs of the deer which can be used for this purpose, the softer hairs from the tail being quite unsuitable.

The usual method is to make several "spinnings" of the hairs along the hook shank, pressing each new one close up to the last until one arrives at the position where one has a hook "palmered" completely with the deer hairs. The "hackle" is then clipped to shape the result being a very close-knit, flue-brush effect with remarkable floating qualities. This is the reason why this type of dressing is used on the bass flies popular in North America, which have to be worked continually on the surface if they are to be effective.

Orange Muddler (Taff Price)

This fly is a variation of the now popular muddler minnow. Fished just under the surface so that it left a wake when retrieved in a medium fast recovery, it accounted for me, three rainbows in succession, then for my friend it took a further five, best of which weighed 2 lb. The rainbows could be seen following the fly in, before the take.

TAIL.   Orange hackle fibres.

BODY.   Flat silver or gold lurex.

WING.   Orange bucktail.

HEAD.   Clipped deer hair as for conventional muddler.

Orange Streamer (Taff Price)

TAIL.   None.

BODY.   Orange floss.

RIB.   Gold tinsel or lurex..

HACKLE.   None.

WING.   Two hot orange hackles back to back, two badger hackles either side of them.

CHEEK.   Jungle cock a quarter the length of wing.

HOOK.   Long-shanked No. 6, 8, 10.

Orange Bucktail (Taff Price)

TAIL.   None.

BODY.   Oval gold tinsel size 8.

WING.   Orange bucktail not too heavily dressed.

HACKLE.   None.

HEAD.   Black with white painted eye and black pupil.

HOOK.   Long-shanked No. 8 to 10.

Sweeney Todd (Richard Walker) (see Plate 14)

HOOK.   Long-shanked No. 10 to 4.

BODY.   Black floss.

RIB.   Fine silver oval tinsel.

THROAT.   Three or four turns of magenta fluorescent wool (D.F.M.).

HACKLE.   Several fibres from a magenta cock or hens hackle tied in as a "false" hackle, i.e. underneath only, in the same way as one ties in the wing.

WING.   Black squirrel tail fibres, or bucktail in the largest sizes.

Texas Rose Muddler Minnow (Richard Walker)

TYING SILK.   Orange.
HOOK.   No. 8 long-shank.
BODY.   Orange floss silk.
RIBS.   Fine oval silver tinsel.
WING.   Yellow bucktail fibres.
HEAD.   Deer body hair as described on page 249.

(A feature of the "Muddlers" made by Dick Walker is the length of the head, as shown in the coloured plate. This is about one-third the length of the body.)

Sweeney Todd Tandem (Richard Walker)

TYING SILK.   Black.
HOOKS.   Two in tandem.
BODY.   Black floss silk.
RIBS.   Fine oval silver tinsel.
THROAT.   Magenta fluorescent wool.
THROAT HACKLE.   Magenta.
WING.   Natural black squirrel tail fibres.

Whisky Fly (see Plate 14)

Designed by the well known and respected casting coach Albert Whillock in the early 70's for fishing Hanningfield, his local reservoir, this lure very quickly gained a reputation for catching large trout. Within a comparatively short time its fame spread, and apart from proving to be a very successful pattern on most waters in the U.K. it is now popular in many other countries, particularly in Canada where it enjoys a great reputation.

HOOK.   D/E No. 6 to 10 long shank.
SILK.   Orange.
TAG OR COLLAR.   D.R.F. Scarlet nylon floss.
RIB.   As above.
BODY.   ⅛″ wide strip of silver sellotape varnished over body and rib.
THROAT HACKLE.   Hot orange cock.
WING.   Hot orange calf's tail.
HEAD.   As for Tag.

Wide silver lures could be used for body, and hot orange bucktail for the wings.

NEW PATTERNS BY THE AUTHOR

THE FLEXIFLY (See Plate 20) (John Goddard)

At certain times it is useful to have a good general pattern, for use on those occasions when the trout do not seem to be feeding on any specific type of food. This pattern has, therefore, been developed for this purpose.

I would not be so bold as to state that this is a completely new pattern, as new discoveries often turn out to be but rediscoveries, however, as far as I am aware it would seem to be new.

With this artificial my main purpose was to provide a pattern that in outline approximated many of the under-water aquatic forms of life on which trout feed. In addition it was essential for it to have the appearance of life even when fished exceedingly slowly. It is of course a relatively simple matter to provide animation with a fly fished fast, by using a soft hen hackle, but after many experiments with different types of hackles I found it was quite impossible to impart any movement at all to any hackle when fishing it very slowly in stillwater.

It was, therefore, necessary to find some other material, and as hair of some type seemed the logical answer, I concentrated on this. To date the very fine hair from a squirrel's tail has proved to be most satisfactory, although I am still looking for an even finer and more flexible hair.

The Flexifly: The body of the fly is formed from one or two strands of ostrich herl for the larger patterns or from condor or heron for the smaller. A narrow collar is then formed on to the front of the body; for this either raffia or a similar material may be used. The purpose of this collar is to provide a sharp edge for the squirrel hair to be tied against, this ensures that the hair then flares out at right angles round the hook, which gives it maximum movement when fished. The hair should be as short as it is possible to tie in, and the minimum amount should be used. It is a little difficult to tie in as it has to be splayed round the hook as it is dressed. The body colour may be varied to suit conditions.

Although this pattern has only been tested out for a short while, in this time it has proved to be a killing pattern. The most effective method of fishing with it is as follows. Mount the fly on its own on the point using a long leader in conjunction with a floating line. After the fly has been cast, allow at least one or two minutes for it to sink to the full depth of the leader, and then retrieve with infrequent jerks as slowly as possible. The very fine hairs used for the hackle are receptive to the slightest movement, and thereby provide animation which seems to be most attractive to the trout, also we have taken trout on the artificial as it has been sinking before commencing the retrieve.

THE GERROFF (See Plate 14)

This new pattern was evolved primarily for fishing on very slow flowing stretches of rivers or small clear stillwater lakes or ponds, and has been designed to bridge the gap between traditional floating nymphs and the relatively fast sinking leaded nymphs. The small body and large hook are the secret of the success of this pattern, as it permits the pattern to sink, but very slowly, and most trout seem to find this irresistible. Takes are often very confident as the pattern loosely represents a shrimp on which most trout are used to feeding. It has proved to be a very killing pattern, and the first time it was used by two rods accounted for twelve trout weighing 49lbs.

Why the odd name? Brian Clarke was testing the fly for me on a slow reach of the river Kennet. At the time there was an abundance of small trout and Clarke spent most of the morning inviting these small intruders to release the nymph, aided by cries of "get off". As the morning wore on and his patience became exhausted this was abbreviated to "GERROFF".

The pattern is extremely simple to dress. The hook size may be between 10 and 14 but slightly longer in the shank than a standard pattern. Wind the brown tying silk a little over half way down the shank and then secure with a slightly tapered strip of P.V.C. or thin latex. Next dub the tying silk with three parts of olive brown seal's fur or sealex to one part of fluorescent pink which should be well mixed. Wind this dubbed silk body material up to the eye and tie off. To complete, stretch the P.V.C. strip over the top of the body material and tie it in with a whip finish.

THE TADPOLLY (See Plate 14)

It has always seemed strange to me that fly dressers apart from one or two isolated exceptions have ignored the common tadpole, as these small creatures are so prolific in many stillwaters during the early part of the summer and are eagerly accepted by the trout.

I sincerely hope that this new dressing will fill this gap, as since I first developed it it has proved to be a very killing pattern. It should be retrieved slowly in the margins of ponds or lakes either on a floating or slow sink line. The round fat body formed from peacock herl may be replaced as an alternative with a section of ethafoam trimmed into an oval shape, pierced with the hook point and slid up to the eye and coloured with a black felt tip pen. This will give you a very buoyant pattern which may be fished on the bottom utilizing a fast sink line.

With this method, which is often effective, you cast out your line and wait till it has sunk to the bed of the lake. At this stage the buoyant artificial will be floating well up from the bottom. You then retreive with a long pull and an even longer pause, which in effect causes the Tadpolly to dive towards the bottom and then slowly float upwards towards the surface. Many trout find this movement irresistible.

This is also a very simple pattern to dress. Take a long shank down eye hook size 10 or 12 and with black tying silk secure three sharp black hackle points about two thirds of the way down the shank to form the tail, or as an alternative a couple of strands of black marabou may be used as this gives a very lifelike appearance to the pattern in the water. Next dub some black seal's fur thickly on the silk and wind up to the eye and secure. The final operation is to wind several strands of peacock herl into an oval shape to give the body the correct silhouette. When dressing the alternative floating pattern with the ball of ethafoam, the black seal's fur may be omitted.

SUSPENDER (A revolutionary new Hatching Midge Pupa)

Reproduced by kind permission of the editor of *Trout Fisherman*.

In the early part of the 1978 season Neil Patterson, a constant fishing companion on the Upper Kennet, introduced me to a new floating nymph pattern with which he was experimenting. The original concept of this unique dressing had been noticed by Neil in an American book *Nymph Fishing for Larger Trout* by Charles E. Brooks. The author called this new pattern the "Natant nylon nymph". The basic dressing of the pattern and materials used were purely traditional as it was intended as a general pattern. However the originality of this nymph lay in the addition of a small ball of polypropylene fibres enveloped in a small ball of nylon net or mesh cut from a lady's stocking. This little ball was tied on top of the body of the nymph well back from the eye, and was intended by the author to represent the emerging wings bulging up through the split nymphal chuck. If desired, the little ball could be anointed with grease to hold the pattern in the surface film where the natural is usually found.

Neil immediately realised the potential of this pattern but soon found in practice that even with the ball well greased there was insufficient flotation either in the grease or the polypropylene fibres within the nylon mesh to float the pattern for more than a few seconds, particularly if the water was fairly turbulent. He then hit upon the brilliant idea of replacing the polypropylene with a small square of foam trimmed into a ball shape and then enclosed in the mesh.

It was at this stage that he showed it to me, and I must admit I was most impressed as it floated extraordinarily well although not quite so high in the film as I would have liked. After much trial and error I eventually hit upon the idea of using ethafoam as this relatively new closed cell foam is the most buoyant of all. This completely solved the problem and we now had a pattern that floated high up on the surface and would float all day, even in the roughest water. From then on it was only a short step to produce an imitation pattern to represent the hatching olive nymphs that were so prevalent on our stretch of river. This olive Poly-nymph proved a great success and during the season accounted for many nice trout from our stretch of river.

What has this new river pattern got to do with a book on stillwater trout flies? The answer is that there is a new stillwater pattern that, for want of a better name, we have decided to call the 'suspender' derived directly from the river pattern we have been describing.

Towards the middle of the season I was sitting beside the river enjoying a leisurely lunch, and at the same time idly studying our new nymph to see if I could think of any further improvements. One of the nymphs happened to be a pattern I had dressed the day before and omitted to colour as usual with a felt tip pen. Therefore the little ball of nylon mesh looked distinctly white, due to the white ethafoam showing through. It immediately reminded me of the bunch of white breathing filaments on the top of the head of the average midge pupa, so I asked myself whether the new pattern could be adapted to represent an emerging midge pupa. If so, would it not solve the age old problem of allowing one to present an artificial that would hang tail down and head up in the surface film without the aid of any grease or floatant on the fly or the leader itself, which up to now has been the only way around the problem? I suggested to Neil we dress some midge pupa patterns but position the ball of etha- foam on top of the shank immediately behind the eye. This was duly accomplished, and we had a pupa that simulated the natural hanging down from the surface almost to perfection. I eventually simplified the original dressing and also found that by tying the net ball of ethafoam out over the eye of the hook an even better silhouette was obtained. Viewed from underwater it was difficult at a quick glance to pick out the naturals from the artificials, as from this medium at least, in the mirror of the under surface, only a portion of the ball could be seen.

We have now proved beyond doubt that this is an exceptionally killing pattern, during a surface rise of trout to the midge pupa or buzzer as it is affectionately known. In August this year, accompanied by two very experienced stillwater fly fishers Stewart Canham and Max King, we tested this new pattern one evening on a local lake where by repute the trout were extremely difficult to catch. Soon after our arrival the trout started to rise, obviously to midge pupa, so the three of us took up a position on one stretch of bank about ten yards apart and began fishing. My companions used standard pupa patterns of various types while I used the new patterns. Within the next 30 minutes I landed six trout and they had not even had an offer. Stewart then took my rod and flies and promptly proceeded to pull in four trout, while Max and I continued casting hard to no avail. Finally just before dusk decended Max took over the new patterns and broke his luck with a couple of nice fish.

I have since used these new patterns on several stillwaters in America and found they were equally effective over there. I mount two or three Suspenders on droppers about 30 inches apart which is much closer than I normally mount my patterns. I like to cast them in the path of a rising trout and if they are closer together there is a better chance he will see at least one of them. They should be fished either with no movement at all or alternatively a particularly productive method is to give the line a small twitch when you estimate they are within the trouts' vision. This slight pull on the line causes the artificials to lift up slightly and take up a horizontal position momentarily before dropping back to the vertical. This simulates to perfection the natural pupa lifting up to search for a weak spot in the film in which to break through. The slight animation with the artificial seems to be irresistible and is only possible with these new patterns. On standard patterns the floatant one has to use on the leader will only serve to scare the trout rather than attract when movement is imparted.

The Suspender (John Goddard). First take some white nylon filaments or several strands of white fluoro wool and tie them well round the bend of the hook, then tie in a length of silver lurex with which to rib the body. Next wind on the body material of seal's fur, or better still the new sealex material of the appropriate colour, two thirds of the way up the shank, rib and tie off. This is followed with a thorax formed from three strands of brown dyed turkey herl.

From a sheet of ethafoam cut a small square between $\frac{1}{8}$in. and $\frac{3}{16}$in. in diameter according to the hook size being used. With practice you will soon be able to judge the desired size, but it should be no larger than required to float the pattern. The square should then be trimmed into a ball with your hackle scissors. We then come to the difficult part, as you now require one lady's stocking which you will have to beg, borrow or purloin. From this cut a small square of nylon about one inch in diameter and wrap the ethafoam ball in it, so that it forms a pouch. Tie the base of the pouch in front of the thorax and behind the eye, and when it is well secured with your tying thread trim off the excess of nylon mesh and finish with a dab of varnish.

Like standard midge pupa you may dress these with different coloured bodies and on different sized hooks. We also had some success with a small white bodied pattern, with the little ball coloured orange with a felt tip pen. This was a good match for the pupa of the phantom fly, and although these naturals are seldom found right in the surface film, except possibly late at night, the trout did not seem to mind.

MODERN BOAT FISHING TECHNIQUES.
TWO NEW METHODS

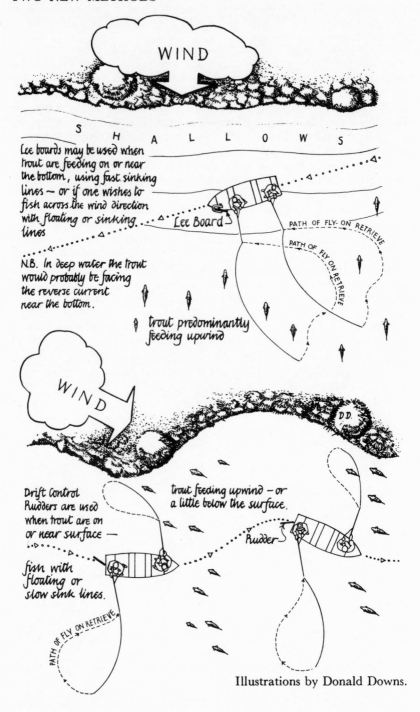

WIND

S H A L L O W S

Lee boards may be used when trout are feeding on or near the bottom, using fast sinking lines — or if one wishes to fish across the wind direction with floating or sinking lines

Lee Board

PATH OF FLY ON RETRIEVE

PATH OF FLY ON RETRIEVE

N.B. In deep water the trout would probably be facing the reverse current near the bottom.

trout predominantly feeding upwind

WIND

D.D.

Drift Control Rudders are used when trout are on or near surface —

trout feeding upwind — or a little below the surface.

Rudder

fish with floating or slow sink lines.

PATH OF FLY ON RETRIEVE

Illustrations by Donald Downs.

BIBLIOGRAPHY

BOOKS

BRIDGETT, R. C. *Loch-Fishing*. Herbert Jenkins.
BROWN, E. S. *Life in Fresh Water*. Oxford University Press. 1955.
BUCKNALL, G. *Fly Fishing Tactics on Stillwater*. Frederick Muller Ltd. 1966.
CLEGG, J. *Pond and Stream Life of Europe*. Blandford Press Ltd. 1963.
CLEGG, J. *Freshwater Life of the British Isles*. Frederick Warne & Co. Ltd. 1952.
COLYER & HAMMOND. *Flies of the British Isles*. Frederick Warne & Co. Ltd. 1951.
FROST, W. E. and BROWN, M. E. *The Trout*. Collins Clear Type Press. 1967.
GODDARD, J. *Trout Fly Recognition*. A. & C. Black Ltd. 1966.
HARRIS, J. R. *An Angler's Entomology*. Collins. 1952.
HENZELL, H. P. *The Art and Craft of Loch Fishing*. Phillip Allan & Co. Ltd. 1937.
HICKIN, NORMAN E. *Caddis Larvae*. Hutchinson & Co. Ltd. 1967.
IMMS, A. D. *Insect Natural History*. Collins. 1947.
IVENS, T. C. *Still Water Fly Fishing*. Andre Deutsch Ltd. 1952.
KITE, OLIVER. *Nymph Fishing in Practice*. Herbert Jenkins. 1963.
LANE, COL. JOSCELYN. *Lake and Loch Fishing*. Seeley Service & Co. Ltd.
LINSSEN, E. F. and NEWMAN, L. H. *Common Insects and Spiders*. Fredk. Warne & Co. Ltd. 1953.
MACAN, T. T. and WORTHINGTON, E. B. *Life in Lakes and Rivers*. Collins. 1951.
MELLANBY, H. *Animal Life in Freshwater*. University Press. 1938.
MOSELY, M. E. *The British Caddis Flies*. George Routledge & Sons Ltd. 1939.
NEEDHAM AND NEEDHAM. *Fresh Water Biology*. Constable & Co. Ltd. 1962.
OATTS, COL. H. A. *Loch Trout*. Herbert Jenkins. 1958.
PHILLIPS, E. *Trout in Lakes and Reservoirs*. Longmans Green & Co.
VENIARD, J. *A Further Guide to Fly Dressing*. A. & C. Black Ltd. 1964.
WALKER, C. F. *Lake Flies and Their Imitation*. Herbert Jenkins. 1969.
WILLIAMS, A. COURTNEY. *A Dictionary of Trout Flies*. A. & C. Black Ltd. 1949.

BOOKLETS AND PAPERS

Fly Fishing on Lakes and Reservoirs—John Henderson. Private Printing.

FRESH-WATER BIOLOGICAL ASSOCIATION SCIENTIFIC PUBLICATIONS

No. 15. *Adults of Ephemeroptera.* D. E. Kimmins.
No. 16. *British Water Bugs.* T. T. Macan, M.A. Ph.D.
No. 17. *Nymphs of the British Stoneflies.* H. B. N. Hynes, D.Sc.
No. 19. *Crustacea and Malacostraca.* Hynes, Macan and Williams.
No. 20. *Nymphs of the Ephemeroptera.* T. T. Macan, M.A., Ph.D.

BOOKLETS BY THE ROYAL ENTOMOLOGICAL SOCIETY OF LONDON

Vol. IX. Part 1. *Diptera. Introduction and Key to Families.* H. Oldroyd.
Vol. IX. Part 2. *Diptera—Nematocera.* Coe, Freeman and Mattingly.
Vol. 109. Part 5. *Ecology of Chironomidae in Storage Reservoirs.* J. H. Mundie.
Vol. 112. Part 12. *A Study of Trichoptera.* M. I. Crichton.
Vol. 113. Part 6. *Diurnal Variation in the Emergence of Some Aquatic Insects.* N. C. Morgan and A. B. Waddell.
Vol. 116. Part 15. *Diurnal Periodicity of Flights by Insects.* T. Lewis and L. R. Taylor.
Vol. 119. Part 10. *Study of Limnophilus lunatus.* A. M. Gower.

TRANSACTIONS OF THE SOCIETY FOR BRITISH ENTOMOLOGY

Vol. 14. Part 11. *Studies of the Larvae of the British Chironomidae.* D. Bryce.

BOOKLETS BY THE FRESHWATER BIOLOGICAL ASSOCIATION

Vol. IV. No. 4—1952. *Taxonomy of the Nymphs of the British Species of Leptophlebiidae.* T. T. Macan.
Vol. III. No. 1—1951. *Taxonomy of the British Species of Siphlonuridae.* T. T. Macan.

BOOKLET BY THE ZOOLOGICAL SOCIETY OF LONDON

Series A. Vol. 108. Part 4—1938. *The Growth of* Caenis Horaria, Leptophlebia vespertina *and* L. marginata. P. H. Moon.

OTHER PAPERS

A Species of Caenis new to Britain—D. E. Kimmins—reprinted from *The Entomologist*, Vol. LXXVI, 1943.
A Key to the Nymphs of the British species of the Family Caénidae— T. T. Macan—*Entomologists Gazette*, Vol. 6, 1955.
British Midges—B. R. Laurence—*A.E.S. Bulletin*, Vol. 11, 1952.
Some Ephemeroptera and Trichoptera collected by mercury vapour light trap—P. H. Ward—*Entomologists Gazette*, Vol. 16.
Insect Emergence from a small Scottish Loch—N. C. Morgan, 1958.
Diel Periodicity of Pupal Emergence in Natural Populations of some Chironomids—E. Palmen, University of Helsinki, 1955.

The Biology of *Leptocerus aterrimus*, with reference to its availability as a food for trout—N. C. Morgan, The Brown Trout Research Laboratory—Pitlochry, 1955.

Some observations on the Biology of the Trout in Windermere—K. R. Allen, The Freshwater Biological Association Laboratory.

Survey of a Moorland Fishpond—T. T. Macan, the Freshwater Biological Association Laboratory, Wray Castle, Ambleside.

INDEX

276